MW01027706

"*Taking Hold of God* is a verita Beeke and Najapfour have brought together in one volume the teaching on prayer of the giants of the Reformation and Puritan eras: Luther, Calvin, Knox, Perkins, Bunyan, Henry, Edwards, and others. I was personally encouraged and stimulated to take my own prayer life to a higher and hopefully more productive level. All believers who have any desire to pray effectively will profit from this book."

— JERRY BRIDGES, a longtime staff member of the
Navigators and author of *The Pursuit of Holiness*

"Together, Beeke and Najapfour have produced a marvelously helpful and instructive volume on prayer drawn from such giants as Martin Luther, John Calvin, John Bunyan, Matthew Henry, and Jonathan Edwards. It is a veritable potpourri of spiritual insight and godly advice. Books on prayer often induce more guilt than help. *Taking Hold of God*, as the title itself suggests, aims at doing the latter. It beckons us, allures us, into the challenge of prayer itself: laying hold of a gracious Father who longs for our presence and delights to commune with His children. If you aim to read just one book on prayer this year, choose this one."

—DEREK W. H. THOMAS, John E. Richards Professor
of Systematic and Practical Theology, Reformed
Theological Seminary, Jackson, Mississippi

"The Protestant Reformation brought a revolution to the life of prayer. This book opens up the story of how the Reformers like Luther and Calvin, followed by the Puritans like William Perkins and Matthew Henry, teach us a surprisingly new approach to the life of prayer."

—HUGHES OLIPHANT OLD, John H. Leith Professor
of Reformed Theology and Worship, Erskine
Theological Seminary, Due West, South Carolina

"Here is a master stroke indeed!—a book on the prayer-filled lives and teaching of nine masters of the Christian life (plus others included for good measure).

"Many of us feel either infants in the school of prayer or intimidated and beaten down by those who accuse us of being prayer-less but do not teach us how to be prayer-full. But here can be found nourishment, example, instruction, encouragement, and, yes, deep challenge, all in one volume. May these pages serve as a tonic for our weakness, a remedy for our sickness, and an inspiration to greater prayerfulness in our churches!"

—SINCLAIR B. FERGUSON, senior minister of First
Presbyterian Church of Columbia, South Carolina,
and professor of Systematic Theology at
Redeemer Theological Seminary, Dallas, Texas

"Here is a great vault of spiritual riches for anyone who wants to learn more about prayer and be encouraged to pray whether you consider yourself Reformed or a student of the Puritans or not.

"But if some of the names in the table of contents are already favorites of yours, you will enjoy this book even more. This is a valuable book, and I am very grateful for those whose work made it possible."

—DON WHITNEY, associate professor of Biblical
Spirituality at The Southern Baptist
Theological Seminary, Louisville, Kentucky

# TAKING HOLD OF
# GOD

∾∾∾∾

## REFORMED AND PURITAN
## PERSPECTIVES ON PRAYER

∾∾∾∾

*edited by*

Joel R. Beeke
and
Brian G. Najapfour

**Reformation Heritage Books**
Grand Rapids, Michigan

*Taking Hold of God*
© 2011 by Joel R. Beeke and Brian G. Najapfour

**Reformation Heritage Books**
3070 29th St. SE
Grand Rapids, MI 49512
616-977-0889
orders@heritagebooks.org
www.heritagebooks.org

*Printed in the United States of America*
21 22 23 24 25 26/12 11 12 10 9 8 7

---

Library of Congress Cataloging-in-Publication Data

Taking hold of God : Reformed and Puritan perspectives on prayer / edited by Joel R. Beeke and Brian G. Najapfour.
      p. cm.
   Includes bibliographical references.
   ISBN 978-1-60178-120-8 (pbk. : alk. paper) 1. Prayer—Reformed Church—History. 2. Reformed Church—Doctrines—History.
3. Prayer—Puritans—History. 4. Puritans—Doctrines—History.
I. Beeke, Joel R., 1952- II. Najapfour, Brian G.
   BV207.T35 2011
   248.3'2—dc22

                              2010052021

---

*For additional Reformed literature, both new and used, request a free book list from Reformation Heritage Books at the above address.*

# Contents

With heartfelt appreciation to prayer warriors
around the globe, including

**Maurice Roberts from Scotland
Changwon Shu from Korea
Josafá Vasconcelos from Brazil**

who have taught me by their example
what it means to take hold of God.

—JRB

With heartfelt appreciation to my dear mother,

**Vergilia A. Golez**
(also known as Mama Dhel),

for her *unceasing* prayers for me.

—BGN

# Preface

*Let him take hold of my strength, that he may make peace with me.*
—Isaiah 27:5

*Take hold of my covenant.* —Isaiah 56:4

*There is none that calleth upon thy name, that stirreth up himself to take hold of thee.*
—Isaiah 64:7

Imagine that you have been invited into a nobleman's castle in ancient times. As the massive doors swing open before you, an involuntary shiver runs down your spine. You step into great marble halls guarded by strong warriors. But you need not fear: you have an invitation from the lord of the castle, stamped with his personal seal of authentication.

A knight escorts you into the great hall, where the regal lord himself warmly greets you. "Would you like to see my treasury?" he asks. Soon he is leading you into the most secure portion of the castle, hemmed in by massive stone walls. He turns a large iron key and opens a door into inky darkness. For a moment you see nothing. Then your host lights a torch on the wall and you gasp. Before you are hundreds of gold coins in open wooden chests. Silver cups of intricate craftsmanship grace the shelves. Diamonds, rubies, and emeralds shine like stars of many colors. On a table to your left is an ancient sword once used by a great champion to win a historic battle. Here on a stand is the diary of a queen whose courage saved her nation from destruction. Hanging on the wall is a harp whose strings were once plucked by a famous musician. Your noble friend leads you from one discovery to another, pausing at each to explain its significance. You could spend hours in the treasury of this castle, so rich are its contents.

The church of Jesus Christ has such a treasury. Among its treasures preserved through the ages are the writings of the Reformers and the Puritans, which we would consider to be among the most valuable. Though sometimes forgotten like ancient gold lying in an underground vault, these writings shine with the glory of God in Christ. In this book, we invite you to enter and explore the contribution these writers made to the church's treasury of prayer.

The chief reason we consider the writings of the Reformers and Puritans to be treasures is that they are full of *biblical truth*. The treasures of the church are made of the gold, silver, and precious stones of divine wisdom revealed in the Bible. In a world in bondage to ignorance, error, confusion, and deceit, here is truth from God, and Jesus taught us that this truth will set us free. The truth about Christ is that the glory of God shines in Him with life-changing power. As you read these chapters, notice how much the Reformers and Puritans meditated on the Word of God and incorporated biblical truth into their writings. No wonder their writings are treasured by people who love the Word of God.

Another reason people delight in these old Reformed writers is that their books are rich in their exploration of *spiritual experience*. They do not merely dissect doctrines as a scientist dissects a frog. These men reveled in Scripture as a hungry man delights in bread, butter, and honey. They did not separate the Word from the Holy Spirit, for the Spirit is the life-giver. Again and again, you will find that their books have hands that grab you and feet that carry you to places you have never been before. Biblical doctrine is eminently practical and relevant to life.

*Reformed experiential writers* are authors in the Reformation tradition whose writings are biblical, doctrinal, experiential, and practical. These writers were also true men of prayer, who "took hold of God" in secret and public prayer (Isa. 27:5; 56:4; 64:7). In these pages you will see how Martin Luther led the Reformation on his knees; John Calvin called men into fellowship with God; John Knox explained biblical principles of prayer; William Perkins unfolded the meaning of the Lord's Prayer; and Anthony Burgess encouraged prayer by pointing to Christ's mediatorial prayer for us. You will see how John Bunyan stood against formalism in prayer by advocating praying in the Spirit, and how the Puritans rejoiced in the Holy Spirit's help in prayer. You will be shown how Matthew Henry offered methods for continual prayer that are both biblical and practical, while Thomas Boston linked prayer to our adoption by God, and Jonathan Edwards taught prayer as an experience of the divine Trinity. All together, these men, with the Spirit's blessing, have much to offer that can make our prayer life more informed, more extensive, more fervent, and more effectual.

So welcome to the Puritan treasury of prayer. Take time to explore the riches of wisdom and insight gathered by our Reformed and Puritan forefathers in Christ, and then avail yourself of these riches as you seek to take hold of God in the way of Christian prayer.

——————>•••<——————

We are grateful to Peter Beck, Michael Haykin, Johnny Serafini, and Stephen Yuille for contributing enlightening chapters to this book. We wish to thank Paul Smalley for his invaluable research and editorial assistance, and Michael Borg for his help on chapters 5 and 9. We also thank Kate DeVries, Annette Gysen, Ray Lanning, Stan McKenzie, and Phyllis Ten Elshof for their editing expertise; Gary and Linda denHollander for their proofreading and typesetting work, and Amy Zevenbergen for the cover design.

May this book whet your appetite to dig more deeply into the church's treasury by reading the Reformers and Puritans for yourself. Most of all, may it lead us all into deeper communion with the God who hears prayer, to whom all flesh must come (Ps. 65:2), so that God will not have to complain of us, "There is none that calleth upon thy name, that stirreth up himself to take hold of thee" (Isa. 64:7).

—Joel R. Beeke and Brian G. Najapfour

*Chapter 1*

# Martin Luther on Prayer and Reformation

BRIAN G. NAJAPFOUR

*Even in the busiest periods of the Reformation Luther averaged two hours of prayer daily.*

—ANDREW W. KOSTEN

Not only was Martin Luther (1483–1546) the great Protestant Reformer,[1] he was a great man of prayer as well. As he explains, prayer was foundational for his soul's well-being: "Prayer includes every pursuit of the soul, in meditation, reading, listening, [and] praying."[2] Andrew Kosten suggests that "to know...Luther at his best, one must become acquainted with him as a man of devotion."[3] Thus, to some degree, to study Luther and his theology apart from his spirituality in general and his practice of prayer in particular is to miss the context of his whole personality both as a Reformer and theologian. After showing that prayer is an important key to under-

---

1. J. A. Morrison, *Martin Luther: The Great Reformer*, rev. and ed. Michael J. McHugh (Arlington Heights, Ill.: Christian Liberty Press, 1994).

2. Martin Luther, "Explanation of the Ninety-Five Theses," in *Luther's Works*, vol. 31, ed. Helmut T. Lehmann (Philadelphia: Muhlenberg Press, 1957), 86 (hereafter only *LW* 31:86). I owe this reference to William R. Russell, "Prayer: The Practical Focus of Luther's Theology," in *Let Christ Be Christ: Theology, Ethics, and World Religions in the Two Kingdoms*, ed. Daniel N. Harmelink (Huntington Beach, Calif.: Tentatio Press, 1999), 295.

3. *Devotions and Prayers of Martin Luther*, trans. Andrew W. Kosten (Grand Rapids: Baker, 1965), 5.

standing Luther as a Reformer and theologian, this chapter will address Luther's basic theology of prayer, his trinitarian emphasis in prayer, and his personal prayer life.

## Prayer: A Key to Understanding Luther

*Prayer and Luther's Reform*

The Reformation that Luther began was undertaken against that backdrop of spirituality, particularly of prayer. For example, when he nailed his Ninety-Five Theses (1517) on the door of Castle Church in Wittenberg, his intent was partly to reform the Roman Catholic Church's view of prayer in relation to indulgences.[4] In the forty-eighth thesis, he said that the pope had become more interested in people's money than in their prayer.[5] Likewise, from the eighty-second to the eighty-ninth theses, he questioned that if the pope, through his prayer "for a consideration of money" of the people, could take their loved ones' souls from purgatory to heaven, why did he not just empty purgatory "for pure love's sake"?[6] Such a question implies that while at this time Luther "did not...yet deny the validity of indulgences or the sacrament of penance out of which they had grown,"[7] he nonetheless felt something was wrong in the attitude of the church toward prayer.

Therefore, William Russell is not exaggerating when he asserts that "for...Luther, the reformation was about how the church prays." Russell argues, "The emphasis on prayer in the context of catechetical instruction is the heart of Luther's reformation theology."[8]

---

4. In these theses, "Luther applied his evangelical theology to indulgences.... [However, here] he did not even mention justification by faith..., although the implications of that doctrine are present and were not lost upon his enemies" (Introduction to "Ninety-five Theses," in *LW* 31:19).

5. *LW* 31:29.

6. *LW* 31:32.

7. *LW* 31:19.

8. William R. Russell, "Luther, Prayer, and the Reformation," *Word & World* 22, no. 1 (2002): 49.

Luther's *Small and Large Catechisms* (1529)[9] were "part of [his]... longstanding attempt to reform the educational practices in the congregations of his day." They were, as far as prayer is concerned, intended not only to inform people about prayer but also to instruct them on how to pray. Luther desired to reform both their doctrine and their practice of prayer because, for him, "the act of Christian prayer 'enacts' doctrine, just as doctrine 'informs' prayer. They are inseparable in Luther's understanding of catechesis."[10]

Russell also points out that even before the birth of the Reformation on October 31, 1517, Luther placed an emphasis on prayer in catechesis in his Reformation agenda. "For example, already in October of 1516, fully a year before he posted the *Ninety-Five Theses*, Luther preached on the Lord's Prayer and published both a Latin and German exposition of it. The reformer returned to this theme again five months later when he preached a series on the Lord's Prayer during Lent of 1517."[11]

Moreover, as we can see from his 1529 catechisms, Luther's focus on prayer continued after the Reformation had begun. In December of 1518, Russell notes that "he preached another series of sermons on the Lord's Prayer...for children and 'simple lay people.'"[12] Afterwards, he published his *Exposition of the Lord's Prayer for Simple Laymen* on April of 1519.[13] Shortly after this publication, he "preached on prayer once again."[14] This was followed by his treatise *A Short Form of the Ten Commandments, a Short Form of the Creed, a Short Form of the Lord's Prayer* (May 1520),[15] which "served to replace the Roman prayer book."[16] Two years later came

---

9. See Martin Luther, "The Small Catechism" and "The Large Catechism," in *The Book of Concord*, ed. Theodore G. Tappert (Philadelphia: Fortress Press, 1959), 337–57.

10. Russell, "Luther, Prayer, and the Reformation," 50.

11. Ibid.

12. Ibid.

13. *LW* 42:19–81.

14. Russell, "Luther, Prayer, and the Reformation," 51.

15. Ibid.

16. Introduction to "Personal Prayer Book," in *LW* 43:6.

his *Personal Prayer Book* (1522),[17] his Reformed version of the old personal prayer books "used in the medieval church for centuries."[18] In the introduction of this book, Luther notes that these old medieval prayer books "need a basic and thorough reformation if not total extermination."[19] He entreats "everyone to break away from using the Bridget prayers[20] and any other which are ornamented with indulgences or rewards and urge all to get accustomed to praying this plain, ordinary Christian prayer [The Lord's Prayer]."[21] And in 1535, Luther produced his treatise, *A Simple Way to Pray*,[22] which "reveals a lifelong use of the catechism…as a daily resource for prayer."[23]

This survey shows that prayer was an essential element of Luther's reform. Russell observes, "Prayer was the point of the theological reform program he envisioned for the church."[24] "Indeed," states Russell, "a, if not *the*, distinctive feature of the Lutheran Reformation program is its consistent emphasis on reforming the way Christians pray."[25] Deanna Carr writes, "Friedrich Heiler has said that it was as a man of prayer that Luther became a great reformer and the 'inaugurator of a new era in the history of Christianity.'"[26]

---

17. *LW* 43:11–45.
18. *LW* 43:5.
19. *LW* 43:11–12.
20. "St. Bridget (1303–1373) was a Swedish saint and mystic who was canonized in 1391. Her literary works include four prayers, but in the flowering of legends around her captivating personality, a set of fifteen prayers was ascribed to her and used frequently in the spiritual exercises of the devout. Personal prayer books promised that the Bridget prayers would gain for the user a) the salvation of forty souls of the same sex as the person offering the prayers, b) the conversion of forty sinners, and c) the strengthening of forty-six righteous persons" (*LW* 43:12).
21. *LW* 43:12–13.
22. *LW* 43:193–211.
23. *LW* 43:190.
24. Russell, "Prayer: The Practical Focus of Luther's Theology," 293.
25. Russell, "Luther, Prayer, and the Reformation," 54.
26. Deanna Marie Carr, "A Consideration of the Meaning of Prayer in the Life of Martin Luther," *Concordia Theological Monthly* 42, no. 10 (1971): 629.

Prayer is an important key to understanding Luther as a Reformer. He was a Reformer of prayer.

*Prayer and Luther as a Theologian*

While prayer is a significant factor for comprehending Luther as a Reformer, it also functions as a framework for interpreting him as a theologian. Russell says, "The theology of...Luther is a theology of prayer." It is then advisable to approach Luther's theology with the understanding that he thinks as a theologian of prayer. For Luther, prayer is "a central component of his theological reflections." When he "considered the intellectual content of the Christian faith, he could not help but include prayer in his deliberations."[27] This point is evident in his 1529 catechisms—Luther's favorite tool in teaching the basics of Christian belief—which have a section on the Lord's Prayer, along with the Decalogue and the Apostles' Creed. In fact, the *Small Catechism* even contains two segments called "Morning and Evening Prayers: How the head of the family shall teach his household to pray morning and evening," and "Grace at Table: How the head of the family shall teach his household to offer blessing and thanksgiving at table."[28]

It is also interesting to note that in his *Small Catechism*, Luther's exposition of the Lord's Prayer is sprinkled with prayers. Under the first petition ("Hallowed be Thy name"), Luther asks, "How is this done?" He answers, "When the Word of God is taught clearly and purely and we, as children of God, lead holy lives in accordance with it. *Help us to do this, dear Father in heaven!* But whosoever teaches and lives otherwise than as the Word of God teaches, profanes the name of God among us. *From this preserve us, heavenly Father!*"[29]

Luther's first published book was *The Seven Penitential Psalms* (1517).[30] Russell writes that this work concerns "a viable—and practical—theology of prayer, as expressed in the psalmist's prayers." He

---

27. Russell, "Prayer: The Practical Focus of Luther's Theology," 293.
28. Luther, "The Small Catechism," 352–53.
29. Ibid., 346 (italics mine).
30. *LW* 14:ix, 137–205.

cites Gerhard Ebeling, who says that it "provides a key to [Luther's] entire theology, and so to his literary work as a whole."[31] Luther's other major works on prayer include *On Rogationtide Prayer and Procession* (1519)[32] and *Appeal for Prayer against the Turks* (1541),[33] which "includes instructions for suitable public worship services and a form for public prayer."[34]

As a practical theologian, Luther sought to share his theology in layman's terms. This interest is best seen in his demonstration of his theology of prayer. Hence came his *Exposition of the Lord's Prayer for Simple Laymen* (1519) and *A Simple Way to Pray for a Good Friend* (1535). In his *Small Catechism*, he reminds his audience that the Lord's Prayer has to be taught in understandable words: "in the plain form in which the head of the family shall teach it to his household."[35] Carr is thus right to pronounce that "the hallmark of Lutheran prayer would be its simplicity."[36]

When Luther was asked to recant his theology at the Dict of Worms in 1521, his famous reply concluded with a short prayer:

> Unless I am convinced by the testimony of the Scriptures or by clear reason (for I do not trust either in the pope or in councils alone, since it is well known that they have often erred and contradicted themselves), I am bound by the Scriptures I have quoted and my conscience is captive to the Word of God. I cannot and I will not retract anything, since it is neither safe nor right to go against conscience. I cannot do otherwise, here I stand, *may God help me, Amen.*[37]

---

31. Russell, "Prayer: The Practical Focus of Luther's Theology," 295.

32. *LW* 42:87–93. Rogation days were days of prayer to receive God's pardon for sin, protection from danger, and prosperity in harvest.

33. *LW* 43:219–41.

34. *LW* 43:216–17.

35. Luther, "The Small Catechism," 346.

36. Carr, "A Consideration of the Meaning of Prayer in the Life of Martin Luther," 623.

37. Luther, "Luther at the Diet of Worms," in *LW* 32:112–13 (italics mine).

Russell comments that "the way Luther prayed and the many differing circumstances in which he prayed—together with his extensive theological deliberations on prayer—form a comprehensive presentation of the reformer's theology, in the form that was perhaps most significant to Luther himself."[38] Therefore, for Luther, prayer and theology were woven together. Martin E. Lehmann also concludes, "It is clear that his understanding of prayer can in no way be isolated from the totality of his theology. Indeed, it can be said that prayer is an integral and significant part of his entire theology."[39] Prayer is one important key to knowing Luther as a theologian, as it provides a background for his theology.

## Luther's Theology of Prayer

Having looked at how prayer operates as a key to understanding Luther both as a Reformer and as a theologian, we will now examine his theology of prayer. It must be remembered that Luther was not a systematic theologian. While he had several works on prayer, he did not write a single book or section of a book that could be considered his comprehensive theology of prayer; rather, it is scattered throughout his writings. In this section our aim is to provide an introduction to Luther's theology of prayer.

### The Meaning of Prayer

1. Prayer as a duty.

Before Luther proceeded to explain the Lord's Prayer in his *Large Catechism*, he first emphasized that "it is our duty to pray."[40] Luther understood prayer, first and foremost, as a duty. Prayer is obligatory because "God has commanded it."[41] Luther attests that "we were

---

38. Russell, "Prayer: The Practical Focus of Luther's Theology," 295.
39. Martin E. Lehmann, *Luther and Prayer* (Milwaukee: Northwestern Publishing House, 1985), x.
40. Luther, "The Large Catechism," 420.
41. Ibid.

told in the Second Commandment, 'You shall not take God's name in vain.' Thereby we are required to praise the holy name and pray or call upon it in every need. For to call upon it is nothing else than to pray. Prayer, therefore, is as strictly and solemnly commanded as all other commandments, such as having no other God, not killing, not stealing, etc."[42]

Here, Luther equates the divine duty to pray with the other duties in the Decalogue. He uses the second commandment to sustain his thesis that prayer is a command. Thus, he could say that not to pray is a sin, just as much as committing murder. The sin of prayerlessness is no less heinous than the sin of adultery. They carry the same weight of criminality, for they both violate God's law. Luther writes, "From the fact that prayer is so urgently commanded, we ought to conclude that we should by no means despise our prayers, but rather prize them highly."[43]

Similarly, he writes, "Now from the fact that we are so solemnly commanded to pray you must conclude and reason that on no account should anyone despise his prayers. On the contrary, he should think much and highly of them."[44] The Reformer exhorts his readers further:

> You are to look closely at this command and stress it that you do not consider prayer an optional work and act as if it were no sin for you not to pray. You should know that praying is earnestly enjoined, with the threat of God's supreme displeasure and punishment if it is neglected. It is enjoined just as well as the command that you should have no other gods and should not blaspheme and abuse God's name but should confess and preach, laud and praise it.[45]

---

42. Ibid., 420–21.

43. Ibid., 422.

44. Ewald M. Plass, ed., *What Luther Says: A Practical In-Home Anthology for the Active Christian* (St. Louis: Concordia Publishing House, 1959), 1076.

45. Ibid., 1075.

Then he bluntly adds, "He who does not do this [i.e., pray] should know that he is no Christian and does not belong in the kingdom of God."[46]

## 2. Prayer as "the hardest work of all."

For Luther, this command to pray is "the hardest work of all...a labor above all labors, since he who prays must wage a mighty warfare against the doubt and murmuring excited by the faintheartedness and unworthiness we feel within us."[47] Luther knew how spiritually demanding it was to pray. He confesses, "There is no greater work than praying."[48] Indeed, for him it is even more laborious than preaching: "Prayer is a difficult matter and hard work. It is far more difficult than preaching the Word or performing other official duties in the church. When we are preaching the Word, we are more passive than active; God is speaking through us, and our teaching is His work. This is the reason why it is also very rare."[49]

Moreover, for Luther, prayer as "the hardest work of all" is "the work of Christians alone; for before we are Christians and believe, we know neither for what nor how we are to pray."[50] He emphasizes that unbelievers "cannot pray at all."[51] He explains,

> And even though [an unbeliever] prays most devoutly, the spirit of grace is not there; for the attitude of the heart is simply this: Dear Lord, take into consideration how well I live and how much I suffer; or the merit of this and that saint, the intercession and good works of pious people, etc. There is no faith in the divine grace and mercy through Christ, and the heart always remains uncertain, unable to conclude that it is heard without fail. It wants to deal with God only in the

---

46. Ibid.
47. Cited in Carr, "A Consideration of the Meaning of Prayer in the Life of Martin Luther," 621–22.
48. Plass, *What Luther Says*, 1088.
49. Ibid.
50. Ibid., 1077.
51. Ibid., 1089.

basis of its own or other people's holiness, without Christ, as though God should humble Himself before us and let us actually oblige Him to grant us grace and help and thus become our debtor and servant. This does not merit grace but wrath; it is not praying; it is mocking God.[52]

3. Prayer as calling upon God's name.

Noteworthy also is Luther's plain perception of prayer. For him, to pray is simply to call upon God's holy name.[53] On one occasion, he avouches that "to speak to God means to pray; this is indeed a great glory that the high majesty of heaven should stoop to us poor worms and permit us to open our mouths to him...but it is still more glorious and more precious that he should speak to us and that we should hear him."[54]

Luther argued that prayer is a command on the basis of the second commandment (not taking God's name in vain).[55] The positive aspect of this law is that God is commanding us to call upon His name accordingly. Or, in Luther's mind, God is requiring us to pray, since calling upon His name is praying to Him. And when we pray or call upon God's name as He requires, His name "is glorified and used to good purpose."[56]

*The Motive of Prayer*

If one asked Luther why he prayed, his immediate answer would be because it is a command. This is his main motive in prayer: "On this commandment, on which all the saints base their prayer, I too, base

52. Ibid., 1077.
53. Luther, "The Large Catechism," 420.
54. Cited in Carr, "A Consideration of the Meaning of Prayer in the Life of Martin Luther," 622.
55. Unlike the Reformed, Lutherans consider the prohibitions against other gods and against worshiping idols to be one commandment, and they find two commandments under "Thou shalt not covet." Thus the Lutheran second commandment is the Reformed third commandment.
56. Luther, "The Large Catechism," 421.

mine."[57] Furthermore, he adds, "Let this be the first and most necessary point to consider: All our prayers must be based and rest on obedience to God, regardless of our person, whether we be sinners or saints, worthy or unworthy."[58] Luther perceived prayer primarily as a duty. As such, to those who make an excuse not to pray, his response is simple—no matter what happens, "everybody should always approach God in obedience to this command."[59] It is our duty to pray; therefore, we ought to pray!

That Luther's vital ground for prayer is God's command is also obvious when he gives reasons to pray:

> They are as follows: first, the urging of God's commandment, who has strictly required us to pray; second, His promise, in which He declares that He will hear us; third, an examination of our own need and misery, which burden lies so heavily on our shoulders that we have to carry it to God immediately and pour it out before Him, in accordance with His order and commandment; fourth, true faith, based on this Word and promise of God, praying with the certainty and confidence that He will hear and help us—and all these things in the name of Christ, through whom our prayer is acceptable to the Father and for whose sake He gives us every grace and every good.[60]

Friedemann Hebart, however, claims that "Luther always bases prayer on God's command to pray and on his promise to hear prayer." In other words, Luther's motivation to pray is twofold—command and promise. Hebart maintains that in Luther's thinking "both command and promise serve the *one* end, as both Catechisms make clear. Both command and promise provide the assurance that our petitions are heard by our Father."[61] We therefore pray to respond not only to God's precept but also to His pledge that He will hear

---

57. Ibid., 422.
58. Ibid.
59. Ibid.
60. Plass, *What Luther Says*, 1075.
61. Friedemann Hebart, "The Role of the Lord's Prayer in Luther's Theology of Prayer," *Lutheran Theological Journal* 18, no. 1 (1984): 7.

our prayers (always according to His will). No wonder, then, that in his list of reasons to pray, Luther put God's promise just after God's command, indicating that the two are intertwined. Luther also highlighted the weaving of these two in his *Large Catechism*. As he encourages his readers to pray, he says to them:

> We should be all the more urged and encouraged to pray because God has promised that our prayer will surely be answered.... This you can hold up to him and say, "I come to thee, dear Father, and pray not of my own accord or because of my own worthiness, but at thy *commandment and promise*, which cannot fail or deceive me." Whoever does not believe this promise should realize once again that he angers God, grossly dishonoring him and accusing him of falsehood.[62]

*The Manner of Prayer*
With respect to the manner of praying, Luther addressed the question of whether one should pray spontaneously or use a prescribed form and what posture one should use in prayer.

1. Spontaneous prayer.
In one of his conversations later recorded as *Table Talk*, Luther expressed his negative feeling toward the manner of prayer the pope had obligated him to perform. He reflects, "Prayer under the papacy was pure torture of the poor conscience and only blabbering and making of words; no praying, but a work of obedience."[63] He goes on:

> The pope commands a threefold manner of praying. The material prayer, in which a person recites words he does not understand, as the nuns do with the psalter. This was merely a prayer to satisfy the pope. The other, the formal prayer, in which one does understand the words. The third, the effectual prayer, the prayer of devotion and meaning. The third is

62. Luther, "The Large Catechism," 423 (italics mine).
63. Cited in Leonhard Ludwig, "Luther, Man of Prayer," in *Interpreting Luther's Legacy*, ed. Fred W. Meuser and Stanley D. Schneider (Minneapolis: Augsburg Publishing House, 1969), 164.

the right essence and quality of prayer. But on this there is no insistence, but only on the material prayer, that the words were recited and read, as a parrot talks. From this sprang a desolate ocean full of hours of prayer, the howling and shouting in convents and monasteries in which the psalms and lections were sung and read without spirit, in a manner that a person neither understood nor retained either words or sentences of meaning.[64]

Later, from Romans 12:7–16, he explains that "prayer must come from the heart spontaneously, without any prepared and prescribed words. It must speak its own language according to the fervor of the heart."[65] He even rebuked "those who simply read the Psalms in a perfunctory manner without putting their heart into it."[66] "Oral praying is not effective unless it corresponds to the desire of the heart."[67] The essence of true prayer, then, comes naturally from the heart: "All teachers of Scripture conclude that the essence and the nature of prayer are nothing else than the raising of the heart, it follows that everything which is not a lifting up of the heart is not prayer."[68] What matters is not the quantity of our prayer but the quality of it: "For God does not ask how much or how long you have prayed, but how good the prayer is and whether it proceeds from the heart."[69] In fact, he proposes that "our prayer must have few words, but be great and profound in content and meaning. The fewer the words, the better the prayer; the more words, the poorer the prayer. Few words and richness of meaning is Christian; many words and lack of meaning is pagan."[70] He also holds that "a person should pray 'not only in the spirit but also with the mind.'"[71] In

---

64. Ibid.
65. Plass, *What Luther Says*, 1086.
66. Lehmann, *Luther and Prayer*, 5.
67. Kosten, *Devotions and Prayers of Martin Luther*, 50.
68. Plass, *What Luther Says*, 1085.
69. Cited in Lehmann, *Luther and Prayer*, 17.
70. Luther, "An Exposition of the Lord's Prayer for Simple Laymen," in *LW* 42:19.
71. Cited in Lehmann, *Luther and Prayer*, 4.

short, Luther wanted prayer to proceed not only from the heart but also from the mind — that is, to pray with understanding.

## 2. Scripted prayer.

While Luther promoted extemporaneous prayer, he also recommended the use of written prayers. For instance, in his section from the *Small Catechism* called "Grace at Table: How the head of the family shall teach his household to offer blessing and thanksgiving at table," he gives these instructions:

> When children and the whole household gather at the table, they should reverently fold their hands and say:
>
>> "The eyes of all look to Thee, O Lord, and Thou givest them their food in due season. Thou openest Thy hand; Thou satisfiest the desire of every living thing."
>
> Then the Lord's Prayer should be said, and afterwards this prayer:
>
>> "Lord God, heavenly Father, bless us, and these Thy gifts which of Thy bountiful goodness Thou hast bestowed on us, through Jesus Christ our Lord. Amen!"[72]

Here Luther provides his readers with set forms of prayers.

Likewise, in *A Simple Way to Pray*, Luther advises Master Peter (his barber to whom he has dedicated this book):

> When your heart has been warmed by such recitation to yourself [of the Ten Commandments, the words of Christ, etc.] and is intent upon the matter, kneel or stand with your hands folded and your eyes toward heaven and speak or think as briefly as you can:
>
>> O Heavenly Father, dear God, I am a poor unworthy sinner. I do not deserve to raise my eyes or hands towards thee or to pray. But because thou hast com-

---

72. Luther, "The Small Catechism," 353.

manded us all to pray and hast promised to hear us
and through thy dear Son Jesus Christ has taught us
both how and what to pray, I come to thee in obedience to thy word, trusting in thy gracious promise. I
pray in the name of my Lord Jesus Christ together
with all thy saints and Christians on earth as he has
taught us: Our Father who art, etc., through the
whole prayer, word for word.[73]

As Luther fleshes out one by one the seven petitions of the Lord's
Prayer, he supplies his barber with prescribed prayers at the end of
each of these petitions. However, not wanting Peter to think he
must pray only these words, Luther reminds him:

You should also know that I do not want you to recite all
words in your prayer. That would make it nothing but idle
chatter and prattle, read word for word out of a book as were
the rosaries by the laity and the prayers of the priests and
monks. Rather do I want your heart to be stirred and guided
concerning the thoughts which ought to be comprehended in
the Lord's Prayer. These thoughts may be expressed, if your
heart is rightly warmed and inclined toward prayer, in many
different ways and with more words or fewer.[74]

For Luther, the recital of written prayers is not wrong as long
as one does not enslave or confine himself to the set forms. Luther
permitted the use of forms of prayer, though he seems to prefer free
prayer. Luther went on to admonish Master Peter, using his own
experience, which shows his attitude toward this matter:

I do not bind myself to such words or syllables, but say my
prayers in one fashion today, in another tomorrow, depending upon my mood and feeling. I stay however, as nearly as I
can, with the same general thoughts and ideas. It may happen
occasionally that I may get lost among so many ideas on one
petition that I forego the other six. If such an abundance of

---

73. Luther, "A Simple Way to Pray," in *LW* 43:194–95.
74. *LW* 43:198.

good thoughts comes to us we ought to disregard the other petitions, make room for such thoughts, listen in silence, and under no circumstances obstruct them.[75]

3. Suggested postures in prayer.

Luther's counsel to his barber implies that he prays either standing or kneeling with hands folded and eyes toward heaven. However, Luther says plainly, "It is of little importance whether you stand, kneel, or prostrate yourself; for the postures of the body are neither forbidden nor commanded as necessary. The same applies to other things: raising the head and the eyes heavenward, folding the hands, striking the breast."[76]

In his "Morning and Evening Prayers: How the head of the family shall teach his household to pray morning and evening," Luther also suggests making the sign of the cross, which later reformers rejected: "In the morning, when you rise, make the sign of the cross and say, 'In the name of God, the Father, the Son, and the Holy Spirit. Amen.'"[77]

Note also Luther's prescription to end every prayer with the word "amen." Luther says to his barber:

Finally, mark this, that you must always speak the Amen firmly. Never doubt that God in his mercy will surely hear you and say "yes" to your prayers. Never think that you are kneeling or standing alone, rather think that the whole of Christendom, all devout Christians, are standing there beside you and you are standing among them in a common, united petition which God cannot disdain. Do not leave your prayer without having said or thought, "Very well, God has heard my prayer; this I know as a certainty and a truth." That is what Amen means.[78]

75. Ibid.
76. Plass, *What Luther Says*, 1087.
77. Luther, "The Small Catechism," 352.
78. Luther, "A Simple Way to Pray," in *LW* 43:198.

For Luther, saying "amen" is important because it indicates that you really believe that God will indeed hear your prayer. It is a token of confidence in God that He will answer your petition according to His will.

*Music and Prayer*
Those who are familiar with Luther know that he was a musician. As a composer and singer, he utilized music in prayer. In this regard, Carr contrasts him with Zwingli, who "rejects as humanly impossible the use of music as prayer (maintaining that no man can pray properly and sing properly at the same time)."[79] Luther held that prayer can be expressed through singing. Here are some selected stanzas from Luther's hymns that show him to be a singer of prayer:

"From Depths of Woe I Cry to Thee" (Psalm 130)

1.  From depths of woe I cry to Thee,
    Lord, hear me, I implore Thee.
    Bend down Thy gracious ear to me,
    My prayer let come before Thee.
    If Thou rememberest each misdeed,
    If each should have its rightful meed,
    Who may abide Thy presence?

"From Heaven Above to Earth I Come" (Luke 2:1–18)

12. And thus, dear Lord, it pleaseth Thee
    To make this truth quite plain to me,
    That all the world's wealth, honor, might,
    Are naught and worthless in Thy sight.

13. Ah, dearest Jesus, holy Child,
    Make Thee a bed, soft, undefiled,
    Within my heart, that it may be
    A quiet chamber kept for Thee.

---

79. Carr, "A Consideration of the Meaning of Prayer in the Life of Martin Luther," 624.

"We Now Implore God the Holy Ghost" (John 16:13)

> We now implore the Holy Ghost
> For the true faith, which we need the most,
> That in our last moments He may befriend us
> And, as homeward we journey, attend us.
> Lord, have mercy!

"Lord, Keep Us Steadfast in Thy Word" (John 8:31)

1. Lord, keep us steadfast in Thy Word;
   Curb those who fain by craft and sword
   Would wrest the Kingdom from Thy Son
   And set at naught all He hath done.

3. O Comforter of priceless worth,
   Send peace and unity on earth.
   Support us in our final strife
   And lead us out of death to life.

"Our Father, Thou in Heaven Above" (The Lord's Prayer)

1. Our Father, Thou in heaven above,
   Who biddest us to dwell in love,
   As brethren of one family,
   To cry in every need to Thee,
   Teach us no thoughtless word to say,
   But from our inmost heart to pray.

9. Amen, that is, So shall it be.
   Confirm our faith and hope in Thee
   That we may doubt not, but believe
   What here we ask we shall receive.
   Thus in Thy name and at Thy word
   We say: Amen. Oh, hear us, Lord! Amen.[80]

---

80. The Lutheran Hymnal Online, http://www.lutheran-hymnal.com/online/tlh_online.html (accessed November 23, 2010).

*The Marrow of Prayer: The Lord's Prayer*

The Lord's Prayer has a crucial place in Luther's theology of prayer. Hebart asserts: "In speaking of the nature of prayer, Luther accordingly reverts again and again to the Lord's Prayer; and conversely, whenever he expounds the Our Father he explains the nature of prayer as such. Furthermore, many of his own prayers are developed on the basis of the petitions of the Lord's Prayer. It is therefore not surprising that Luther is able to develop his entire theology of prayer on the basis of his understanding of the Lord's Prayer."[81]

Luther called the Lord's Prayer "the very best prayer, even better than the psalter, which is so very dear to... [him]."[82] "Thus, "there is no nobler prayer to be found on earth [than the daily Lord's Prayer], for it has the excellent testimony that God loves to hear it."[83] It was one of his encouragements in prayer. He knew that if he prayed it, God would be pleased because God Himself gives it: "We should be encouraged and drawn to pray because, in addition to this commandment and promise, God takes the initiative and puts into our mouths the very words we are to use. Thus we see how sincerely he is concerned over our needs, and we shall never doubt that our prayer pleases him and will assuredly be heard. So this prayer is far superior to all others that we might ourselves devise."[84]

Furthermore, in his *Table Talk*, Luther speaks of the Lord's Prayer as "a prayer above all prayers, the very highest prayer taught by the very highest master. In it is contained all spiritual and physical need; and it is the most excellent comfort in all trials, distress, and in the last hour."[85] No wonder then that Luther repeatedly used it both as the basis of his praying and as his own prayer. He asserts, "I am convinced that when a Christian rightly prays the Lord's Prayer at any time or uses any portion of it as he may desire, his

---

81. Hebart, "The Role of the Lord's Prayer in Luther's Theology of Prayer," 6.
82. Luther, "A Simple Way to Pray," in *LW* 43:198.
83. Luther, "The Large Catechism," 423.
84. Ibid.
85. Cited in Hebart, "The Role of the Lord's Prayer in Luther's Theology of Prayer," 6.

praying is more than adequate."[86] Thus, he urges "all to get accustomed to praying this plain, ordinary Christian prayer."[87]

The Lord's Prayer is so close to Luther's heart that he laments when people defile and spoil it:

> What a great pity that prayer of such a master is prattled and chattered so irreverently all over the world! How many pray the Lord's Prayer several thousand times in the course of a year, and if they were to keep on doing so for a thousand years they would not have tasted nor prayed one iota, one dot, of it! In a word, the Lord's Prayer is the greatest martyr on earth (as are the name and word of God). Everybody tortures and abuses it; few take comfort and joy in its proper use.[88]

## Prayer and the Trinity

Luther accentuated the Trinitarian dimension of prayer. Prayer is addressed to God the Father, in the name of Jesus, with the help of the Holy Spirit. The triune God commands us to pray, helps us to pray, and hears and answers our prayers.

### Prayer to God the Father

In the preliminary section of his *An Exposition of the Lord's Prayer*, Luther broaches his subject: "The best way to begin or introduce the prayer is to know how to address, honor, and treat the person to whom we submit our petition, and how to conduct ourselves in his presence, so that he will be gracious towards us and willing to listen to us."[89] Then he comments on the name of God the Father, to whom prayer is to be addressed: "Now, of all names there is none that gains us more favor with God than that of 'Father.' This is indeed a friendly, sweet, intimate, and warm-hearted word. To speak the words 'Lord' or 'God' or 'Judge' would not be nearly as gracious

---

86. Luther, Introduction to "Personal Prayer Book," in *LW* 43:12.
87. *LW* 43:13.
88. Luther, "A Simple Way to Pray," in *LW* 43:200.
89. Luther, "An Exposition of the Lord's Prayer for Simple Laymen," in *LW* 42:22.

and comforting to us. The name 'Father' is of our nature and is sweet by nature. That is why it is the most pleasing to God, and why no other name moves him so strongly to hear."[90]

"With this name," explains Luther, "we likewise confess that we are the children of God, which again stirs his heart mightily; for there is no lovelier sound than that of a child speaking to his father."[91] This name "refers to a confidence that we can place solely in God. No one can assist us to get to heaven than this one Father." In fact, Luther regarded the simple utterance "our Father" "to be the best prayer, for then the heart says more than the lips."[92] This is not startling because, as discussed previously, for Luther to call upon God's name is nothing but to pray. Even if we just say "our Father," we have already prayed.

Luther also stressed that in calling upon God as Father, we must not be selfish. That is, prayer ought not to be egotistic. He pointed out that Jesus "does not want anyone to pray only for himself, but for all mankind. He does not teach us to say 'My Father,' but 'Our Father.'" Luther explains further, "Since prayer is a spiritual good which is held in common by all, we dare not deprive anyone of it, not even our enemies. For since God is the Father of us all, he also wants us to be like brothers to each other, who love each other dearly and who pray for one another as each does for himself."[93]

*Prayer in the Name of God the Son*
Prayer is addressed to the Father and is offered in the name of Jesus, as this name is "the prime factor and foundation on which prayer is to stand and rest."[94] In other words, no prayer can come to God that is not offered in the name of Christ. Here Luther applied the Reformation principle of *solus Christus* to prayer: "that apart from

90. Ibid.
91. Ibid.
92. *LW* 42:23.
93. *LW* 42:26.
94. Plass, *What Luther Says*, 1076.

Christ no one is able to pray a single letter that is worth anything before God and acceptable to Him."[95]

Jesus is "our only Mediator and High Priest before God." When we pray in Christ's name, our prayer becomes "pleasing to God and is heard by Him 'as surely as the name of Christ, God's own dear Son, is pleasing to Him, and as surely as God must say yea and amen to all that Christ asks for.'"[96] In his exposition of John 15:7, Luther further insists: "Christians do not base their prayer on themselves but on the name of the Son of God, in whose name they have been baptized; and they are certain that praying in this way is pleasing to God because He has told us to pray in the name of Christ and has promised to hear us." Hence, Luther writes, "Asking in the name of Christ, really means relying on Him in such a way that we are accepted and heard for His sake, not for our own sake."[97] Therefore, "Our prayer must be centered in Him alone."[98]

*Prayer with the Help of God the Holy Spirit*
Prayer is to be addressed to the Father, through the Son, with the help of the Holy Spirit. Luther was convinced that though unbelievers may pray, "the spirit of grace is not there,"[99] and consequently their prayers will not be heard by God, because it is the Holy Spirit, "the Spirit of grace and supplication," who "urges them to cry to God in every need; and in their hearts…assures them that their prayers will be heard."[100] Thus, prayer is impossible without the Spirit. Luther shares his own experience about this matter. He says that before his conversion, he prayed but felt no assurance that God would answer his prayer: "We used to pray much every hour in all

---

95. Ibid., 1077.
96. Cited in John Peter Pelkonen, "Martin Luther's Theology of Prayer, Its Systematic Structure and Its Significance for Michael Agricola" (Ph.D. diss., Duke University, 1971), 123.
97. Plass, *What Luther Says*, 1077.
98. Cited in Pelkonen, "Martin Luther's Theology of Prayer," 123.
99. Plass, *What Luther Says*, 1077.
100. Cited in Pelkonen, "Martin Luther's Theology of Prayer, Its Systematic Structure and Its Significance for Michael Agricola," 147.

the churches and cloisters, yet our prayers were never answered. We could not hope for God's grace, and we felt no assurance that He would grant our requests. We said: 'It is my duty to chant my canonical hours and to count my beads in this way, but I do not know whether God is pleased with this, takes delight in it, and will hear my prayers.'"[101]

Therefore, for Luther, a person needs to be regenerated before he can truly pray to God. And who can effect this regeneration but the Spirit, who also moves and helps us to pray. As Thomas Smuda notes, "[The Spirit] actively and ceaselessly vivifies and moves man's heart in prayer. Even as the Christian carries out his normal, every-day chores, even as he sleeps, the Holy Spirit is always engaged in prayer within the Christian's heart. Whether the Christian is aware of it or not, prayer continues." Then Smuda cites the Reformer: "Luther compares it to man's pulse: 'The pulse is never motionless; it moves and beats constantly, whether one is asleep or something else keeps one from being aware of it.'"[102]

So for Luther, prayer is offered to the Father, in the name of the Son, with the guidance and help of the Spirit. But does that mean that prayer cannot be addressed to Jesus or the Spirit? Here is Luther's opinion:

> When you call upon Jesus Christ and say: O my dear Lord, God, my Creator, and Father, Jesus Christ, Thou one eternal God, you need not worry that the Father and the Holy Spirit will be angry on this account. They know that no matter which Person you call upon, you call upon all three Persons and upon the One God at the same time. For you cannot call upon one Person without calling upon the others, because the one, undivided divine Essence exists in all and in each Person. Conversely, you cannot deny any Person in particular without denying all three and the One God in His entirety, as 1 John

---

101. Cited in ibid., 148.
102. Thomas E. Smuda, "The Effectual Nature of Confident Prayer Expressed in Selected Writings of Martin Luther" (M.Div. thesis, Concordia Theological Seminary, 1980), 11.

2:23 says: "Whosoever denieth the Son, the same hath not the Father."[103]

## Luther's Prayer Life

Ludwig describes Luther as a man of prayer: "When it comes to prayer, Luther was not a theoretician, but a practitioner. He does not furnish a speculative treatment of a topic but the powerful demonstration of a life steeped in prayer."[104] He practiced what he believed. He taught his students how to pray and showed them as well. Veit Dietrich, Luther's friend, reported that Luther used to pray at least three hours a day: "I cannot sufficiently admire the singular steadfastness, the happy attitude, the faith and hope of this man in serious times. But he nurtures this without surcease by diligent occupation with the divine Word. There is not a day on which he does not devote at least three hours, the very ones most suitable for studying, to prayer."[105]

This is amazing, for Luther was preoccupied with many things as a husband and father, pastor, teacher, and writer, and yet he was still able to give so much time to prayer. "Even in the busiest periods of the Reformation," notes Kosten, "Luther averaged two hours of prayer daily."[106] Undoubtedly, an essential part of the Reformer's triumph and achievement was prayer. He accomplished much because he prayed much. For Luther, everything must be attained through prayer:

> Let this be said as an exhortation to pray that we may form the habit of praying with all diligence and earnestness.... Moreover, prayer is in truth highly necessary for us; for we must, after all, achieve everything through prayer: to be able to keep what we have and to defend it against our enemies, the devil and the world. And whatever we are to obtain, we must seek here in prayer. Therefore prayer is comfort, strength, and

---

103. Plass, *What Luther Says*, 1082.
104. Ludwig, "Luther, Man of Prayer," 163.
105. Cited in ibid., 166.
106. Kosten, *Devotions and Prayers of Martin Luther*, 5.

salvation for us, our protection against all enemies, and our victory over them.[107]

As previously mentioned, Luther, as a man of prayer, was not self-centered. He did not spend his two or three hours praying only for himself. In fact, he says that "a man who prays for himself only does not offer a good prayer" and that praying for Christendom "is better than praying for ourselves only."[108] Luther prayed for his family, his congregation, and for other Christians. As a pastor, he was especially concerned with the conversion of sinners, which can be seen in his sermons: "You would be doing real Christian works if you interested yourself in sinners and went into your private room and earnestly implored God, saying: O my God, this is what I hear of so-and-so; that man is lying in sin, and that other one has fallen; O Lord, help him to rise, etc.—In this way you would assist him and would serve him."[109]

In his exposition of John 17:9, Luther also admonishes his readers to pray even for the salvation of their enemies: "So far as the person is concerned, we should pray for everybody; our prayer should be general and should embrace both friend and foe. We should pray that our enemies be converted and become our friends and, if not, that their doing and designating be bound to fail and have no success and that their persons perish rather than the Gospel and the kingdom of Christ."[110] However, Luther admits that when he thinks of his antagonists, he cannot pray without cursing them at the same time:

> I cannot pray without cursing at the same time. If I say: "Hallowed be Thy name," I must thereby say: May the names of the papists and all who blaspheme Thy name be accursed, condemned, and dishonored. If I say: "Thy kingdom come," I must thereby say: May the papacy, together with all king-

107. Plass, *What Luther Says*, 1094.
108. Ibid., 1099.
109. Ibid., 1100.
110. Ibid.

doms on earth that are opposed to Thy kingdom, be accursed, condemned, and destroyed. If I say: "Thy will be done," I must thereby say: May the plans and plots of the papists and of all who strive against Thy will and counsel be accursed, condemned, dishonored, and be brought to naught. Truly, thus my lips and heart pray day in, day out; and all who believe in Christ are praying in this way with me.[111]

One should not be quick to judge Luther, because his imprecatory prayer was intended to protect God's glory from His adversaries. It grieved Luther's heart to see people profane God's holy name. This shows Luther's concern for God's glory, which is the ultimate end of his prayer. This is why, for him, when the first petition ("Hallowed be Thy name") is prayed wholeheartedly, "God becomes everything and man becomes nothing."[112] In short, by treating God's name as holy, we give God all the praise and glory. Contrarily, when we defile His name, we make God nothing and ourselves everything. In this light one can understand that Luther, when thinking of those who blaspheme God, could not pray for them without cursing them.

What is noteworthy here is Luther's consistent prayer life. He prayed regularly, day and night. His life revolved around prayer. Even when he worked, he prayed. Kosten comments, "His daily work was a prayer and prayer was his daily work."[113] Luther's life was infused with prayer. He was a man who simply could not live without prayer; he was a true prayer warrior. When he prayed, he prayed as if God had already answered him. His prayer life also displays how much he depended on the grace of God. He prayed to God because he knew that only God could help him. In return, the Lord blessed Martin Luther tremendously, and, even though he is long dead, his life, labors, and prayers still continue to be a blessing to many throughout the world.

---

111. Ibid., 1101.
112. Cited in Lehmann, *Luther and Prayer*, 37.
113. Kosten, Preface to *Devotions and Prayers of Martin Luther*, 5.

*Chapter 2*

# John Calvin on Prayer as Communion with God

─────────── ∞Ͼ∞ ───────────

JOEL R. BEEKE

> *It is, therefore, by the benefit of prayer that we reach*
> *those riches which are laid up for us with the Heavenly*
> *Father. For there is a communion of men with God....*
>
> —JOHN CALVIN

John Calvin (1509–1564), renowned preacher and theologian, was also a pastor who wanted Christ's sheep to grow in the Christian life.[1] His pastoral emphases are abundantly evident in his writing on prayer.

Calvin focuses more on the practice of prayer than on its doctrine, which shows how practical his theology is.[2] For Calvin, prayer is the essence of the Christian life; it is a precious gift, not an academic problem.[3] He writes warmly and experientially[4] about prayer in his sermons and commentaries — especially on the Psalms — and

---

1. This chapter is a slightly expanded version of Joel R. Beeke, "The Communion of Men with God," in *John Calvin: A Heart for Devotion, Doctrine, and Doxology,* ed. Burk Parsons (Orlando: Reformation Trust, 2008), 231–46.

2. Wilhelm Niesel, *The Theology of Calvin,* trans. Harold Knight (London: Lutterworth Press, 1956), 156.

3. Charles Partee, "Prayer as the Practice of Predestination," in *Calvinus Servus Christi,* ed. Wilhelm H. Neuser (Budapest: Pressabteilung des Raday-Kollegiums, 1988), 246.

4. Robert Douglas Loggie stresses that it is particularly Calvin's discussion of prayer in the *Institutes,* 3.20, that contributes to the experiential flavor of his third

in one of his longest chapters of the *Institutes* (3.20), which spans seventy pages in the Battles-McNeill edition.[5] Editor John T. McNeill notes, "This thoughtful and ample chapter, with its tone of devout warmth, takes its place in the forefront of historically celebrated discussions of prayer."[6]

In this chapter, I would like to look at Calvin's thought on prayer: what it is; how effective it is; its purposes, methods, and rules; how it is built on a trinitarian foundation; and how prayer promotes authentic piety. Throughout, we will notice that though Calvin sets high standards for prayer, even acknowledging that praying rightly is a "peculiar gift,"[7] he assures his readers that these standards are not his but God's, as taught in His Word. As such, these standards are not attainable by our sinful human natures,[8] but God is pleased to help His children pray (Rom. 8:26).

## The Definition and Effectiveness of Prayer

In the final edition of his *Institutes*, Calvin defines prayer as "a communion of men with God by which, having entered the heavenly sanctuary, they appeal to him in person concerning his promises in order to experience…that what they believed was not in vain."[9] Elsewhere, he writes that prayer is "a communication between God and us whereby we expound to him our desires, our joys, our sighs, in a word, all the thoughts of our hearts."[10]

---

book ("Chief Exercise of Faith—An Exposition of Calvin's Doctrine of Prayer," *The Hartford Quarterly* 5, 2 [1965]:67).

5. Only Calvin's chapter on faith is longer in the original *Institutes*.

6. John Calvin, *Institutes of the Christian Religion*, ed. John T. McNeill; trans. Ford Lewis Battles (Philadelphia: Westminster Press, 1960), 2:850 n. 1 (hereafter, Inst.).

7. Inst. 3.20.5.

8. John Calvin, *Commentaries of Calvin* (Grand Rapids: Eerdmans, 1948–50), on Jeremiah 29:12.

9. Inst. 3.20.2.

10. John Calvin, *Instruction in Faith*, trans. Paul T. Fuhrmann (Philadelphia: Westminster, 1949), 57.

Calvin considered prayer as holy and familiar conversation with God, our heavenly Father; reverently speaking, it is family conversation, or even intimate covenantal conversation in which the believer confides in God as a child confides in his father.[11] Prayer is "an emotion of the heart within, which is poured out and laid open before God."[12] In prayer we both communicate and commune with our Father in heaven, feeling our transparency in His presence. Like Christ in Gethsemane, we cast our "desires, sighs, anxieties, fears, hopes, and joys into the lap of God."[13] Through prayer, a Christian puts his "worries bit by bit on God."[14] We are "permitted to pour into God's bosom the difficulties which torment us, in order that he may loosen the knots which we cannot untie."[15] Prayer is the outpouring of the soul, the deepest root of piety, the bedrock of assurance. Prayer is the most important part of the Christian life; it is the lifeblood of every true believer.[16]

A fundamental aspect of Calvin's thought on prayer is that prayer was not primarily instituted for God, but rather for man. Prayer is a means given to man so that he might, by faith, "reach those riches which are laid up for us with the Heavenly Father."[17] Calvin demonstrates how prayer works in the life of the believer. He says that prayer allows the believer to appeal to the providence, predestination, omnipotence, and omniscience of God the Father. Prayer calls down the Father's tender mercy and care for His children because having prayed, we have a sense of peace that God knows all and that He "has both the will and the power to take the best care of us."[18]

---

11. *Commentary* on Psalm 10:13; cf. Herman J. Selderhuis, *Calvin's Theology of the Psalms* (Grand Rapids: Baker, 2007), 219.

12. Inst. 3.20.29; cf. Ronald S. Wallace, *Calvin's Doctrine of the Christian Life* (London: Oliver and Boyd, 1959), 281–82.

13. *Commentary* on Psalm 89:38–39.

14. *Commentary* on Psalm 86:6.

15. *Commentary* on Genesis 18:25.

16. *Commentary* on Psalm 14:4.

17. Inst. 3.20.3.

18. Inst. 3.20.2.

The childlike outpouring of the soul before its heavenly Father involves entreaties and thanksgiving.[19] Proper requests include "those things which make for the extension of his [God's] glory and the setting forth of his name, and those benefits which conduce [serve] to our own advantage." Proper thanksgivings "celebrate with due praise his [God's] benefits toward us, and credit to his generosity every good that comes to us."[20] Owing to our spiritual needs and poverty as well as God's liberality, "we must assiduously use both kinds of prayer."[21]

Two objections often surface about Calvin's understanding of prayer. First is that when the believer obediently submits to God's will, he relinquishes his own will. To that objection, Calvin would respond that through the act of submissive prayer, the believer invokes God's providence to act on his behalf. Thus, under the Spirit's guidance, man's will and God's will work together.

Second is that prayer seems superfluous in light of God's omniscience and omnipotence. To that objection, Calvin responds that God ordained prayer not for Himself, but as an exercise of piety for man. Our prayers do not get in the way of providence because God, in His providence, ordains the means along with the end. Prayer is thus a means ordained to receive what God has planned to bestow.[22] What God "has determined to give of His own free will, even before He is asked, He promises to give all the same in response to our prayers."[23] Prayer is a way in which believers seek and receive what God has determined to do for them from eternity.[24]

Prayer does not change God or His decrees for three reasons: first, God is immutable; second, God's good pleasure governs

19. Calvin, *Instruction in Faith*, 5–59.
20. Inst. 3.30.28.
21. Calvin, *Instruction in Faith*, 58–59; Wallace, *Calvin's Doctrine of the Christian Life*, 284–86.
22. Inst. 3.20.3.
23. *Commentary* on Matthew 6:8.
24. Partee, "Prayer as the Practice of Predestination," 254; cf. David Crump, *Knocking on Heaven's Door: A New Testament Theology of Petitionary Prayer* (Grand Rapids: Baker Academic, 2006), 297.

everything; and third, God is in control of everything, including our prayers. If prayer could change God or His decrees, the human will would usurp from God at least part of His control of history, which would deny God's all-controlling grace and would destroy our faith.[25] Rather, "prayer is something we do with God's help on the basis of what God has done for us in eternal election."[26]

Nevertheless, prayer is still effective, for these two truths must never be forgotten: "first, that in His divine wisdom God anticipates our prayers; and second, that in His divine love God responds to them."[27] It is against God's nature not to hear and answer the prayers of His people. God feels drawn to help us and not to disappoint us in His grace.[28]

Bruce Ware summarizes Calvin's view of effective prayer as follows: "While prayer never coerces God to act other than his infinite wisdom has willed, it nevertheless is one important and necessary condition which must be present for certain aspects of God's work to be carried out. Prayer, then, is not contrary to divine sovereignty but is a divinely ordained instrument functioning within the sphere of God's sovereign wisdom and power in carrying out his will."[29] Ultimately, God's response to prayer is a "divine response to a divine initiative in the elect."[30] Prayer is effective because it is grounded in God and flows out of His sovereign, loving grace at work in us.

**The Purposes and Method of Prayer**

According to Calvin in Book 3, chapter 20, there are at least six purposes of prayer: (1) to fly to God with every need and gain from

25. Inst. 1.17.12; 3.20.43; Partee, "Prayer as the Practice of Predestination," 252.
26. Ibid., 254.
27. *Commentary* on Psalm 119:38.
28. *Commentary* on Psalm 65:2; Selderhuis, *Calvin's Theology of the Psalms*, 225.
29. Bruce A. Ware, "The Role of Prayer and the Word in the Christian Life According to John Calvin," *Studia Biblica et Theologica* 12 (1982):90. Cited in David Calhoun, "Prayer: 'The Chief Exercise of Faith,'" in *A Theological Guide to Calvin's Institutes: Essays and Analysis,* ed. David W. Hall (Phillipsburg, N.J.: P&R, 2008), 352.
30. Partee, "Prayer as the Practice of Predestination," 255.

Him what is lacking in ourselves to live the Christian life; (2) to
learn to desire wholeheartedly only what is right as we place all
our petitions before God; (3) to prepare us to receive God's benefits and responses to our petitions with humble gratitude; (4) to
meditate on God's kindness to us as we receive what we have asked
for; (5) to instill the proper spirit of delight for God's answers in
prayer; and (6) to confirm God's faithful providence so that we may
glorify Him and trust in His present help more readily as we witness His regularly answering our prayers.[31] All of these purposes are
designed to foster communion with God so that "the promises of
God should have their way with us."[32]

These purposes should be pursued in a biblically directed way.
For Calvin, faith and prayer are inseparable. Faith nourishes and
compels prayer, and prayer nourishes and confirms faith.[33] "The true
test of faith lies in prayer," for "we cannot pray to God without
faith."[34] Prayer that proceeds from faith is the only way to invoke
God. "It is faith that obtains whatever is granted to prayer."[35]

The Bible teaches that prayer is the chief and perpetual exercise of faith, Calvin says.[36] Prayer cannot help but express the hope
and joy that are inevitably attached to faith.[37] As Walter Stuermann
says: "One may say that prayer is a catalyst for faith, a condition
under which the transaction between man and God progresses
swiftly toward perfection.... It is the principal means by which the
faithful are armed to do battle with Satan and by which they are
enabled to enjoy a confidence, peace, and joy in spite of the warfare
in which they are engaged."[38]

31. Inst. 3.20.3.
32. Cited in Niesel, *Theology of Calvin*, 157.
33. *Commentary* on Zephaniah 3:7; Acts 8:22.
34. *Commentary* on Matthew 21:21; Romans 8:26.
35. Inst. 3.20.11.
36. *Commentary* on Matthew 21:21.
37. *Commentary* on Psalm 91:15.
38. Walter Earl Stuermann, *A Critical Study of Calvin's Concept of Faith* (Tulsa,
Okla.: Edwards Brothers, 1952), 303, 313, 314.

Prayer must be rightly grounded in God's Word by faith. "Prayer rightly begun springs from faith, and faith, from hearing God's Word."[39] The content of our prayers must be shaped, controlled, and restrained by Scripture. This faith provides boldness and confidence in prayer. As Ware says, "This progression from the Word to faith to prayer is, for Calvin, the key to apprehending from God all that is necessary to live the Christian life."[40]

Such prayer leans on God's promises.[41] Calvin writes: "Let us learn that God in his promises is set before us as if he were a willing debtor."[42] God's promises supply meditation and fuel for prayer.[43] "We testify by prayer, that we hope to obtain from God the grace which he has promised. Thus anyone who has no faith in the promises, prays dissemblingly."[44] Furthermore, through Christ's intercession, prayer obtains what God promises by faith. "We dig up by prayer the treasures that were pointed out by the Lord's gospel [promises], and which our faith has gazed upon."[45]

The promises of God buttress our faith because God has bound Himself to fulfill them. Those covenant promises invite and allure us to prayer.[46] God would deny Himself and His covenant were He not to fulfill them.[47]

## The Rules of Prayer

For Calvin, prayer is not some undisciplined habit of Christians. He writes, "Unless we fix certain hours in the day for prayer, it easily

---

39. Inst. 3.20.27.

40. Ware, "The Role of Prayer and the Word," 88.

41. *Commentary* on Psalm 85:5.

42. *Commentary* on Psalm 119:58.

43. Wallace, *Calvin, Geneva, and the Reformation,* 211.

44. *Commentary* on James 1:6.

45. Inst. 3.20.2.

46. *Commentary* on Psalm 50:14; 36:13; cited in Selderhuis, *Calvin's Theology of the Psalms,* 220.

47. For covenantal prayer in Calvin, see Peter Lillback, *The Binding of God: Calvin's Role in the Development of Covenant Theology* (Grand Rapids: Baker, 2001), 26–69.

slips from our memory."[48] Calvin prescribes several rules to guide believers in offering effectual, fervent prayer.[49] The first is *a heartfelt sense of reverence.* In prayer we must be "disposed in mind and heart as befits those who enter conversation with God."[50] Our prayers should arise from "the bottom of our heart."[51] Calvin calls for a disciplined mind and heart, asserting that "the only persons who duly and properly gird themselves to pray are those who are so moved by God's majesty that, freed from earthly cares and affections, they come to it."[52]

The second rule is *a heartfelt sense of need and repentance.* We must "pray from a sincere sense of want and with penitence," maintaining "the disposition of a beggar."[53] Calvin does not mean that believers should pray for every whim that arises in their hearts, but that they must pray penitently in accord with God's will, keeping His glory in focus, yearning for every request "with sincere affection of heart, and at the same time desiring to obtain it from him."[54]

The third rule is to have *a heartfelt sense of humility and trust in God.* True prayer requires that "we yield all confidence in ourselves and humbly plead for pardon," trusting in God's mercy alone for blessings both spiritual and temporal,[55] always remembering that the least drop of faith is more powerful than unbelief.[56] Any other approach to God will only promote pride, which will destroy us; "if we claim for ourselves anything, even the least bit," we will be in grave danger of destroying ourselves in God's presence.[57]

---

48. *Commentary* on Daniel 6:10.
49. Inst. 3.20.4–16.
50. Inst. 3.20.4–5.
51. John Calvin, *Sermons on the Epistle to the Ephesians* (Edinburgh: Banner of Truth Trust, 1973), 679.
52. Inst. 3.20.5.
53. Inst. 3.20.6–7.
54. Inst. 3.20.6; cf. Wallace, *Calvin's Doctrine of the Christian Life*, 280–81.
55. Inst. 3.20.8–10.
56. Inst. 3.2.17.
57. Inst. 3.20.8.

The final rule is to have *a heartfelt sense of confident hope.*[58] The confidence that our prayers will be answered does not arise in ourselves but through the Holy Spirit working in us. In believers' lives, faith and hope conquer fear so that we are able to "ask in faith, nothing wavering" (James 1:6). True prayer is confident of success, owing to Christ and the covenant, "for the blood of our Lord Jesus Christ seals the pact which God has concluded with us."[59] Believers thus approach God boldly and cheerfully because such "confidence is necessary in true invocation...which becomes the key that opens to us the gate of the kingdom of heaven."[60]

These rules may seem overwhelming—even unattainable—in the face of a holy, omniscient God. Calvin acknowledges that our prayers are fraught with weakness and failure. "No one has ever carried this out with the uprightness that was due," he writes.[61] But God tolerates "even our stammering and pardons our ignorance," allowing us to gain familiarity with Him in prayer, though it be in "a babbling manner."[62] In short, we will never feel like worthy petitioners. Our checkered prayer life is often attacked by doubts,[63] but such struggles show us our ongoing need for prayer itself as a "lifting up of the spirit"[64] and continually drive us to Jesus Christ who alone will "change the throne of dreadful glory into the throne of grace."[65] Calvin concludes that "Christ is the only way, and the one access, by which it is granted us to come to God."[66]

---

58. Inst. 3.20.11–14.

59. Cited in Niesel, *The Theology of Calvin*, 153.

60. *Commentary* on Ephesians 3:12; for a helpful explanation of Calvin's four rules of prayer, see Don Garlington, "Calvin's Doctrine of Prayer," *The Banner of Truth*, no. 323–24 (Aug.–Sept. 1990):45–50, and Stephen Matteucci, "A Strong Tower for Weary People: Calvin's Teaching on Prayer," *The Founders Journal* (Summer 2007):21–23.

61. Inst. 3.20.16.

62. Ibid.; *Commentary on the Psalms*, 2:171.

63. *Commentary* on Matthew 21:21.

64. Inst. 3.20.1, 5, 16; cf. Joel R. Beeke, *The Quest for Full Assurance: The Legacy of Calvin and His Successors* (Edinburgh: Banner of Truth Trust, 1999), 49.

65. Inst. 3.20.17.

66. Inst. 3.20.19.

## The Trinitarian Focus of Prayer

Calvin stresses the trinitarian aspect of prayer. Prayer originates with the Father, is made possible through the Son, and is worked out in the soul by the Spirit, through whom it returns via Christ to the Father. The triune God gives, hears, and answers prayer.

Prayer is given by the Father, who graciously invites us to pray through Christ, buttressing that invitation with His promises. Apart from Christ, it is "folly and rashness for mortals to presume to address God."[67] They should, rather, wait for the Father's call that He implements through His Word, "for when he promises to be our Savior he shows that he will always be ready to receive us. He does not wait till we come seeking him; rather, he offers himself and exhorts us to pray to him—and in doing so, tests our faith."[68] He draws us to prayer by the very sweetness of His name *Father*.

Calvin devotes considerable attention to the work of Christ in prayer.[69] In His walk on earth, Jesus counseled His disciples to ask anything in His name (John 16:23). Only by His name can we have access to the Father, Calvin says. God will hear our prayers for the sake of His Son when we pray in His name.[70] Calvin also gives a stern warning that if we do not approach God in the name of Jesus Christ, "no way and no access to God remain; nothing is left in his throne but wrath, judgment, and terror."[71]

Christ is the nexus between the believer and God; He is the junction where the believer's sinful prayers are purified "by sprinkled blood" and presented to the Father.[72] "Let us learn to wash our prayers with the blood of our Lord Jesus Christ," Calvin counsels.[73]

---

67. Sermon on 1 Timothy 2:8, in *Grace and Its Fruits: Selections from John Calvin on the Pastoral Epistles*, ed. Joseph Hill (Darlington, England: Evangelical Press, 2000), 259–60, cited in Hesselink, *On Prayer*, 4.

68. Ibid.

69. E.g., Inst. 3.20.17–20.

70. Inst. 3.20.17.

71. Inst. 3.20.19.

72. Inst. 3.20.18.

73. John Calvin, *Sermons on Election and Reprobation*, trans. John Fields (Audubon, N.J.: Old Paths, 1996), 210.

Christ is also our intercessor in heaven, the "only way, and the one access, by which it is granted us to come to God."[74] "God can listen to no prayers without the intercession of Christ."[75] Christ's finished work and the "power of his death [avail] as an everlasting intercession in our behalf."[76] We come through Christ and with Christ to the Father, so that "Christ becomes the precentor who leads the prayers of his people."[77]

The Holy Spirit also plays a crucial role in the prayer life of believers, Calvin says. He is "our teacher in prayer, to tell us what is right and [to] temper our emotions."[78] He intercedes for us with groans that are unutterable (Rom. 8:26). Calvin explains that He "arouses in us assurance, desires, and sighs, to conceive which our natural powers could scarcely suffice."[79] He affects our heart in such a way that these prayers "penetrate into heaven itself by their fervency."[80]

Calvin further addresses the believers' response when the Spirit is not present in prayer. He says that this is no excuse to cease praying until they feel the Spirit come upon them, but rather they must importunately "demand that they be inflamed with the fiery darts of his Spirit so as to be rendered fit for prayer."[81] We should never cease to pray for the increase of the Spirit.[82]

---

74. Inst. 3.20.19.

75. *Commentary* on Exodus 29:38.

76. Inst. 3.20.20.

77. T. H. L. Parker, *Calvin: An Introduction to His Thought* (Louisville: Westminster John Knox Press, 1995), 110. A "precentor" (Latin, "first singer" or "singer before") is a person who leads worship.

78. Inst. 3.20.5.

79. Ibid.

80. *Commentary* on Romans 8:26.

81. Geneva Catechism, Q. 245, Reid trans., 131, cited in Hesselink, *On Prayer*, 10.

82. *Commentary* on Acts 1:14; cf. Wallace, *Calvin's Doctrine of the Christian Life*, 286–87.

## Prayer as Part of Piety

Calvin's concept of piety (*pietas*) includes attitudes and actions that are directed to the adoration and service of God. Prayer is the principal and perpetual exercise of faith and the chief element of piety, Calvin says.[83] Prayer shows God's grace to the believer even as the believer offers praises to God and asks for His faithfulness. Prayer expresses piety both privately and corporately.[84] Herman Selderhuis says that Calvin's commentary on the Psalms stresses that "prayer is not so much about moving God to a responsive action so much as it is given to bring a believer to greater confidence" in God. This, in turn, promotes a lifestyle of authentic piety.[85] An increased piety requires prayer, for prayer diminishes self-love and multiplies dependence on God. Prayer unites God and man, not in substance, but in will and purpose. Like the Lord's Supper, prayer lifts the believer to Christ and renders glory to God.

That glory is the purpose of the first three petitions of the Lord's Prayer as well as other petitions dealing with His creation. Since creation looks to God's glory for its preservation, the entire Lord's Prayer is directed to God's glory.[86] The Lord's Prayer, which Calvin dwells on at length in the *Institutes*, is a model prayer for us; we are bound by its pattern, not its words. Our words may be "utterly different, yet the sense ought not to vary."[87] The Lord's Prayer shows us how all our prayers must be controlled, formed, and inspired by the Word of God.[88] Only the Word can provide holy boldness in prayer,

---

83. See Loggie, "Chief Exercise of Faith," 65–81; H.W. Maurer, "An Examination of Form and Content in John Calvin's Prayers" (Ph.D. diss., Edinburgh, 1960); Joel R. Beeke, *Puritan Reformed Spirituality* (Darlington, England: Evangelical Press, 2006), 1–33.

84. Cf. Thomas A. Lambert, "Preaching, Praying, and Policing the Reform in Sixteenth Century Geneva" (Ph.D. diss., University of Wisconsin-Madison, 1998), 393–480.

85. Selderhuis, *Calvin's Theology of the Psalms*, 224–26.

86. Inst. 3.20.11.

87. Inst. 3.20.49.

88. Joel R. Beeke, "Calvin on Piety," *The Cambridge Companion to John Calvin*, ed. Donald K. McKim (Cambridge: University Press, 2004), 125–52.

"which rightly accords with fear, reverence, and solicitude."[89] I. John Hesselink says that Calvin's writing on the Lord's Prayer includes four things: (1) it revolves around the reconciling work of Christ, (2) is corporate in nature, (3) unveils the nature of God's kingdom, and (4) involves our daily physical needs.[90]

We must be disciplined and steadfast in prayer, for prayer keeps us in fellowship with Christ. Without His intercessions, our prayers would be rejected.[91] Thus, prayer is the channel between God and man. It is how the Christian expresses his praise and adoration of God and asks for God's help in submissive piety.[92]

There is also a corporate element of piety in prayer. Upon Christ's ascension, the church now has "a surer advocate,"[93] Calvin says. Christ is an individual advocate as well as a corporate advocate to whom the church can apply for strength and comfort. Consequently, Calvin counsels us "to direct all intercessions of the whole church to that sole intercession" of Christ.[94]

Furthermore, Christ has entered into the heavens before the saints, "and thus the mutual prayers for one another of all members yet laboring on earth rise to the Head."[95] Thus the corporate church and the individual believer pray for one another through and in Christ's name. The best way that we can love one another as believers is to pray for each other and to identify with each other so that we weep and rejoice together. Our prayers should include the universal church and all mankind, even generations unborn.[96]

89. Inst. 3.20.14; Wallace, *Calvin's Doctrine of the Christian Life*, 276–79.
90. Hesselink, *On Prayer*, 26–30.
91. *Commentary* on Hebrews 7:26.
92. Lionel Greve, "Freedom and Discipline in the Theology of John Calvin, William Perkins, and John Wesley: An Examination of the Origin and Nature of Pietism" (Ph.D. diss., The Hartford Seminary Foundation, 1976), 143–44. For how Calvin's emphasis on prayer impacted the Reformed tradition, see Diane Karay Tripp, "Daily Prayer in the Reformed Tradition: An Initial Survey," *Studia Liturgica* 21 (1991):76–107, 190–219.
93. Inst. 3.20.18.
94. Inst. 3.20.19.
95. Inst. 3.20.20.
96. *Commentary* on Psalm 90:16.

In intercessory prayer, we forgo our propensity for selfishness and "clothe ourselves with a public character," sharing with Christ in His intercession.[97]

The prerequisite of effective, corporate prayer is effective, private prayer, Calvin says. Individual piety must be learned and nurtured so that the church's corporate piety can grow. Calvin refers to the Old Testament temple as bearing the God-given title of "house of prayer" and that therefore "the chief part of his [God's] worship lies in the office of prayer." By this corporate prayer, the "unity of the faith" is nurtured so that "the prayers of the church are never ineffectual."[98]

In his commentary on the Psalms, Calvin focuses on singing as a part of prayer that helps lift up the heart to God. The Psalms are, in themselves, a prayer book, for they are "an anatomy of all the parts of the soul." In the commentary's preface, Calvin says that prayer proceeds "from a sense of our need, and next, from faith in the promises of God." He says that the Psalms are particularly helpful in making believers aware of their need, and they also tell where to find the "remedies for their cure."[99] The Psalms, whether sung individually or corporately, teach us to place our trust in God and to find remission of our sins in Jesus Christ.[100]

The singing of Psalms gives access to God and freedom "to lay open before him our infirmities."[101] Calvin includes singing as a way to "exercise the mind in thinking of God and keep it attentive." Singing allows believers to glorify God together, and it allows "all men mutually, each one from his brother [to] receive the confession of faith and be invited and prompted by his example."[102]

---

97. *Commentary* on Psalm 79:6.

98. Inst. 3.20.29.

99. *Commentary on the Psalms,* "The Author's Preface," 1:xxxvii.

100. Ibid., 1:xxxix; cf. Ross J. Miller, "Calvin's Understanding of Psalm-Singing as a Means of Grace" and "Music and the Spirit: Psalm-Singing in Calvin's Liturgy," in *Calvin Studies VI* (Colloquium on Calvin Studies at Davidson College, 1992), 35–58.

101. *Commentary on the Psalms,* 1:xxxviii.

102. Inst. 3.20.31.

Singing greatly aids prayer, not only because it glorifies God but also because it promotes corporate piety towards God.

## Persevering for Precious Communion in Prayer

Throughout his writings, Calvin offers a theology on prayer. He presents the throne room of God as glorious, holy, and sovereign while also accessible, desirable, and precious in and through Christ. Given the rich blessings accessible to us through prayer, those who refuse to pray "neglect a treasure, buried and hidden in the earth, after it had been pointed out"[103] to them. They also commit idolatry by defrauding God, since prayerlessness is a blatant denial that "God is the author of every good thing."[104]

We must persevere in pursuing precious access to God in prayer, Calvin concludes.[105] Discouragements may abound and almost overwhelm us: "Our warfare is unceasing and various assaults arise daily." But that gives all the more reason to discipline ourselves to persevere in prayer, even if "we must repeat the same supplications not twice or three times only, but as often as we need, a hundred and a thousand times."[106] Ceasing to pray when God does not answer us quickly is the surest mark that we have never become a believer.[107]

Calvin counsels believers not only to better methods of prayer but to a deeper devotion and a surer access to the triune God who has given the gift of prayer. He modeled this prayer life by accompanying every public act with prayer, providing forms of prayer,[108] and appointing days of prayer for a variety of occasions—as well as

103. Inst. 3.20.1.
104. Inst. 3.20.14.
105. Inst. 3.20.51–52.
106. Cited in Hesselink, *On Prayer*, 19.
107. *Commentary* on Psalm 22:4; Wallace, *Calvin, Geneva, and the Reformation*, 214.
108. John Calvin, *Treatises on the Sacraments of the Church of Geneva, Forms of Prayer, and Confessions of Faith*, trans. by Henry Beveridge (reprint, Grand Rapids: Reformation Heritage Books, 2002); Charles E. Edwards, *Expositions and Prayers from Calvin* (Philadelphia: Presbyterian Board of Publication, 1897); Clyde Manschreck, ed., *Prayers of the Reformers* (Philadelphia: Muhlenberg Press, 1958); W.

privately in his own life.[109] These merge well in the last prayer he records in the commentary on Ezekiel, which, due to failing health, he was not able to complete:

> Grant, Almighty God, since we have already entered in hope upon the threshold of our eternal inheritance, and know that there is a certain mansion for us in heaven after Christ has been received there, who is our head, and the first-fruits of our salvation: Grant, I say, that we may proceed more and more in the course of thy holy calling until at length we reach the goal, and so enjoy that eternal glory of which thou affordest us a taste in this world, by the same Christ our Lord. Amen.[110]

Ultimately, for Calvin, prayer is a heavenly act, a holy and precious communing with the triune God in His glorious throne room, grounded in an assured, eschatological hope.[111]

"Lord, teach us to pray" (Luke 11:1).

---

de Greef, *The Writings of John Calvin: An Introductory Guide* (Grand Rapids: Baker, 1989), 126–31.

109. Elsie McKee, *John Calvin: Writings on Pastoral Piety* (New York: Paulist Press, 2001), 29, 167ff.

110. *Commentary* on Ezekiel 20:44.

111. Wallace, *Calvin, Geneva, and the Reformation*, 214.

*Chapter 3*

# John Knox:
# A Theologian of Prayer
━━━━━━━━━━━━━━━━━cↄ✠ↄↄ━━━━━━━━━━━━━━━━━

## BRIAN G. NAJAPFOUR

*I fear the prayer of John Knox more than the combined
armies of Europe.*
　　　　　　　　　　　　—MARY, QUEEN OF SCOTS

John Knox, born about 1514 in or near Haddington, Scotland,[1]
is pictured in various ways. W. Stanford Reid portrays him as the
"trumpeter of God," an epithet that Knox used to depict himself.[2]
David D. Murison calls him "the writer" or "the pamphleteer."[3]
Lemuel B. Bissell refers to him as "the father of Presbyterianism
in Scotland."[4] However, the designation "theologian of prayer" can
also be rightfully conferred on him. This chapter considers a variety
of aspects of Knox's theology of prayer and will conclude with a
cursory look at his life of prayer.

---

1. The place of Knox's birth is uncertain. If the Gifford-gate was Knox's place
of birth, then he was born *in* Haddington, but if he was born in the village Gifford,
then *near* Haddington. For this reason, historians say "in or near Haddington," an
expression that I have adopted.

2. See W. Stanford Reid, *Trumpeter of God: A Biography of John Knox* (New
York: Charles Scribner's Sons, 1974).

3. See David D. Murison, *Knox: The Writer* (Edinburgh: The Saint Andrews
Press, 1975).

4. Lemuel B. Bissell, "Introduction" to *The Presbyterian Pulpit, A Volume of
Sermons by Ministers of the Synod of Michigan* (Monroe, Mich.: Sermon Printing
House, 1898), 5.

## Knox's Theology of Prayer

Knox's theology of prayer can best be seen in *A Treatise on Prayer, or A Confession, and Declaration of Prayers,*[5] also called *A Declaration of The True Nature of Prayer* (hereafter *Treatise on Prayer*), which he usually used in his sermons in the congregations where he preached.[6] He wrote this treatise in 1553 before he left England for Dieppe and after King Edward VI died. But it was not published until July 1554, a year after Mary Tudor became queen of England.[7]

The *Treatise on Prayer*, as its subtitle shows, purposely addresses three basic questions about prayer: (1) what true prayer is, (2) how we should pray, and (3) for what we should pray.[8] In its entirety, however, this treatise may be divided into five major segments that can be difficult to detect because the treatise's structure is not always obvious. The first division requires that prayer be made with utmost reverence because of the character of God.[9] The second section, on the same basis, stresses the need of repentance in prayer.[10] The third rebukes hypocrisy in prayer,[11] while the fourth castigates unbelief.[12] The fifth emphasizes that godly prayer presupposes "the perfect [complete] knowledge of the Advocate, Intercessor, and Mediator."[13] This is then followed by practical considerations and applications.[14]

5. John Knox, "A Treatise on Prayer, or A Confession, and Declaration of Prayers," in *Selected Writings of John Knox: Public Epistles, Treatises, and Expositions to the Year 1559*, ed. Kevin Reed (Dallas: Presbyterian Heritage Publications, 1995), 71–100. For the standard critical edition of this treatise, see *The Works of John Knox*, ed. David Laing (Edinburgh: Printed for the Bannatyne Club, 1854–1864), 3:81–107. Since the Reed edition reflects modern spelling, punctuation, and grammar, subsequent quotations from *Treatise on Prayer* will be taken from this edition, which is also based on the definitive edition of Laing.

6. Thomas M'Crie, *Life of John Knox* (Edinburgh: W. Blackwood and Sons, 1855), 55.

7. Ibid.

8. Knox, "A Treatise on Prayer," in *Select Writings*, 73.

9. Ibid., 74–76.

10. Ibid., 76–79.

11. Ibid., 79–80.

12. Ibid., 80–85.

13. Ibid., 85–90.

14. Ibid., 90–98.

Since it is in the *Treatise on Prayer* that Knox reveals his doctrinal position on prayer, it will be the focus of this study of Knox's theology of prayer, but I will interact with his other writings as well. I will look at the following: description of prayer; encouragement to pray, place, time, object, and method of prayer; the Spirit's work and Christ's role in prayer; and the issue of delay and denial in prayer.

*Description of Prayer*

1. Prayer as an indication of true faith.

Knox opens his treatise by emphasizing the necessity of "the right invocation of God's name, otherwise called perfect prayer."[15] By "perfect prayer," Knox does not mean perfect in an absolute sense, but rather "perfect" in the sense that it is right. If a man is not acquainted with this perfect or right prayer, his being a Christian is in question since prayer "is the very branch which springs forth of true faith."[16] Prayer is an inherent fruit of saving faith; if a man does not continually pray, he may not have been born again. As Knox argues, if he does not pray, even if he is "endued with whatsoever other virtues, yet, in the presence of God, is he reputed for no Christian at all."[17] "It is a manifest sign, that such as are always negligent in prayer do understand nothing of perfect faith; for if the fire be without heat, or the burning lamp without light, then true faith may be without fervent prayer."[18]

Knox saw a close connection between true faith and perfect prayer. Perfect prayer emanates from true faith, and true faith produces perfect prayer. In this way, prayer becomes an indication of true faith.

2. Prayer as "an earnest and familiar talking with God."

Knox defines prayer as "an earnest and familiar talking with God, to whom we declare our miseries, whose support and help we implore

---

15. Ibid., 73.
16. Ibid.
17. Ibid.
18. Ibid.

and desire in our adversities, and whom we laud and praise for our benefits received."[19] As such, prayer "contains the exposition of our dolours [sorrows], the desire of God's defence, and the praising of his magnificent name."[20]

Since prayer is conversing with God, we must realize who God is and that this God we are speaking to is the "omnipotent Creator of heaven and earth, and of all the contents thereof; whom a thousand thousand angels assist and serve, giving obedience to his eternal majesty."[21] This realization, according to Knox, should provoke us to pray "most reverently," to flee assiduously from things that "offend his godly presence," and to ask for things "which may be pleasant and acceptable in God's presence," and "which may be most to his glory, and to the comfort of our conscience."[22] Otherwise, states Knox, "all our prayers are in vain."[23] God does not hear sinners—those who "do glory and continue in iniquity. So that of necessity, true repentance must needs be had, and go before perfect, or sincere invocation of God's name."[24]

## Encouragement to Pray

People sometimes do not want to pray to God or are ashamed to do so because they have feelings of unworthiness arising from what they have done against Him in the past. Knox advises such persons that they should rather flee to God with "a sorrowful and a repenting heart, saying with David, 'Heal my soul, O Lord, for I have offended against thee. Before I was afflicted, I transgressed, but now let me observe thy commandments.'"[25] Moreover, Knox reminds them of a twofold encouragement they have in God to pray: "To mitigate or ease the sorrows of our wounded conscience,

---

19. Ibid.
20. Ibid., 73–74.
21. Ibid., 74.
22. Ibid.
23. Ibid., 76.
24. Ibid., 77.
25. Ibid., 82.

our most prudent Physician has provided two plasters to give us encouragement to pray (notwithstanding the knowledge of offences committed): that is, a *precept* and a *promise*."[26]

1. The precept of God.

"The precept or commandment to pray," writes Knox, "is universal, frequently inculcated and repeated in God's scriptures."[27] He quotes several verses to support this: Psalm 50:15; Matthew 7:7 and 26:41; 1 Thessalonians 5:17; and 1 Timothy 2:1–2, 8.[28] For Knox, therefore, the mandate to pray is not only an encouragement but also a reason for us to pray. We ought to pray because God commands us to do so, even if we feel unworthy of being heard. After all, no one is worthy to come to God, but since He commands us to pray, we should pray regardless of circumstances. Knox cites the eighth commandment, "Thou shalt not steal," as an example to elucidate this point. He says, "For in this commandment, 'Thou shalt not steal,' is a precept *negative*; so, 'Thou shalt pray,' is a commandment *affirmative*. And God requires equal obedience of all and to all his commandments."[29] The sin of prayerlessness is not less sinful than the sin of theft. They incur the same guilt, for they both violate God's sacred law.

This indicates Knox's high regard for prayer. Indeed, he affirms, "Yet more boldly will I say: He who, when necessity constrains, desires not support and help of God, does provoke his wrath no less than such as make false gods or openly deny God."[30] Here Knox's point is that if we need to pray and we do not pray, we actually inflame God's holy fury, just as when we break His first two commandments. It is not, therefore, surprising when Knox declares, "Not to pray is sin most odious. Oh why cease we then to call instantly to his mercy, having his commandment so to do? Above all our

---

26. Ibid. (italics mine).
27. Ibid.
28. Ibid.
29. Ibid., 82–83.
30. Ibid., 83.

iniquities, we work manifest contempt and despising of him, when by negligence, we delay to call for his gracious support. Whoso does call upon God obeys his will, and finds therein no small consolation, knowing nothing is more acceptable to his Majesty than humble obedience."[31]

2. The promise of God.

People who have a strong sense of unworthiness to come to God should be encouraged to pray not only because of God's precept but also because of His promise. Despite our grievous sins against God, we may still hope that He will hear us if we come to Him with a repentant spirit. Knox explains: "That we shall not think God will not hear us, Isaiah says, 'Before ye cry I shall hear, and while they speak I shall answer.' And also 'if at even come sorrow or calamity, before the morning spring, I shall reduce and bring gladness.' And these most comfortable words does the Lord speak not to carnal Israel only, but to all men sorely oppressed, abiding God's deliverance."[32] Knox further insists that "the hope to obtain our petitions should depend upon the promises of God,"[33] and not on ourselves:

> Oh, hard are the hearts whom so manifold, most sweet, and sure promises do not mollify [make soft or tender]; whereupon should depend the hope to obtain our petitions. The indignity or unworthiness of ourselves is not to be regarded; for albeit we are far inferiors to the chosen who are departed in holiness and purity of life, yet, in that part we are equal, in that we have the same commandment to pray, and the same promise to be heard. For his Gracious Majesty esteems not prayer, neither grants the petition for any dignity of the person that prays, but for his promise sake only.[34]

31. Ibid.
32. Ibid., 84.
33. Ibid.
34. Ibid.

Knox shows that David, for this reason, relied on God's promise when he said, "Thou hast promised unto thy servant, O Lord, that thou wilt build a house for him; wherefore thy servant hath found in his heart to pray in thy sight, now even so, O Lord, thou art God, and thy words are true. Thou hast spoken these things unto thy servant; begin, therefore, to do according to thy promise; multiply, O Lord, the household of thy servant."[35]

God does not accept our petitions on the ground of our good works. Knox warns his readers, "Let us not think that we should be heard for anything proceeding of ourselves; for such as advance, boast, or depend anything upon their own justice, [God] repels from the presence of his mercy, and holds with the high proud Pharisee."[36] To bolster his point, Knox provides examples of prayers from David, Jeremiah, Isaiah, and Daniel (Psalm 79:8–9; Isaiah 64:5–6, 8–9; Jeremiah 14:7; Daniel 9:5, 18–19).[37] He concludes,

> Behold, that in these prayers is no mention of their own merits; but most humble confession, proceeding from a sorrowful and penitent heart; having nothing whereupon it might depend, but the free mercy of God alone, who had promised to be their God (that is, their help, comfort, defender, and deliverer).... Wherefore it is plain, that such men as, in their prayers, have respect to any virtue proceeding of themselves, thinking thereby their prayers are accepted, never prayed aright.[38]

The merciful God hears our prayers in response to His faithful promise to us in His Word, never in response to our good deeds toward Him. Noteworthy here is the way Knox intertwines the appeals to God's mercy and His promise. To depend on God's promise is but to depend on His mercy. However, if God does not regard our righteous works, why did David pray this way: "Preserve my soul; for I am holy: O thou my God, save thy servant that trust-

---

35. Ibid.
36. Ibid., 77.
37. Ibid.
38. Ibid., 78.

eth in thee" (Ps. 86:2)? Hezekiah prayed similarly: "I beseech thee, O LORD, remember now how I have walked before thee in truth and with a perfect heart, and have done that which is good in thy sight" (2 Kings 20:3). At first glance, David and Hezekiah seem to be asking God to listen to them on the basis of their holy and righteous doings, as if God is obliged to hear them. Knox anticipated this kind of question from his readers, so he immediately addresses it: "These words are not spoken of men glorious, neither yet trusting in their own works. But herein they testify themselves to be the sons of God, by regeneration; to whom he promises always to be merciful, and at all times to hear their prayers."[39]

In short, when David and Hezekiah brought up their good works to God, they were expressing their confidence that He would hear them because they were His children. It was their expression of faith in God that their prayers would be answered in accord with His promise. Knox puts it this way:

> And so their words spring from a wonted, constant, and fervent faith, surely believing that, as God of his infinite mercy had called them to his knowledge, not suffering them to walk after their own natural wickedness, but partly had taught them to conform themselves to his holy law; and that for the promised Seed's sake; so might he not leave them destitute of comfort, consolation, and defence in so great and extreme necessity. And so they allege not their justice to glory thereof, or to put trust therein, but to strengthen and confirm them in God's promises.
>
> And this consolation I would wish all Christians in their prayers; a testimony of a good conscience to assure them of God's promises.[40]

Here again we see Knox's twofold encouragement to pray: God's precept and promise. However, Knox seems to add one more encouragement, namely, God's blessing. According to Knox, there

---

39. Ibid.
40. Ibid., 79.

are some who say that we do not have to pray since God already knows what we need and that we do not have to understand what we pray because, after all, God understands the secrets of our hearts. But for Knox, "such men verily declare themselves never to have understood what perfect prayer meant, nor to what end Jesus Christ commanded us to pray."[41] Then Knox gives two reasons the Lord has commanded us to pray:

> First, that our hearts may be inflamed with continual fear, honour, and love of God, to whom we run for support and help whensoever danger or necessity requires; that we so learning to notify [make known] our desires in his presence, he may teach us what is to be desired, and what not. Second, that we, knowing our petitions to be granted by God alone (to him only we must render and give laud and praise), and that we, ever having his infinite goodness fixed in our minds, may constantly abide to receive that which with fervent prayer we desire.[42]

Knox shows here that even if God already knows our necessities, we must still pray, not only because it is a command but also because there is a blessing that follows. Prayer inflames our hearts "with continual fear, honour, and love of God." It thus draws us closer to God and keeps our eyes focused on Him. In short, it strengthens our souls. God instructs us to pray not only for His own pleasure but for our profit as well. Prayer is an instrument through which God showers His blessings upon us. When we ask why we should pray if God already perceives our needs, Knox answers that we should do so for the good of our souls.

*Place, Time, and Object of Prayer*
1. Place of prayer.
For Knox, the issues of place, time, and object of prayer are of great significance and are "not to be passed over with silence."[43] With

---

41. Ibid., 75.
42. Ibid.
43. Ibid., 94.

regard to the place of private prayer, there is no required or specific place, "although Jesus Christ commands us to enter into our chamber, and to close the door, and so to pray unto our Father secretly." This does not mean that we should pray only behind a closed door when we seek personal communion with God. Knox understands the words of Jesus figuratively—"that we should choose for our prayers such places as might offer least occasion to call us back from prayer; and also that we should expel forth of our minds, in time of our prayer, all vain cogitations."[44] "For otherwise," Knox reasons, "Jesus Christ himself does observe no special place of prayer; for we find him sometimes praying in Mount Olivet, sometimes in the desert, sometimes in the temple, and in the garden."[45] As far as private prayer is concerned, we can pray anywhere, but we should strive to find a place where we can solemnly commune with God. However, whenever danger or necessity requires us to pray, we should pray wherever we are: "Paul prayed in prison, and was heard by God. Who also commands men to pray in all places, lifting up unto God pure and clean hands; as we find that the prophets and most holy men did, whensoever danger or necessity required."[46]

Knox, on the other hand, believes that insofar as public or common prayer is concerned, there is an appointed place to be kept:

> But public and common prayers should be used in [the] place appointed for the assembly, from whence whosoever negligently extracts himself is in no wise excusable. I mean not, that to be absent from that place is sin, because that place is more holy than another; for the whole earth created by God is equally holy. But the promise made, that, "Wheresoever two or three be gathered together in my name, there shall I be in the midst of them," condemns all such as contemn the congregation gathered in his name. But mark well this word "gathered"; I mean not, to hear piping, singing, or playing; nor to patter upon beads, or books whereof they have no understanding;

44. Ibid.
45. Ibid., 94–95.
46. Ibid., 95.

nor to commit idolatry, honouring that for God which is no god indeed.[47]

Two things can be noted here. First, in public prayer, it is not the *place* that matters the most but the *promise* that Jesus will be present with those who assemble together in His name. The main issue is neglecting this promise. Thus, it is still God's promise that should motivate us to pray corporately. This again demonstrates that God's promise is crucial to Knox's theology of prayer. Second, also obvious is Knox's criticism of the Roman Catholic Church's practice of prayer. When Knox composed his *Treatise on Prayer*, Queen Mary, a staunch supporter of Roman Catholicism, was already trying to resurrect Catholicism in England. Knox was aware of this, so he emphatically reminded his readers that they were to gather in order to pray, and not to pipe, sing, play, or "patter upon beads, or books," such as the Breviary.

2. Time and object of prayer.

Beyond affirming that we should pray "for all men, and at all times,"[48] Knox advises that we should pray for "the household of faith as suffer persecution, and for commonwealths tyrannically oppressed…that God, of his mercy and power, will withstand the violence of such tyrants."[49] Obviously, as Knox was writing his treatise, he was anticipating possible persecution from the hand of the newly proclaimed Queen Mary.[50] Indeed, by 1554, a few months after the composition of this treatise, all Protestants were accused of heresy. It is with this circumstance in mind that Knox exhorts his readers to seriously pray for the protection of the persecuted as well as for the conversion of the persecutors. Knox himself, at the end of his discourse, prayed for this:

---

47. Ibid.

48. Ibid., 96.

49. Ibid.

50. Knox's *Treatise on Prayer* seems to have been composed in August 1553, a month after Mary became queen.

Behold our trouble and apparent destruction, and stay the
sword of thy vengeance before it devours us. Place above us,
O Lord, for thy great mercy's sake, such as a head, with such
rulers and magistrates as feareth thy name, and willeth the
glory of Christ Jesus to spread. Take not from us the light of
thy evangel [gospel], and suffer thou no Papistry to prevail in
this realm. Illuminate the heart of our sovereign lady Queen
Mary, with pregnant gifts of thy Holy Ghost; and inflame the
hearts of her council with thy true fear and love. Repress thou
the pride of those that would rebel; and remove from all hearts
the contempt of the word. Let not our enemies rejoice at our
destruction, but look thou to the honour of thy own name,
O Lord; and let thy gospel be preached with boldness in this
realm.... Mitigate the hearts of those that persecute us; and let
us not faint under the cross of our Saviour, but assist us with
the Holy Ghost, even to the end.[51]

This prayer reveals something about Knox's political character. As
a nineteenth-century editor of Knox's publications wrote, "He was
the friend of peace and order, instead of tumult and revolution; and
whatever might be his own personal sentiments, he was ready to
submit to every constitutional authority, even though it might be
impersonated in a 'female regime.'"[52]

Knox's views regarding the time and object of prayer may also
be found in *The Form of Prayers and Ministration of the Sacraments,
etc., used in the English Congregation at Geneva* (1556),[53] which Knox
himself, along with four other ministers, prepared.[54] The *Form*,
though not written solely by Knox, is essential to understanding
his theology of prayer since he employed it in his own congregation at Geneva. Later in 1564, the Church of Scotland approved

51. Ibid., 100.
52. *Select Practical Writings of John Knox* (Edinburgh: Printed for the Assembly's Committee, 1845), xvi.
53. John Knox, "The Form of Prayers and Ministration of the Sacraments,
etc., used in the English Congregation at Geneva," in *Works*, 4:141–214.
54. *Works*, 4:146–47. The other four ministers were William Whittingham,
Anthony Gilby, John Foxe, and Thomas Cole.

and received this same *Form* with slight alterations and additions;[55] henceforth, it became known as the *Book of Common Order* (1565).[56] The *Book* is also a good source for examining Knox's theology of prayer. Although it was not written entirely by him, it, as David Laing observes, "was sanctioned, if not partially prepared by" him.[57]

Some of the titles of the prayers in the *Book of Common Order* reflect Knox's sentiment toward the time and object of prayer:

- "A Prayer for the Whole State of Christ's Church"
- "Another Manner of Prayer After the Sermon"
- "Prayers Used in the Churches of Scotland, in the Time of Their Persecution by the Frenchmen: but Principally When the Lordes Table Was to Be Ministered"
- "A Thanksgiving unto God After Our Deliverance from the Tyranny of the Frenchmen; with Prayers Made for the Continuance of the Peace Betwixt the Realmes of England and Scotland"
- "A Prayer to Be Said in Visiting of the Sicke"
- "A Forme of Prayers to Be Used in Private House Everie Morning and Evening"
- "A Prayer to Be Said of the Childe, Before He Studie His Lesson"
- "A Prayer to Be Said Before a Man Begin His Worke"
- "A Prayer in Tyme of Affliction"
- "A Prayer for the King"[58]

---

55. Added to the *Form* are various prayers, Calvin's Catechism, and Sternhold and Hopkins's *Psalms in English Meter*.

56. *Works*, 4:148. See also John Knox, "The Book of Common Order: or the Form of Prayers and Ministration of the Sacraments, etc., approved and received by the Church of Scotland," in *Works*, 6:277. It is also known as *Knox's Psalms and Liturgy* or just *Knox's Liturgy*.

57. *Works*, 6:283. This *Book of Common Order* continued to be used until it was superseded by the *Directory* of the Westminster Divines.

58. Knox, "The Book of Common Order," in *Works*, 6:298–380.

*The Method of Prayer*

Are the prayers in the *Book of Common Order* intended to be read in worship? Did Knox favor the use of forms of prayer? Before we can answer these questions, we need to explore the views of some historians who have considered Knox an Anglican. Historians such as C. L. Warr and Gordon Donaldson advocate this view.[59] This would suggest that Knox was a supporter of the *Book of Common Prayer*, which contains prayers designed to be read in worship, and also that Knox practiced set forms of prayer. The *Book of Common Prayer*, first published in 1549, underwent three revisions: in 1552, 1559, and 1662. However, the idea that Knox was an Anglican has been convincingly disproved in W. Stanford Reid's article, "Knox's Attitude to the English Reformation." Reid argues on the basis of common sense that if "Knox had really favoured acceptance of the Anglican orders, confession and liturgy, one wonders why the Scots bothered preparing their own [i.e., *The Form of Prayers and Ministration of the Sacraments*]—but they did."[60] However, Reid admits that "undoubtedly some individuals [i.e., followers of Knox] employed the second Book of Common Prayer in their services..., but this did not mean that they felt that they should employ the prayer book in the same manner as did the English church. Whether they used it was a matter of freedom."[61] Reid further admits that at one point even Knox "advised his Berwick congregation to use the second Prayer Book [albeit on certain conditions] for the sake of peace, but at the same time under protest."[62]

James Stalker shares Reid's view: "There is some evidence that the English Book of Common Order, issued in the reign of Edward VI, was occasionally employed in the earliest stages of the Reformation in Scotland; and there is nothing surprising in this taking place at a time when Knox himself was officiating as a minister of

---

59. W. Stanford Reid, "Knox's Attitude to the English Reformation," *Westminster Theological Journal* 26, no. 1 (1963): 2, 6.

60. Ibid., 6.

61. Ibid., 28.

62. Ibid., 24, 31.

the Church of England."[63] As Reid explains, "Since the magistrates were truly Christians and the times were difficult and dangerous they [i.e., Knox and his supporters] should submit for the sake of peace."[64] Thus, Reid comes to the conclusion that "despite his dislike of the Book of Common Prayer, Knox would have conformed if he were living in England."[65] But as David Laing observes concerning the occasional use of the *Book of Common Prayer* as the Reformation dawned in Scotland: "Such arrangements, however, were merely prospective, to suit the exigencies of the times; and if we admit that the English Liturgy was actually adopted, it could have only been to a partial extent, and of no long continuance."[66]

There are significant differences between the intended use and content of the Scottish *Book of Common Order* and the English *Book of Common Prayer*. Laing writes,

> In reference to the *Book of Common Order*, it may be remarked that there was this marked difference in its use when compared to the *Book of Common Prayer*, that while the latter was in England prescribed as a ritual which admitted of no change, the other in Scotland was enjoined to be used chiefly as a guide or directory. Thus, in some of the rubrics, it is distinctly stated that "the minister was not expected to repeat these things, but he had the option, after closing his sermon, either to use these prayers, or to pray in the Spirit if God shall move his heart, framing the same according to the time and matter which he hath intreated of."[67]

Laing also notes, "In no instance do we find Knox himself using set forms of prayer."[68] Furthermore, the Scottish liturgy, in an attempt to avoid ceremonies not prescribed in Scripture, did not call for kneel-

---

63. James Stalker, *John Knox: His Ideas and Ideals* (London: Hodder and Stoughton, 1905), 217.

64. Reid, "Knox's Attitude to the English Reformation," 24–25.

65. Ibid., 31.

66. *Works*, 6:278.

67. *Works*, 6:281.

68. *Works*, 6:283.

ing during prayer or for those taking the Lord's Supper, avoided frequent repetitions of the Lord's Prayer, and replaced English chanting, instrumental music, and choral anthems with congregational singing of metrical Psalms.[69]

The contrast between adhering to a prescribed form of prayer versus praying in the Holy Spirit leads us to another emphasis in Knox's theology of prayer, one he shared with later Puritan writers.

### The Holy Spirit in Prayer

In his *Treatise on Prayer*, Knox briefly discusses the Spirit's role in prayer. He insists that without the Spirit of God, "there is no hope that we can desire anything according to God's will," because it is the Spirit who makes "intercession for us with unceasing groans (Rom. 8:26), which cannot be expressed with tongue."[70] However, Knox explains that this does not mean "that the Holy Ghost does mourn or pray, but that he stirs up our minds, giving unto us a desire or boldness to pray, and causes us to mourn when we are extracted or pulled therefrom."[71] In other words, for Knox, the Spirit's role is not really to pray for us but to assist us in prayer. This implies that if we are able to pray, it is because of the help of the Spirit who dwells in us. Thus, for those who do not possess the Spirit, true prayer is impossible. This goes back to Knox's assertion that true prayer is an indication of true faith and regeneration. Since the unregenerate do not have the Spirit they cannot pray, for it is the Spirit who aids us in our prayers. Yes, the unregenerate may be able to pray, but not to please God, who calls for right and true prayer, which is only possible through the work of the Spirit.

### The Mediation of Christ in Prayer

Knox also highlights the work of Christ in prayer. If the Spirit is our helper, Christ is our mediator. Knox presses upon his readers

---

69. Ibid.
70. Knox, "A Treatise on Prayer," in *Select Writings*, 75.
71. Ibid.

the necessity that we must have a mediator. First, we are not in our-selves "worthy to compear or appear in God's presence, by reason" of our sin that so offends our God.[72] Thus God has given us His beloved Son to be a mediator between us and Him, in whom if "we faithfully believe, we are so clad that we may with boldness compear and appear before the throne of God's mercy; doubting nothing but whatsoever we ask, by our Mediator, we shall obtain most assuredly that same."[73]

Second, "without our Mediator…, we enter not into prayer; for the incalling of such as pray without Jesus Christ is not only in vain, but also they are odious and abominable before God."[74] Knox remarks that just like in the Old Testament, when only the high priest could enter into the most Holy Place, "and as all sacrifices offered by any other than by priests only, provoked the wrath of God upon the sacrifice maker, so whoever does intend to enter into God's presence, or to make prayers without Jesus Christ, shall find nothing but fearful judgment and horrible damnation."[75] On this basis, Knox affirms that while Turks and Jews pray fervently to God, "their prayers are never pleasing unto God; neither honour they his holy Majesty in anything, because they acknowledge not Jesus Christ; for whoso honours not the Son, honours not the Father."[76]

Third, the precept of God makes it indispensable that we have Jesus alone as our mediator. Knox says, "For as the law is a statute that we shall call upon God, and as the promise is made that he shall hear us, so are we commanded only to call by Jesus Christ, by whom alone we obtain our petitions; for in him alone are all the promises of God confirmed and complete."[77] Here, Knox repeats his precept-promise concept, showing how important it is in his theol-ogy of prayer. We must have Jesus as our only mediator because it is

---

72. Ibid., 85.
73. Ibid.
74. Ibid., 85–86.
75. Ibid., 86.
76. Ibid.
77. Ibid.

God's precept or command and because there is a promise attached to it that God will hear us. Notice here Knox's application of the Reformation *solus Christus* principle to prayer—that without Christ no one can come to God. Knox further explains, "It is plain, that such as have called, or call presently upon God, by any other name than by Jesus Christ alone, do nothing regarding God's will, but obstinately prevaricate, and do against his commandments. And, therefore, they obtain not their petitions, neither yet have entrance to his mercy. 'For no one cometh to the Father,' says Jesus Christ, 'but by me.' He is the right way; whoso declines from him errs, and goes wrong."[78]

*Delay and Denial in Prayer*
Why is it that sometimes even if we pray aright, with the Spirit's help and through Christ, the answer seems to be delayed or denied?

1. Delay in prayer.
Why does God delay in answering our prayer? Knox gives two reasons: First, "for the exercise and trial of our faith, and not that he sleeps or is absent from us at any time."[79] In this sense, delay becomes a means through which we can exercise greater faith toward God. The longer our prayer is delayed, the more we will have an opportunity to exercise our faith. Also, delay is one means by which God tests the sincerity and eagerness of our faith when we pray to Him. Delay should not stop us from praying but should stir us up more to continue praying: "If God defers or prolongs to grant our petitions, even so long that he seems apparently to reject us, yet let us not cease to call; prescribing him either time, neither manner of deliverance; as it is written, 'Let not the faithful be too hasty, for God sometimes defers and will not hastily grant, to the probation of our continuance,' as the words of Jesus Christ testify."[80]

78. Ibid.
79. Ibid., 76.
80. Ibid., 91–92.

Second, delay can make us more glad and appreciative when God answers our prayer. God sometimes delays "that with more gladness we might receive that which, with long expectation, we have abidden [been praying for]; that thereby we, assured of his eternal providence…, doubt not but that his merciful hand shall relieve us in most urgent necessity and extreme tribulation."[81] Knox cited Hannah, Sarah, and Elizabeth, who, "after great ignominy of their barrenness and sterility, receive fruit of their bosoms with joy."[82]

## 2. Denial in prayer.

Not only does God delay in answering our prayer but sometimes He even denies it. Why? According to Knox, one reason is our own hypocrisy—that is, "when men do ask of God things whereof they have no need."[83] Knox was convinced that such prayer offends God:

> In such cases a great number do offend, principally the mighty and rich of the earth, who for a common custom, will pray this part of the Lord's prayer, "Give us this day our daily bread": that is, a moderate and reasonable sustenance; and yet their own hearts will testify that they need not so to pray, seeing they abound in all worldly solace and felicity. I mean not that rich men should not pray this part of the Lord's prayer, but I would they understood what they ought to pray in it…, and that they ask nothing whereof they feel not themselves marvelously indigent and needy. For unless we call in verity, he shall not grant; and except we speak with our whole heart, we shall not find him.[84]

Another reason that Knox gives for God's denying our prayer is unbelief: "For nothing more offends God, than when we ask doubting whether he will grant our petitions; for in so doing, we doubt if God be true, if he be mighty and good."[85] Thus there must be

---

81. Ibid., 76.
82. Ibid., 92.
83. Ibid., 79.
84. Ibid., 80.
85. Ibid.

"a sure hope to obtain what we ask."[86] Jesus Himself, Knox notes, "commands that we firmly believe to obtain whatsoever we ask; for all things are possible to him that believes. And, therefore, in our prayers, desperation always is to be expelled."[87]

But this does not mean that "any man in extremity of trouble can be without a present dolour [sorrow], and without a greater fear of trouble to follow."[88] Nevertheless, even our troubles can become the spurs to stir us to pray. Knox beautifully writes, "Trouble and fear are the very spurs to prayer; for when man, compassed about with vehement calamities, and vexed with continual solicitude (having, by help of man, no hope of deliverance, with sorely oppressed and punished heart, fearing also greater punishment to follow), does call to God for comfort and support from the deep pit of tribulation, such prayer ascends into God's presence, and returns not in vain."[89]

Moreover, with regard to troubles, Knox bluntly asserts that "he that prays not in trouble, denies God. For like as it is to know no physician or medicine, or in knowing them, to refuse to use and receive the same; so not to call upon God in your tribulation, is like as if you did not know God, or else utterly denied him."[90] Troubles, then, should not become an excuse for not praying but rather an encouragement to pray.

After all, even if the Lord is pleased to deny our prayer, He still has commanded us to pray. We should obey that command no matter what happens or what the Lord does in response to our praying. David, "desiring [or praying] to be restored to his kingdom, offers to God obedience, saying, 'If I have found favour in the presence of the Lord, he shall bring me home again; but if he shall say, 'Thou pleasest me not longer to bear authority,' I am obedient; let him do what seemeth good unto him.'"[91] For Knox, then, what matters the most

86. Ibid.
87. Ibid.
88. Ibid.
89. Ibid., 80–81.
90. Ibid., 83.
91. Ibid., 92.

is our obedience to God, which is expressed when we pray to Him. This again shows how God's precept and His promise are central to Knox's theology of prayer. Indeed, his concept of prayer is anchored in these two elements.

## Knox's Piety and Practice of Prayer

Knox was not only a theologian of prayer but a practitioner as well. He put doctrine into application. He acted on what he believed. Thus, as previously mentioned, his own *Treatise on Prayer* includes prayer at the end, which is characteristic of his piety—that, contrary to what other people think, he was a lover of peace. He desired tranquility and not anarchy. He prayed for the queen as well as for her kingdom. He prayed for her salvation, not for her destruction: "Illuminate the heart of our sovereign lady Queen Mary [i.e., Mary Stuart, Queen of Scots] with pregnant gifts of thy Holy Ghost; and inflame the hearts of her council with thy truth and love. Repress thou the pride of those that would rebel [against her kingdom]."[92]

Knox later became hostile to the queen, refusing to pray for her. However, he did this to show that even in his prayer he could not tolerate the queen's wickedness. In 1571, Knox was accused "of sedition, of railing against the Queen, etc.—from his pulpit in St. Giles's." Knox "admitted that he had boldly called wickedness by its own terms, as he called a spade a spade. As for not praying for the Queen, he answered, 'I am not bound to pray in this place, for sovereign to me she is not; and I let them understand that I am not a man of law that has my tongue to sell for silver or favour of the world.'"[93] On one occasion Knox prayed, "'Give me Scotland or I die;' and the queen said: 'I fear the prayer of John Knox more than the combined armies [of Europe].'"[94] Bissell comments on this

---

92. Ibid., 100.

93. G. Barnett Smith, *John Knox: The Scottish Reformation* (Edinburgh: The Religious Tract & Book Society of Scotland, 1905), 143.

94. Cited in Bissell, Introduction to *The Presbyterian Pulpit, A Volume of Sermons by Ministers of the Synod of Michigan*, 5.

prayer: "Such prayer goeth not out but from faith and such faith
cometh not but by prayer."[95]

As a pastor, Knox prayed for his congregation, and as a father,
for his family. He was truly a man of "perfect prayer," which he also
called "godly prayer."[96] As prayer is an indication of true faith, so it
is a sign of true godliness. For Knox, a truly pious person is one who
prays aright. He further maintains that "godly prayer requires the
perfect [complete] knowledge of" Christ.[97] Pious prayer is rooted
in right Christology.

Indeed, piety and prayer are inseparable in Knox's mind. This
truth is also evident in the *Book of Common Order,* which is com-
prised of two prayers titled "A Godlie Prayer to Be Said at All
Times" and "A Godlie Prayer,"[98] showing that people behind this
*Book* are very much concerned with piety in prayer. In fact, one purpose for the composition of the prayers in *The Form of Prayers and
Ministration of the Sacraments* is to promote piety among the people,
to "use prayers and other orders...to the increase of Godes glorye,
and edification of his holye people."[99]

Knox remained prayerful even unto death. John Howie wrote
that while Knox was in his dying hours, "he was much engaged in
meditation and prayer," often saying,

Come, Lord Jesus. Sweet Jesus into Thy hand I commend my
spirit. Be merciful, Lord, to Thy Church, which Thou hast
redeemed. Give peace to this afflicted commonwealth. Raise
up faithful pastors who will take charge of Thy Church. Grant
us, Lord, the perfect hatred of sin, both by evidences of Thy
wrath and mercy.[100]

95. Ibid., 5–6.
96. Knox, "A Treatise on Prayer, or A Confession, and Declaration of
Prayers," 85.
97. Ibid.
98. Knox, "The Book of Common Order," in *Works,* 6:357, 370.
99. Knox, "The Form of Prayers," in *Works,* 4:164.
100. John Howie, *The Scots Worthies According to Howie's Second Edition, 1781:
With Explanatory Notes, Supplementary Matter, a Full Index of Persons and Places,*

"Grant us, Lord, the perfect hatred of sin"—a prayer truly characteristic of John Knox. After he died on November 24, 1572, one of his contemporaries, Thomas Smeaton, said of him, "I know not if ever God placed a more godly and great spirit in a body so little and frail."[101]

*and an Appendix of Sermons*, ed. Andrew A. Bonar (Glasgow, Melbourne, and Dunedin: McGready, Thomson, & Niven, 1879), 61.

101. Ibid., 63.

*Chapter 4*

# William Perkins on the Lord's Prayer

———————————coɔcoɔ———————————

## J. STEPHEN YUILLE

*Do we not dissemble with God when we say with our tongues, Thy will be done, and yet in life and conversation, have no regard to square our works thereby?*

—WILLIAM PERKINS

Elizabeth I is undoubtedly one of England's most famous monarchs. She was born in 1533, the fruit of that fateful union between Henry VIII and Anne Boleyn. In 1558, after the death of her Protestant half-brother, Edward, and the death of her Catholic half-sister, Mary, she ascended the throne. Immediately, she was besieged from all sides. Domestically, she struggled with the religious establishment, seeking a *via media* between Catholics (who denied the legitimacy of her birth) and Puritans (who rejected prelacy, which she viewed as essential to the governance of her realm).[1] Internationally, she had to contend with countless enemies, culminating in the Spanish Armada's thwarted invasion in 1588. Admirably, Elizabeth withstood it all and turned England into the foremost Protestant power by the time of her death in 1603.

---

1. The meaning of the term *Puritan* is multifaceted in the sixteenth and seventeenth centuries. Here, it refers to those who desired to remove all remnants of Roman Catholicism from the Church of England and reform its government on the basis of Presbyterianism. Strictly speaking, Perkins was not a Puritan in that sense of the word, for he refused to align himself with the more militant figures of his era.

Coinciding with the years of Elizabeth's illustrious reign is the life of one of England's most influential theologians, William Perkins (1558–1602). He was born in the village of Marston Jabbett, in Bulkington parish, in Warwickshire.[2] As a young man, he enrolled at Christ's College, Cambridge University, where he soon made a name for himself, but not for the reasons we might expect. By his own admission, he was given to recklessness and drunkenness. His spiritual state was desperate, but God soon began to work in his heart. Burdened with the weight of his sin, he turned to Christ, the Savior of sinners.

Applying himself to his studies, Perkins received his B.A. in 1581 and his M.A. in 1584. After graduation, he was appointed lecturer at St. Andrew's Church—a position he held until his death. He wielded great influence as a preacher. According to Benjamin Brook, "[Perkins] used to apply the terrors of the law so directly to the consciences of his hearers that their hearts would often sink under the convictions; and he used to pronounce the word *damn* with so peculiar an emphasis, that it left a doleful *echo* in their ears a long time after."[3] Around the time of his appointment to St. Andrew's, Perkins was also elected to a fellowship at Christ's College. This placed him in a position whereby he influenced a generation of students. During the next decade, his reputation as a teacher was unrivalled. When Thomas Goodwin enrolled at Cambridge in 1613, a full ten years after Perkins's death, he wrote, "The town was then filled with the discourse of the power of Mr. Perkins's ministry, still fresh in most men's memories."[4]

---

2. For an account of Perkins's life, see *The Dictionary of National Biography*, s.v. "Perkins, William." Also see Joel Beeke and Randall Pederson, *Meet the Puritans* (Grand Rapids: Reformation Heritage Books, 2006), 469–80; and Benjamin Brook, *The Lives of the Puritans* (1813; reprint, Morgan, Pa.: Soli Deo Gloria, 1996), 2:129–36.
3. Brook, *Lives of the Puritans*, 2:130.
4. As quoted in Ian Breward, ed., *The Works of William Perkins* in The Courtney Library of Reformation Classics: Vol. III (Appleford, U.K.: Sutton Courtnay Press, 1970), 9.

By the time of his death, Perkins's writings had begun to "displace" those of John Calvin, Theodore Beza, and Heinrich Bullinger.[5] His widespread appeal was the result of his "ability to clarify and expound complex theological issues which aroused the respect of fellow scholars," and his "gift for relating seemingly abstruse theological teaching to the spiritual aspirations of ordinary Christians."[6] Due to the popularity of his writings, Perkins became instrumental in the development of English Reformed theology and the piety to which it gave rise: Puritanism. Given the negative connotation in his day, Perkins would never have referred to himself as a Puritan, yet it is the very term that others used (favorably or not) to describe that piety so prevalent in his life and ministry. With a hint of frustration, he declared, "Who are so much branded with vile terms of Puritans and Precisians, as those that most endeavor to get and keep the purity of heart in a good conscience?"[7] It is this fervent pursuit of godliness that marked Perkins's piety and defined the entire Puritan movement that followed—a movement that profoundly shaped Christianity on both sides of the Atlantic.

This towering influence merits Perkins's inclusion in the present work. Unsurprisingly, prayer occupies a prominent place in his collected writings. His exposition of the Lord's Prayer, in particular, lends many valuable insights into the piety of the one who is the father of English Puritanism.

## Sincerity, the Prerequisite of True Prayer

The English word *sincere* comes from two Latin words: *sine* (without) and *cera* (wax). In the ancient world, dishonest merchants would use wax to hide defects, such as cracks, in their pottery so that they could

---

5. Ian Breward, "The Significance of William Perkins," *Journal of Religious History* 4 (1966): 116.

6. Ibid., 113.

7. William Perkins, *A Godly and Learned Exposition Upon Christ's Sermon on the Mount* in *The Works of William Perkins* (London, 1631), 3:15 [hereafter, *Works*]. Unless otherwise indicated, all quotations are from this treatise.

sell their merchandise at a higher price.[8] More reputable merchants would hang a sign over their pottery—*sine cera* (without wax)—to inform customers that their merchandise was genuine.

In Matthew 6:1–18, Christ teaches us to be sincere in our practice of godliness. This means that we are to be motivated by a desire to please God, not man, in our performance of spiritual duties. Christ conveys this message by way of three examples: giving, praying, and fasting. Perkins summarized Christ's aim as follows: "We must learn this one thing which Christ principally intends, to wit, in all holy duties to avoid hypocrisy, endeavoring to do them with all simplicity and sincerity of heart, whereby we truly desire to have God and not man the seer and approver of them."[9]

When it comes specifically to prayer, Christ gives two warnings against hypocrisy. First, "When thou prayest, thou shalt not be as the hypocrites are: for they love to pray standing in the synagogues and in the corners of streets, that they may be seen of men" (Matt. 6:5). This is not a condemnation of all public prayer. As Perkins made clear, Christ's rebuke is directed at those who pray "nowhere else, but in the open and public places."[10] To counter this hypocrisy, Christ commands, "But thou, when thou prayest, enter into thy closet, and when thou hast shut thy door, pray to thy Father which is in secret; and thy Father which seeth in secret shall reward thee openly" (Matt. 6:6). According to Perkins, Christ is here speaking metaphorically; therefore, we are not to take His words as implying that we must always pray in private, but that we must always pray as though we were in private.[11]

Second, Christ warns, "When ye pray, use not vain repetitions, as the heathen do: for they think that they shall be heard for their much speaking" (Matt. 6:7). Here, Christ condemns what Perkins

---

8. James M. Boice, *Romans: The New Humanity* (Grand Rapids: Baker, 1995), 1591.
9. *Works,* 3:163.
10. *Works,* 3:110.
11. *Works,* 3:113.

calls the sin of "babbling."[12] In a word, babblers focus on needless repetition, while ignoring the weightier matters of the soul. While refusing to give their hearts to God, they think they will be heard because of their many words. To counter this hypocrisy, Christ commands, "Be not ye therefore like unto them: for your Father knoweth what things ye have need of, before ye ask him" (Matt. 6:8). Here, Christ points to God's omniscience, as the Father who knows all things, which makes such repetition both needless and useless, or truly vain.

Having issued these two warnings against hypocrisy, Christ proceeds to teach us how to pray in sincerity, thus bringing us to one of the most beloved portions of God's Word: the Lord's Prayer.[13] For Perkins, it "is the most excellent form of prayer that is, or can be made by any creature: for it was indeed indited and propounded by the Son of God, who is the wisdom of the Father."[14] In his analysis, he divides it into three parts—preface, petitions, and conclusion—and expounds each part under two headings: meaning and instructions.

### The Preface to the Lord's Prayer

Christ begins, "Our Father which art in heaven" (Matt. 6:9). Perkins identified the Father as the first person of the Trinity, "who is first and chiefly the Father of Christ; and in Christ our Father."[15] God is "our Father," explained Perkins, "not by nature, or in regard of personal union, but by the grace of adoption in Christ."[16] By adoption, God has made us part of His family, and He has granted us

---

12. *Works*, 3:115. For seven abuses condemned under babbling, see ibid., 116.

13. Perkins believed that Christ, in the Lord's Prayer, describes both the manner (form) and the matter (content) of our prayers. He places great importance on the prayer's form as a model for us. For his thoughts on set prayers, see *Works*, 3:119–20.

14. *Works*, 3:120.

15. *Works*, 3:121.

16. Ibid. See John 1:12; Gal. 3:26; Eph. 1:4–6.

all the rights and privileges of membership in that family.[17] Perkins
derived four lessons from this precious truth: (1) It teaches us to
pray to God.[18] (2) It teaches us to pray to God as He reveals Himself in His Word. (3) It teaches us to pray with boldness because of
our position in Christ. (4) It teaches us to pray "as children towards
their Father" with reverence, humility, repentance, and a sincere
desire to mortify sin.[19] Next, Perkins defined the term *heaven*. In
what sense is God in heaven? Perkins explained, "God is said to
be in heaven, not as though he were in the circles of the heavens…
(1 Kings 8:27), and indeed he is neither included nor excluded any
place, being infinite, and so every where; but because his majesty
and glory is most eminent[ly displayed] in the highest heavens to
his saints and angels."[20]

Having thus explained the meaning of the preface, Perkins
turned to instructions (or "uses"). (1) Given that God is "our
Father," we must approach Him with confidence. "When we come
to God in prayer," wrote Perkins, "we must ground upon this covenant in Christ, and so shall we go boldly unto the throne of grace.…
God is thy Father, and so thou shalt be welcome."[21] (2) Given that
God is in heaven, we must approach Him with reverence. Perkins
commented, "When we pray we must come before God with all
reverence, fear, and trembling; for he is in heaven a most glorious
God, full of majesty and power."[22]

---

17. As our Father, God loves us (Matt. 10:29–32), hears us (Matt. 7:11), disciplines us (Heb. 12:6), comforts us (2 Cor. 1:3), protects us (Rom. 16:20), forgives
us (Rom. 8:1), blesses us (1 Cor. 2:9), and keeps us (Rom. 8:30). For more on these
blessings, see Thomas Watson, *The Lord's Prayer* (1692; reprint, Edinburgh: Banner
of Truth, 1999), 15–25.

18. Perkins did not believe the words "Our Father" rule out praying to the
Son or the Holy Spirit, commenting, "Though the Father alone be here named,
yet the other two persons are not hereby excluded.… We must pray to all, though
we name but one, having in that one relation to the rest in our mind and heart"
(*Works*, 3:121).

19. *Works*, 3:121–22.

20. *Works*, 3:121.

21. *Works*, 3:122.

22. *Works*, 3:123.

On occasion, we lack confidence in prayer. Why? Because we have lost sight of "our Father." On other occasions, we lack reverence in prayer. Why? We have lost sight of "our Father which art in heaven." To sum up, then, in the preface, Christ teaches us how to approach God in a right attitude of heart.

## The Petitions of the Lord's Prayer

Following the preface, there are six petitions. Of these, three focus on God's glory while three focus on man's need. The order is significant, for, as Perkins put it, "God's glory is the absolute end of all things"—even our needs. [23]

### *The First Petition*

In the first petition, we pray, "Hallowed be thy name" (Matt. 6:9). It raises three questions. First, what is God's name? Perkins replied, "God himself."[24] He is the "I AM" (Ex. 3:14), meaning He is infinite, eternal, and immutable. Second, what does it mean to hallow God's name? It means, in Perkins's estimation, to give to God "the highest honor."[25] Third, how do we hallow God's name? For Perkins, the answer is twofold. First, we hallow God's name in His person: with our minds, acknowledging Him as He reveals Himself in His Word; with our hearts, loving, fearing, and trusting Him above all; and with our lips, praising His name for His goodness.[26] Second, we hallow God's name in His creatures: acknowledging His power and wisdom in creation; esteeming the creature according to its proper place, and sanctifying our use of the creature by prayer.[27] In short, God's name is hallowed when we fear Him with a godly fear.

When we speak of the fear of God, it is important to distinguish between ungodly and godly fear. Perkins affirmed that these

---

23. *Works*, 3:124.
24. *Works*, 3:124.
25. Ibid.
26. *Works*, 3:125.
27. Ibid.

two are distinguished by our perception of God. Ungodly fear is the result of viewing God as a potential source of harm, and it causes people to take steps to minimize the perceived threat while continuing steadfast in their sin. For Perkins, this ungodly fear occurs when people fear only God's punishment. In marked contrast, godly fear is the result of viewing God as the greatest good. This may include a fear of God's wrath, but it is not limited to this; on the contrary, it focuses on God's majesty. Perkins maintained that this fear is synonymous with fearing God's name — the fullest revelation of His glory.[28] It is a fear that grips the affections, thereby making a divide between the soul and sin. In other words, it is a fear that manifests itself in the pursuit of holiness.

By way of instructions arising from the first petition, Perkins spoke of: (1) "wants to be bewailed," such as lack of zeal, hardness of heart, and profaneness of life; (2) "graces to be desired," such as knowledge, holiness, reverence, gratitude, and moderation; and (3) "duties to be practiced," such as forsaking sin and serving God. In all of these, his point is clear: the hallowing of God's name implies a change in heart, which expresses itself in a change in conduct.

### The Second Petition

In the second petition we pray, "Thy kingdom come" (Matt. 6:10). In expounding this request, Perkins made a distinction between God's "general" kingdom and "special" kingdom.[29] The first is "God's absolute power and sovereignty, whereby he ruleth all things in heaven, in earth, and in hell." The second is God's rule over "his elect and chosen people." This special kingdom has two aspects: (1) the present kingdom of grace, "wherein God makes men willingly subject to his written word"; and (2) the future kingdom of glory, which is "the blessed estate of God's elect in heaven, whereby God in Christ becomes all things unto them immediately."[30] These two do

---

28. *Works*, 3:125–26.
29. *Works*, 3:127.
30. *Works*, 3:127–28.

not differ in nature but in degree, meaning the kingdom of grace is the beginning of the kingdom of glory. And so when we pray "Thy kingdom come," what are we asking? We are not asking for the effective governance of God's general kingdom[31] but for the expansion of the kingdom of grace and the arrival of the kingdom of glory.

When applying this petition by way of instruction, Perkins made a threefold division. (1) In terms of "wants to be bewailed," we must mourn for our own sins and for the sins of the whole world, "whereby God is dishonored." (2) In terms of "graces to be desired," we must pray for—among other things—the preaching of the gospel, the enlightening of minds, the glorifying of Christ, and the enlarging of the church. (3) In terms of "duties to be practiced," we must seek to produce the fruit of the kingdom, learn to be content in our calling, and labor to bring others into the kingdom.[32]

## The Third Petition

Next, we pray, "Thy will be done in earth, as it is in heaven" (Matt. 6:10). What is the relationship between this and the preceding petitions? Perkins answered, "This petition dependeth on both the former thus; as a means whereby we do that which we desire in the first petition: for God's name is glorified, when his will is done: and as a manifestation of that which we desire in the second petition, for there we pray, that God's kingdom may come unto us, and he rule in our hearts by his word and spirit: now here we crave that we may do his will, and so testify ourselves to be his loyal subjects."[33]

Perkins made it clear that God's will is "considered in itself, as God is one." However, for our better understanding, he believed it is helpful to distinguish between God's "absolute" will and "revealed" will.[34] The first refers to the rule of God's actions, or decrees: "God's absolute will is the will of his good pleasure, whereby according to

---

31. *Works*, 3:127.
32. *Works*, 3:128–30.
33. *Works*, 3:131.
34. Ibid.

his eternal counsel, he determines all things, what shall be done, or what shall not be done, and in what manner." The second refers to the rule of man's actions, or God's precepts: "God's revealed will is the sacred doctrine of God in his word, whereby he signifieth unto man, so far as concerns his happiness and salvation, what he ought to do, or what he ought not to do." This distinction is rooted in Scripture. We see it, for example, when Joseph's brothers sell him as a slave. This act was not in accord with God's revealed will, but it was the outworking of His absolute will, for Joseph says to his brothers, "It was not you that sent me hither, but God" (Gen. 45:8; cf. 50:20). Likewise, we see it in the Jews' crucifixion of Christ. Again, this act was a transgression of God's revealed will, but it was determined by His absolute will, for Peter declares, "Him, being delivered by the determinate counsel and foreknowledge of God, ye have taken, and by wicked hands have crucified and slain" (Acts 2:23).

When we pray "Thy will be done," which will do we have in view? Perkins replied, "We mean not the absolute, but the revealed will of God."[35] Why? "The absolute will of God is always done, and cannot be resisted." We pray, therefore, for help to obey God's revealed will "as the blessed angels and glorified saints do it in heaven."[36] God commands us to love one another; to abstain from what is evil; to pursue righteousness; to be holy; to submit to one another in the fear of Christ; to submit to those in authority; to be patient; to be humble; to love our spouse; to share with those in need; to make disciples; to abstain from immorality; to resist the evil one; to be faithful stewards; to be diligent servants; to worship Him; to be strong; to love our neighbor; and to love Him with all our heart, soul, mind, and strength. We are incapable of doing any of these things in and of ourselves. And so we pray.[37]

---

35. Ibid.

36. *Works*, 3:133. For Perkins's thoughts on what this looks like, see *Works*, 3:133–34.

37. Turning to instructions, Perkins again speaks of "wants to be bewailed," "graces to be desired," and "duties to be practiced" (*Works*, 3:132–33).

Before moving on, Perkins emphasized the fact that "we must seek to practice that which we ask in prayer."[38] In the present context, this means that "we must seek to cut off all things that hinder us from doing God's will."[39] Perkins primarily has sin in view. If we are serious about doing God's will, then we will be serious about forsaking sin. By way of motivation, Perkins appealed to the fact "that our old man is crucified with [Christ], that the body of sin might be destroyed, that henceforth we should not serve sin" (Rom. 6:6). When we are united with Christ, we share in the merit of His death. Therefore, our old man has been condemned, judged, and crucified. Sin is no longer the governing principle in us because the Holy Spirit dwells within. As a result, we must "reckon" ourselves "to be dead indeed unto sin, but alive unto God through Jesus Christ our Lord" (Rom. 6:11). Perkins's concern was that we strive for consistency between what we ask and how we act. He warned, "Do we not dissemble with God when we say with our tongues, *Thy will be done*, and yet in life and conversation, have no regard to square our works thereby?"[40]

*The Fourth Petition*

"Hitherto," said Perkins, "we have handled the petitions that concern God's glory; now we come to the petitions that concern ourselves."[41] They build on the third petition ("Thy will be done"), in that we do God's will when we (1) "depend upon his providence for the blessings of this life," (2) "rely upon his mercy for the pardon of our sins," and (3) "trust in his power for strength against temptation and deliverance from evil."[42]

In the fourth petition specifically we pray, "Give us this day our daily bread" (Matt. 6:11). What does Christ mean by bread? For Perkins, "It must be taken in a general sense, not only for bread,

---

38. *Works*, 3:132.
39. *Works*, 3:133.
40. *Works*, 3:132.
41. *Works*, 3:135.
42. Ibid.

but for all other necessary food, and for raiment also, with health, peace, liberty, and all other things that are meet and needful for the good outward estate of man, or family, or commonwealth."[43] In other words, "bread" refers to whatever serves for our physical being and well-being: food, shelter, work, family, health. What does Christ mean by "daily" bread? "Such bread," said Perkins, "as serves to preserve health and life from day to day."[44] This does not imply that we neglect to make provision for the future. It simply means that we trust God to meet our daily material needs.

### The Fifth Petition

Having taught us to pray for temporal blessings, Christ now teaches us to pray for spiritual blessings, the first of which is "remission of our sins."[45] Hence, we pray, "Forgive us our debts" (Matt. 6:12). Christ attaches a condition to this petition: "As we forgive our debtors." "This Christ addeth," said Perkins, "for weightiness, even to cross the fraud and hypocrisy off our corrupt hearts, who would have forgiveness of God, and yet would not forgive our brethren, nor yet leave off the practice of sin ourselves."[46] He further explained, "Our forgiving is a sign that God hath forgiven us, being indeed a fruit of our reconciliation with God; for it is a sign of true repentance, which is a fruit of faith, whereby we apprehend the mercy of God for the pardon of our sins in Christ."[47] As for how we are to forgive others, Perkins spoke of the forgiveness of revenge, punishment, and judgment.[48] In this context, he believed Christ intends the first. In other words, we must forgive others by withholding revenge, mortifying anger, cultivating love, and rendering good. According to Perkins,

---

43. *Works*, 3:136. Perkins divided the petition into six points: (1) "what we ask: bread"; (2) "what bread we ask: daily bread"; (3) "whose bread: ours"; (4) "for what time: this day"; (5) "to whom: to us"; and (6) "to whom must we look: God."
44. *Works*, 3:136.
45. *Works*, 3:139.
46. *Works*, 3:141.
47. *Works*, 3:155.
48. *Works*, 3:142.

those who forgive in this way know God's forgiveness—"a free and full discharge from sin and the punishment thereof, without any satisfaction on our part: and this God doth, when he is content for Christ's sake, not to impute sin unto us, but to account it as not committed; and the punishment thereof as not due unto us; being fully and freely contented with the all sufficient satisfaction made by Christ in his death and passion."[49]

At this point Perkins anticipated an obvious question: "But of what sins do we here ask pardon?" After all, does not God forgive us all our sins at conversion? If so, why do we need to ask repeatedly for forgiveness? By way of reply, we must think of God's forgiveness in two ways. First, there is the removal of condemnation. When we believe in Christ, God forgives us our sin. As Paul makes clear, "There is therefore now no condemnation to them which are in Christ Jesus" (Rom. 8:1). Second, there is the renewal of fellowship. As Christians, we still sin; hence, we must seek God's forgiveness continually (1 John 1:9). "The child of God," said Perkins, "hath his sins past fully pardoned at once on God's part, upon his true repentance; yet he is not able so to receive pardon as God gives it, but must receive it by little and little, and as it were drop by drop."[50]

Perkins presented a number of instructions arising from this petition: we must bewail our carnal security, look to God's mercy in Christ, repent daily of our sins, see that we cannot fulfill the law, pursue those means by which God gives assurance of forgiveness, and pray for the pardon of our brother's sins.[51] In addition, he believed this petition provides "a notable remedy against despair, wherewith the devil assaults many a child of God, when through infirmity they fall into some grievous sin, or commit the same sin often, which greatly wounds the conscience."[52] Because of our sin, we often doubt God's willingness to forgive. The only solution for such despair is Christ. Perkins made it clear that it is Christ's

---

49. *Works*, 3:140.
50. Ibid.
51. *Works*, 3:140–41.
52. *Works*, 3:141.

entrance into God's presence that guarantees the sinner's acceptance with God. For this reason, those who despair must look to Christ. In a word, they must meditate upon this wonderful truth: "We have such an high priest, who is set on the right hand of the throne of the Majesty in the heavens" (Heb. 8:1).

Christ's priesthood consists of two parts: oblation and intercession.[53] In simple terms, Christ's oblation is His sacrifice. It was offered to make atonement by giving God a full and adequate satisfaction for the sins of His people. The second part of Christ's priesthood is His intercession. In heaven, Christ presents Himself before God on behalf of His people. In this way, He guarantees the application of all that He procured by His crucifixion and resurrection. It is particularly this ministry of intercession that Perkins had in view when He spoke of Christ's priesthood. As Paul asks and then answers, "Who shall lay any thing to the charge of God's elect? It is God that justifieth. Who is he that condemneth? It is Christ that died, yea rather, that is risen again, who is even at the right hand of God, who also maketh intercession for us" (Rom. 8:33–34). Here, Paul mentions four inseparable works: (1) Christ's crucifixion: it is He who died. In so doing, He paid the penalty for our sin. (2) Christ's resurrection: it is He who was raised. This testifies to God's acceptance of Christ's substitutionary sacrifice. (3) Christ's ascension: it is He who is "at the right hand of God." He has entered God's presence on our behalf. (4) Christ's intercession: it is He who "is interceding for us." His presence in heaven guarantees the application of all He accomplished by His death, burial, and resurrection. In short, it guarantees the forgiveness of our sins.

*The Sixth Petition*
In the final petition we pray, "Lead us not into temptation, but deliver us from evil" (Matt. 6:13). Who are most subject to temptation? According to Perkins, "The children of God, that set

---

53. William Perkins, *A Golden Chain; or, The Description of Theology Containing the Order of the Causes of Salvation and Damnation* in *Works*, 3:27–31.

themselves to seek his glory, to advance his kingdom, to do his will, to depend upon his providence, and to rely upon his mercy for the pardon of their sins."[54] Having thus reminded us to expect temptation, Perkins was careful to note that it consists of two "sorts." There is "good and holy" temptation—"an action of God whereby he proveth and trieth man, to make manifest unto himself and unto others, what is in his heart."[55] There is also "evil" temptation—"a wicked motion, allurement, or persuasion, whereby man is provoked to sin against God in the transgression of some commandments."[56] When we pray, "Lead us not into temptation," we ask God to keep us from the second. In short, "We pray against Satan's sleights and policies which he exerciseth against God's children, for their ruin and destruction."[57]

As we pray, we should be encouraged by the fact that Satan is shackled. Perkins remarked, "Satan can go no further than God permits him: he could not touch Job's goods, his children, nor his body, until God gave him leave."[58] This is a source of great comfort. When Adam and Eve disobeyed, they, along with all their posterity, fell into bondage to sin and death. By consequence, they fell under Satan's dominion. At that time, God ordained Satan to be the executioner of the sentence of death. The obligation of man to death is what gives Satan all his power. Obviously, the removal of that obligation is the termination of Satan's power, and that is precisely what Christ accomplished at the cross. He paid our debt by His death. In so doing, He destroyed Satan's power. That is what Paul has in mind when he says that Christ "spoiled principalities and powers" (Col. 2:15). By His death, Christ stripped them of their power. Having done so, He "made a shew of them openly." When it comes to our salvation, therefore, there is no match for God. Salvation is a work of God's limitless power from start to finish. Nothing can oppose Him.

---

54. *Works*, 3:143.
55. *Works*, 3:144. Perkins gave Abraham as an example (Gen. 22:1–2).
56. Ibid.
57. *Works*, 3:147. For six policies, see *Works*, 3:147–48.
58. *Works*, 3:146.

For Perkins, this truth is an unwavering source of encouragement as we pray, "Lead us not into temptation, but deliver us from evil."

## Conclusion

Christ ends the Lord's Prayer as follows: "For thine is the kingdom, and the power, and the glory, forever. Amen" (Matt. 6:13). In Perkins's opinion, "These words contain the reason of the former six petitions...to persuade the child of God that prayeth thus, that God will grant his requests."[59] We pray in faith because the kingdom belongs to God forever. We approach Him who freely disposes all things for the good of His people. We pray in faith because the power belongs to God forever. "By *power*," said Perkins, "is meant an ability in God whereby he can do whatsoever he will, and more than he will do."[60] We pray in faith because the glory belongs to God forever. "By glory," said Perkins, "is meant excellency and majesty."[61]

It is important to remember that the Lord's Prayer is set in a specific context. There is a sin condemned (practicing our righteousness before others to be seen by them) and a sentence pronounced (the loss of reward) (Matt. 6:1). In three simple examples (giving, praying, and fasting), Christ makes it clear that we are to avoid hypocrisy (a desire to please man) and pursue sincerity (a desire to please God) in our practice of spiritual duties. He also makes it clear that we do so by living in the reality of God's presence. Three times He refers to the fact that "thy Father...seeth in secret" (Matt. 6:4, 6, 18). The significance of this recurring statement was not lost on Perkins, who wrote, "God sees and beholds things that no man can see, even the secret thoughts and desires of man's heart."[62] An awareness of this truth is, for Perkins, the key to praying with a sincere heart.

---

59. *Works*, 3:150.
60. *Works*, 3:151.
61. Ibid.
62. *Works*, 3:109.

*Chapter 5*

# Anthony Burgess on Christ's Prayer for Us
────────────ᴄᴏꝛᴄᴏꝛ────────────

## JOEL R. BEEKE

*To pray is such a solemn worship of God, that it requireth the whole man, the intellectual part, all our judgment, invention, and memory is to be employed therein, as also the whole heart, the will and affections, yea, and body also.*
— ANTHONY BURGESS

Anthony Burgess (d. 1664) was a Puritan pastor and writer known for his piety, scholarship, and skill as a preacher, teacher, and apologist. He worked for a time as a teaching fellow at Emmanuel College, Cambridge. Then, from 1635 to 1662, he served as pastor of the church at Sutton-Coldfield in Warwickshire. His ministry was interrupted for several years in the 1640s, first when the Civil War between the king and Parliament forced him to flee, and then by the Westminster Assembly, where he played a significant role in helping craft the Westminster Standards. Burgess returned to Sutton-Coldfield in 1649 and served there until he was ejected from public ministry by the Act of Uniformity (1662). Burgess retired to Tamworth, Staffordshire, where he attended a parish church until his death two years later.[1]

---

1. For a biography and overview of the writings of Anthony Burgess, see Joel R. Beeke, *Puritan Reformed Spirituality* (Darlington: Evangelical Press, 2006), 172–74; Joel R. Beeke and Randall J. Pederson, *Meet the Puritans: With a Guide to Modern Reprints* (Grand Rapids: Reformation Heritage Books, 2006), 112–17.

During a fifteen-year span (1646–1661), Burgess wrote at least a dozen books based largely on his sermons and lectures. His writings reveal a scholar's acquaintance with Aristotle, Seneca, Augustine, Aquinas, Luther, and Calvin. He used many Greek and Latin quotations, but judiciously. He also reasoned in the plain style of Puritan preaching. This cultured scholar and experimental preacher produced astute, warm, devotional writing. His works show that he was a faithful steward of the mysteries of God. He wrote a vindication of the Puritan view of God's law, a defense of justification by faith alone, a treatise on original sin, and massive discourses on 1 Corinthians 3 and 2 Corinthians 1. He also wrote *Spiritual Refining*, a work of more than a thousand pages on saving grace and assurance.[2] Burgess excelled in applying the Scriptures to the heart and distinguishing between the true believer and the unsaved, fulfilling his goal to "endeavor the true and sound exposition…so as to reduce all doctrinals and controversials to practicals and experimentals, which is the life and soul of all."[3]

Although Burgess never wrote a treatise on prayer, he did preach 145 sermons on the prayer of Christ in John 17. His sermons cover a broad range of doctrinal and experiential subjects, while consistently focusing on Christ.[4] He regarded John 17 as a mountaintop of divine revelation, "a pearl in the gold" of the Bible.[5] The Lord

---

2. Reprinted as Anthony Burgess, *Spiritual Refining*, 2 vols. (Ames: International Outreach, 1996–1998).

3. Anthony Burgess, *An Expository Comment, Doctrinal, Controversial and Practical Upon the whole First Chapter of The Second Epistle of St Paul to the Corinthians* (London: Abraham Miller for Abel Roper, 1661).

4. This work includes such topics as God the Father and God the Son; the love of God; providence over death; election; the deity of Christ; the Mediator as teacher, priest, and king; union with Christ; knowledge of God; eternal life; justification; sanctification; obedience; separation from the world; faith; prayer; perseverance; worship; Christian unity; gospel ministry; the glory of heaven, etc., all discussed according to the order of the text of John 17.

5. Anthony Burgess, *CXLV Expository Sermons Upon the Whole 17th Chapter of The Gospel According to St. John: or Christs Prayer Before his Passion Explicated, and Both Practically and Polemically Improved* (London: Abraham Miller, 1656), 2 (I). The pagination is irregular, so the sermon number will also be cited in parentheses.

offers this prayer in the presence of His disciples so that those who hear it (and later, those who read it) might be filled with joy (John 17:13).[6] Burgess writes,

> This prayer of Christ may be compared to a land flowing with milk and honey, in respect to that treasure of consolation which is contained therein…. Seeing therefore this is such a fountain for healing and refreshing, come with a spiritual thirst to be replenished thereby. Seeing here is the honey and the honeycomb, do not with Jonathan taste a little honey only, but eat freely and abundantly thereof. Thou wilt by a serious and constant meditation find this heavenly matter in Christ's prayer make thee heavenly also, and assimilate thee into his own likeness. How vain and empty will all the glory of the world appear to thee, when thou shalt be lifted up upon this Mount of Transfiguration! They that live under the torrid zone never feel any cold, and thou who shalt find this prayer of Christ active and vigorous in thy breast, wilt never have cause to complain of that dullness, formality and coldness which many other groan under.[7]

The prayer in John 17 is especially significant because Jesus utters it the night before His crucifixion, which is the climax of His earthly work. Burgess thus asks his readers, "If the words of a dying man are much to be regarded, how much more of a dying Christ?"[8] In this light, Anthony Burgess expounds John 17 as the prayer of Christ, both as our mediator—if we are believers—and as the model of a godly man.

## The Prayer of Christ Our Mediator

In John 17:4, Jesus prayed, "I have finished the work which thou gavest me to do." Burgess says Christ Jesus "came not into the world to have his ease and pleasure and outward glory, but to work"—to

---

6. Burgess, *Expository Sermons*, 400 (LXXVI).

7. Burgess, *Expository Sermons*, "The Epistle to the Reader."

8. Burgess, *Expository Sermons*, 1 (I).

do the will of the Father who sent Jesus to earth (John 4:34). Christ came not "as a glorious Lord and Lawgiver" but as a servant under a law. Indeed, He not only had to obey the moral law but also a specific mandate given to Him in covenant with the Father (John 10:18) "to be a Mediator for those his Father had given him," Burgess says.

On the eve of His crucifixion, Christ speaks in anticipation of completing His mission from God.[9] He opens His prayer by offering His obedience to the Father, which is "not merely obedience, but a meriting obedience," Burgess says. Christ's prayer thus stands upon His finished work as "a Mediator and a Surety," meaning that He has paid the debt owed by others to satisfy divine justice on their behalf.[10] Burgess says, "Christ satisfied God as a just Judge.... Christ by his blood and satisfaction, undertook that the justice of God should never fall upon us to punish us."[11] That does not imply that Christ won over an angry Father, for Christ was sent by the loving Father for this very mission (John 17:18).[12] Rather, Christ died as the representative and substitute of His people. As Isaiah 53:5 says, "But he was wounded for our transgressions, he was bruised for our iniquities: the chastisement of our peace was upon him; and with his stripes we are healed." He laid upon Him the iniquities of us all, and by His stripes we are healed. Thus everywhere His death is said to be for us. Nothing in Christ made Him a curse upon the cross; it was for us and our sins that He was cursed and died.[13]

---

9. In another sermon, Burgess noted that Jesus said in the present tense, "I am no more in the world" (John 17:11), though His departure from the world was obviously in the future (Burgess, *Expository Sermons*, 271 [L]).

10. Burgess, *Expository Sermons*, 119–20 (XXII).

11. Anthony Burgess, *The True Doctrine of Ivstification Asserted, and Vindicated* (London: Robert White, 1648), 101.

12. Burgess, *Expository Sermons*, 487–88 (XCV). Burgess here noted how all three persons in the Trinity cooperated in the redemption of sinners. The Father in His love sent the Son to purchase redemption. The Father and the Son sent the Holy Spirit to apply salvation.

13. Burgess, *Expository Sermons*, 193–94 (XXXV).

Jesus Christ is the only mediator between God and man. He is not merely an example for us to follow when we pray to God; He is the foundation on which to build our relationship to God. Burgess writes,

> Christ is to be set up the only foundation, in respect of mediation and intercession with God. We can have no approach to God without him, because of the great gulf sin hath railed between him and us. He is a consuming fire, and we are stubble, without Christ.... God is an enemy to me, and I to God. And for this end were all those sacrifices appointed in the old administration, to show, that by Christ was all reconcilement and atonement.[14]

Understanding that Christ's mission was to reconcile sinners to God profoundly shapes how we view His prayer and its application to ourselves.

*The Intercessions of the High Priest*
Burgess insists that the prayer in John 17 is a special kind of prayer. It is the prayer of One appointed by God to give eternal life to a definite group of people (John 17:2). It is the prayer of the One who declared that if men would have eternal life, they must not only know God but also Jesus Christ through the gospel (John 17:3).[15] Burgess writes,

> It's a mediatory prayer, and so differs from all the prayers of other men. As they are bare mere men, so their prayers are bare mere prayers. There is no merit, no mediation in them, but Christ's prayer is of a far more transcendent nature, even as the blood of the martyrs came far short of Christ's. Their blood was not expiatory, it was not by way of a sacrifice for sins, whereas Christ's was. Thus there is a vast difference between

---

14. Anthony Burgess, *The Scripture Directory for Church-Officers and People. Or, A Practical Commentary Upon the Whole third Chapter of the first Epistle of St Paul to the Corinthians* (London: Abraham Miller, 1659), 147.

15. See Burgess, *Expository Sermons*, sermons X, XI, and XVIII.

prayers and prayers…but yet the prayer of Christ as in the office of a Mediator doth far surmount all. So then in Christ's prayer we are especially to look to the mediatory power, to the impetratory efficacy[16] of it. It's not a mere supplication as ours are, but a powerful obtaining of what is desired. His prayer can be no more refused than his blood.[17]

The prayers of the Mediator are powerful because He is both God and man. His divine nature imparts infinite worth to His prayers in God's sight. He is the only begotten Son of the Father, and God listens to His Son with great love. The Lord Jesus prays with perfect trust, love, and zeal to God. Burgess says, "The sea is not fuller of water than his soul was of such enlargements." Christ also prays in accordance with God's will, for He asks for the glory appointed for Him from the beginning.[18] And He prays as a man "whose affections and compassions are larger to thee than any of thy dearest friends can be." His heart is full of compassion because He suffered, was tempted, and experienced human weakness like we do (Heb. 4:15).[19]

Christ also prays specifically in the mediating office of a priest.[20] Jesus says, "For their sakes I sanctify myself" (John 17:19). He is a priest whose sacrifices were consecrated to God.[21] His office as priest of His people requires two works: offering and prayers.[22] In Christ the types of the Old Testament priesthood find their fulfillment, for those priests were mortal sinners, but Christ is the sinless, immortal intercessor (Heb. 7:25–27).[23] Burgess explains,

---

16. "Impetratory efficacy" is the power to obtain what you request.
17. Burgess, *Expository Sermons*, 10 (II).
18. Burgess, *Expository Sermons*, 10–12 (II).
19. Burgess, *Expository Sermons*, 225 (XLII).
20. Burgess, in continuity with Reformed tradition going back to Calvin, saw a threefold mediatorial office—prophet, priest, and king—corresponding to our threefold need: our ignorance, blindness, and darkness; our guilt under the wrath of God; and our bondage and captivity to sin and Satan (Burgess, *Expository Sermons*, 503–504 [XCVIII]).
21. Burgess, *Expository Sermons*, 501 (XCVIII).
22. Burgess, *Expository Sermons*, 508 (XCIX).
23. Burgess, *Expository Sermons*, 227 (XLII).

This prayer Christ poured forth, so far as it relateth to the Church of God and all believers, is part of his priestly office, for the priest was to do two things, first to pray, then to offer a sacrifice. Now Christ in this chapter he prayeth and afterwards offereth up himself an holy and unspotted sacrifice for the sins of his people, and as the High Priest was to carry the names of the twelve tribes in his breast to present them to God, so doth Christ here, he presents all his children unto God the Father by this prayer. There is no godly man so mean, so weak, so inconsiderable but he is commended unto the Father, and may justly expect the fruit of this prayer.[24]

Christ's intercession bridges the gap between obtaining the right to all spiritual blessings by His blood and His application of those blessings by His Spirit. Christ did not merely purchase salvation and then leave the application of that salvation to man's free will, for then He might have suffered and died for nothing, which was unthinkable to Burgess, in light of the dishonor it would cast upon God.[25] Christ intercedes for everyone for whom He died. Believers will certainly receive the blessings for which He paid so dearly (Rom. 8:34).[26]

*The Scope of Christ's Mediatorial Prayer*
Jesus Christ prays to His Father, "I pray for them: I pray not for the world, but for them which thou hast given me; for they are thine" (John 17:9). Christ prays for those given to Him by the Father. In this Burgess notes that Christ's people are also called His "sheep," some of which are still enemies of God and are sheep "only in respect of God's purpose and election" (John 10:16). Others are "actually put into a possession of Christ, having new natures, and so enjoying a title and right to him." Both are covered under Christ's mediating prayers, though the latter group more so. Just as our Lord prayed for His sheep while on earth, so He continues to intercede

---

24. Burgess, *Expository Sermons*, 8 (II).
25. Burgess, *Expository Sermons*, 225–26 (XLII).
26. Burgess, *Expository Sermons*, 233 (XLIII).

for them in heaven, though now in a state of exaltation instead of with the cries and tears of His humiliation.[27]

Burgess says, "All the children of God are under the fruit and benefit of Christ's mediatory prayer." All believers have Christ as their advocate with the Father (1 John 2:1). Christ has not set aside His love and affection for the good of His people, but lives to intercede for them (Heb. 7:25). Burgess writes, "It's good to have this friend in the court of heaven.... Oh the unspeakable dignity and happiness to be under Christ's intercession. If we do so much esteem the prayer of a godly man on earth...what then will the prayer of Christ himself do?"[28]

Furthermore, the Lord Jesus prays "for them also which shall believe on me through their word" (John 17:20). Burgess observes, "That such is Christ's care and love to his, that they are remembered in his prayer and death, even before they had a being." Christ's intercession comes out of the divine decree and purpose made from all eternity (Eph. 1:4; 2 Tim. 1:9).[29] He writes later, "The foundation of Christ's intercession is because they were given by election to Christ as a people to be saved through him."[30]

Christ says He does not pray for everyone—not the world, which Burgess says refers to those whom the Father has not given to Christ. They are the reprobate. Burgess says, "Christ's mediatory prayer, and so his death is not for all the world but only some certain persons who are given by the Father to Christ." Burgess understands that the doctrine of limited or particular atonement is controversial.[31] He does not deny that "all mankind, even reprobates themselves, do obtain a world of mercies through Christ's

27. Burgess, *Expository Sermons*, 226 (XLII).
28. Burgess, *Expository Sermons*, 8 (II).
29. Burgess, *Expository Sermons*, 532–33 (CV).
30. Burgess, *Expository Sermons*, 536 (CVI).
31. The Synod of Dort (1618–1619) had rejected the Arminian doctrine of universal atonement just a few decades earlier. John Cameron (ca. 1579–1625) and Moses Amyraut (1596–1664) were also promoting a combination of particular election and universal atonement in Reformed circles in France. Burgess alluded to both the Arminians and the Amyraldians in *Expository Sermons*, 241 (XLIV).

death." But when Christ died for sinners, He died not merely for their benefit but as their substitute, "in their stead to suffer all that anger of God which was due them." Those for whom God gave His Son will receive all of God's blessings, from justification to glorification (Rom. 8:30–32). Those for whom Christ died receive Christ's intercession so that no one can condemn them (Rom. 8:34). Burgess preaches particular redemption not to stir controversy but to establish the peace and joy of the flock of Christ, so that they might have full confidence in Christ's mediation.[32]

While Burgess limits the priestly mediation of Christ to the elect, he exults in the broad scope of His blessings, for every spiritual blessing comes through Christ's death and intercession. He writes, "Though it was once uttered by him upon the earth, and he ceaseth to pray any further, yet it liveth in the efficacy and power of it, yea that continual intercession of his in heaven, what is it but the reviving of this prayer? So that by the virtue of this prayer through his blood we are sanctified, we are justified, and shall hereafter be for ever glorified."[33] Burgess says that Christ prays for the conversion of His people: "There is no man to be converted by the word but Christ prayed for that man's conversion." He also prays for "pardon and forgiveness of sin, and that as oft as it is committed," for "preservation from sin…that their faith may not fail," and for "their glorification…that they may enjoy that glory which Christ had purchased for them." In short, the Lord Jesus prays "for the accomplishing of all grace here and glory hereafter. There is no heavenly or spiritual mercy but Christ hath prayed for it."[34]

---

32. Burgess, *Expository Sermons*, 232–34 (XLIII). Sermons XLIII and XLIV explain and defend this doctrine.

33. Burgess, *Expository Sermons*, 702 (CXLV).

34. Burgess, *Expository Sermons*, 9, (II). See also ibid., 326–27 (XLII). Burgess's point is substantiated by the specific requests Jesus made for His own with respect to their preservation (John 17:11, 15), sanctification (John 17:17), conversion out of the world (John 17:20–21, cf. v. 6), and future enjoyment of His glory (John 17:24).

Far from discouraging sinners from coming to God through Christ, Burgess teaches that Christ's death has a sufficiency or "value enough to redeem thousands of worlds," even though its effectual application is limited to the elect.[35] The greatness of one's sins cannot compare to the greatness of Christ's sufferings. So Burgess says, "If thou art a believer, if thou repenteth, question not but that Christ's death extends to thee. It is for such as hunger and thirst, and therefore whatsoever soul lieth under any burden of sin, and doth desire the grace of God through Christ, let him not stagger but confidently go unto him." The sacrifice and prayers of this Priest are sufficient to cover all human need.[36]

*The Exalted Position of Our Intercessor*
Jesus Christ says to His Father in John 17:11, "I come to thee." Of this, Burgess writes, "He goeth to the Father, and there will be a potent favorite in the court of heaven for them." Jesus' promise is for the comfort of His disciples and for believers today. Burgess refers to the shadow of Christ in Joseph, writing, "Our Saviour comforts their troubled hearts with this, that he was going to the Father, not merely for his own glory and honour, but also for their good—even as Joseph was advanced in Pharaoh's court for the good of his father and his brethren as for his own glory." But Burgess also notes that Christ came to the Father through the death of the cross. The lowest humiliation must precede the highest exaltation so that divine justice is satisfied and men are redeemed.[37]

Burgess then says of Christ's ascension into heaven, "Herein is implied, that state of glory and honour he shall have in heaven....

35. This classic distinction may be traced back to Peter Lombard (d. 1160), who said that Christ offered himself "for all, with respect to the sufficiency of the ransom, but for the elect alone with regard to its efficiency, because it effects salvation for the predestined alone." *Sententiae in IV Libris Distinctae* 3.20.5, cited by Raymond A. Blackster, "Definite Atonement in Historical Perspective," in *The Glory of the Atonement*, ed. Charles E. Hill and Frank A. James III (Downers Grove, Ill.: InterVarsity, 2004), 311.
36. Burgess, *Expository Sermons*, 233–34 (XLIII).
37. Burgess, *Expository Sermons*, 289–90 (LIII).

Now he was no more to be like a servant but to be made the Prince of glory.... In this is the whole treasury of a Christian. The fountain of all our comfort is in this, that Christ is gone to the Father." Burgess lists some of these comforts of the ascended Christ:

1) "Hereby his Holy Spirit is given in, more plentifully and abundantly (John 7:39)."

2) "A second benefit of Christ's going to the Father is enabling us with all holy and heavenly gifts, either in a sanctifying way or a ministerial way (John 14:12; Eph. 4:8–12)."

3) "The third benefit of Christ going to the Father is to prepare a place for his children (John 14:3)."

4) "Christ goeth to the Father, to be an Advocate and plead our cause, 1 John 2. Heb. 7. He ever liveth to make intercession for us. Christ is not so affected with that glory and honour God hath put upon him, that he should forget the meanest [or least] of his children. He dealeth not as Pharaoh's butler that forgot poor Joseph, when he was promoted. No, when we are not and cannot think or mind ourselves, yet Christ is commending our estate to the Father. So we have this glorious friend speaking for us in the court of heaven, whensoever any accusation is brought against us."

5) "Christ's departure from the Father is not an eternal departure. He does not leave us forever, but he will come again and take us to the Father also."[38]

Overflowing with joy over the exaltation of our sacrificial and praying Priest, Burgess continues: "Oh then what glad tidings should this be in our ears. Christ hath ascended to the Father, for that is as much as to say, neither sin or devil or grave could prevail over him, and therefore he hath fully discharged the work of a Redeemer. He

---

38. Burgess, *Expository Sermons*, 290–92 (LIII).

hath paid to the utmost farthing,[39] so that the love and justice of God cannot but be satisfied by the atonement he hath made."[40]

In heavenly intercession, Jesus Christ prays for His people as "one authorized and appointed thereunto" far above any earthly priest ordained by God. The prayers of our Lord stand upon His completed mission from the Father, His finished work of atonement. Our Lord prays for those whom He died for, so that "what he obtained for his people should be applied to them." These prayers are "of him who is the beloved Son of the Father, so that nothing can be in justice denied to Christ's prayer, because it is a meriting and an obliging prayer."[41]

### Praying through Christ's Mediation

We must therefore draw near to God by believing that God sent Christ as mediator. Burgess says that "resting the soul upon Christ" is the only way to please God. Such faith in Christ is just as acceptable to God as if we had ourselves fulfilled His law because it is "the most evacuating grace"—it empties us wholly of ourselves, and God delights in humility. "Now nothing humbleth us and takes us off all our seeming worth like faith in Christ, for therefore I wholly trust in him for righteousness, because I have none of my own,"[42] Burgess says. Faith is the only grace suited to receive Christ and His benefits. "As the hand of all parts of the body taketh a treasure when given, and thereby a man is enriched.... It is not the hand but the treasure taken by the hand that enricheth." Faith is the hand that receives Christ in His fullness in both justification and sanctification.[43] Prayer without faith in the Mediator is futile; prayer that relies upon Christ enters the treasuries of heaven.

---

39. A farthing was a small British coin worth a quarter of a penny.

40. Burgess, *Expository Sermons*, 292 (LIII).

41. Burgess, *Expository Sermons*, 508 (XCIX).

42. Burgess, *Expository Sermons*, 211, 214 (XXXVIII).

43. Burgess, *Expository Sermons*, 217 (XXXIX). Burgess rejected any so-called faith that tries to receive "some things of Christ but not the whole Christ. They think it's only believing on him as a Saviour for pardon of sin. They do not choose him as a Lord to whom in all obedience they resign themselves"(ibid., 213 [XXXVIII]).

God's people should consciously depend upon Christ's intercession for the acceptance of their own prayers to God. This brings great comfort to those struggling to pray. Burgess writes, "This prayer of Christ sanctifieth all our prayers. They become accepted of God through him…. As our tears need washing in his blood, so our prayers need Christ's prayer. He prayed that our prayers may be received…. Though I am unworthy yet Christ is worthy to be heard."[44] He also says,

> This mediatory prayer of Christ is the ground of all the acceptance of our prayers. Our prayers if not found in him are provocations rather than appeasements. If a godly man's prayer availeth much, it is because Christ's prayer availeth much. He is the altar upon which all the oblations are sanctified, and from hence it is that the incense of their prayers are perfumed, so that God finds a sweet savour in them…. This may unspeakably support thee under sad temptations, when thou canst not pray. Thy heart is bound up. Thy affections are faint and cold. Thou criest out, Oh the sins and infirmities of thy prayers, yet Christ's prayer is full and fervent for thee. There is no imperfection, no fault to be found with him. Oh it's a good refuge to run unto, when thou are almost overwhelmed because of thy dull, formal and distracted prayers![45]

Why does a chapter about prayer dwell so much upon Christ and His work? Because Jesus is the only way to God. Without the prayer of Christ our mediator, we could pray to no one but an angry judge whose law demands our punishment. Burgess reminds us that the Mediator's work is a strong foundation for praying with faith and peace.

---

44. Burgess, *Expository Sermons*, 12 (II).
45. Burgess, *Expository Sermons*, 227, 225 (XLII). These pages immediately follow each other in this order in the book.

## The Prayer of Christ as the Model of a Godly Man

Christ's prayers as mediator are offered as human prayers because God cannot pray, being omnipotent and supreme in authority.[46] Christ prays as a man with limited power, subject to the law of God, using the divinely appointed means of seeking grace for His people as an act of worship and the model or example of a godly man for us to follow.[47] Let us turn to Burgess's comments on John 17 as the exemplary prayer of the perfect man, Christ Jesus.

### The Necessity and Benefits of Prayer

After stressing the absolute sovereignty of God and complete sufficiency of Christ, Burgess asks, "But if Christ's prayer be thus all in all, what need we pray? Are not our prayers superfluous?" He answers by reminding us that our prayers do not serve the same purposes as Christ's prayers, namely, "for merit or mediation." Our prayers have other objectives, such as "to set up God," that is, to exalt Him as the God to whom we pray; "to debase ourselves," that is, to humble ourselves; "to quicken our graces," or stir up our souls to lively faith, hope, and love; "to give us an holy communion and fellowship with him"; and "to show our obedience to his command."[48]

Burgess strongly affirms the Reformed doctrines of predestination and sovereign providence. He says it is false and sinful for a man to pray thinking he can change God's mind and make Him alter His will. God is immutable and unchangeable. Yet even those things God has promised to give to His people must be accomplished by our praying for them, for God's purposes and promises require our supplications. Burgess says this is the order God has appointed: "Ask and ye shall have, seek and ye shall find, knock and it shall be opened to you, Matt. 7." Burgess says some acts of God are independent of prayer, such as God's sending Christ into the world to save sinners and the initial workings of grace in the beginning of

---

46. Burgess, *Expository Sermons*, 519 (CII).
47. Burgess, *Expository Sermons*, 520 (CII). See also ibid., 8 (II).
48. Burgess, *Expository Sermons*, 12 (II).

our conversion. He explains, "Our prayers are not meritorious. They deserve not [anything] at God's hand." God does not give mercy because we pray, but He stimulates us to pray so that He may give us the mercy He intends for us. Our prayers are part of God's grace to us, for He gives us not just the opportunity to pray but our actual prayers. At the heart of Burgess's understanding of the necessity of prayer is the doctrine of God's sovereign use of means to accomplish His ends. He writes, "God in the wonderful things he hath predestined or promised for his people hath appointed means for the performance of them. Hence as he converts by the Word, so he bestoweth his mercy upon a praying people."[49]

God's people must thus pray for the success of the Word. John 17:1 says, "These words spake Jesus, and lifted up his eyes to heaven." From this Burgess infers that prayer is necessary for the good effect of all instructions and consolations. "Christ himself doth not think it enough to plant, but he prays there may be a watering from above." Thus all ministers are to take Christ's way, which may mean spending the day in preaching and the night in praying.[50] God is the source of all grace, and He commands men to pray that He might receive all the glory for the effects of His Word. Men are utterly unable to do any good thing from their own fallen nature. So, in all ministry, "we are to be as the little child who leaneth only upon his father."[51]

God has reasons for requiring our prayers to accomplish His purposes:

1) God will have us pray to Him because "hereby he is acknowledged the author and fountain of all the good we have.... He that liveth without prayer liveth as if there were no God."

2) God graciously honors us when we pray, in "that we may be admitted into his presence, and have holy

49. Burgess, *Expository Sermons*, 137–39 (XXV).
50. Burgess, *Expository Sermons*, 2 (I).
51. Burgess, *Expository Sermons*, 2–4 (I).

communion[52] with him.... Prayer is heavenly commerce with God."

3) "God will have us pray because prayer is an appointed means by him as well as faith and repentance. Now God's purposes and promises must never be opposed to, or separated from the means.... As Augustine said, If Stephen had not prayed for his persecutors, the church had never had such a glorious doctor as Paul was."

4) "God hath appointed prayer not only for our honour but also for our spiritual advantage and profit. By praying fervently the heart is raised up, made more heavenly, and lifted up even into the third heavens.... When we come into God's presence and pray effectually, a divine Spirit, a heavenly frame of heart, may come upon us. We shall go from prayer ravished with the church, saying, My Beloved is the chiefest of ten thousand."

5) "God will have us pray because hereby we must testify our desire and high esteem we have of the mercy prayed for. Do we not say that is little worth which is not worth asking?... Hence it is that God loveth wrestling and fervent prayers."

6) God has made prayer necessary "because hereby faith is drawn out in all the choice and excellent effects of it. Prayer without faith is like a musical instrument without a hand to make a sound melodious."[53]

Burgess says, "In our earnest petitions we do not bring God's will to ours but ours to him. Prayer is a golden chain that reacheth from heaven to earth, and although we think to move God to us, yet we move our selves to him. As the ship that is fastened with the

---

52. Burgess here does not use "holy communion" with respect to the Lord's Supper, but sacred fellowship with the Lord.
53. Burgess, *Expository Sermons*, 139–141 (XXV).

cable doth not bring the haven to it, but its self to the haven, so the change prayer makes is not in God, but in our selves."[54] In light of the necessity and benefits of prayer, Burgess asks pointed questions:

> Why in these latter days [is it that] the Word preached makes no more wonderful works? At first propagation of the gospel, so many fish were caught in the net that it was ready to break. And at the first Reformation out of Popery, the kingdom of God suffered violence, but now he that is profane is profane still, the blind are blind still, the proud still proud. What is the matter? Is not the Word of God as powerful as ever? Is not the Lord's arm as strong as ever? Yes, but the zeal of people is grown cold. There are not such fervent prayers, such high esteems of the means of grace. Men do not besiege heaven, giving God no rest day or night till he come with salvation into their souls, and truly the Spirit of prayer is a sure forerunner of spiritual mercies to be bestowed.[55]

*The Heavenly Manner of Prayer*

Christ "lifted up his eyes to heaven" and prayed, says John 17:1. From this Burgess infers that all our prayers should come from a spiritual and heavenly heart. The very definition of prayer is lifting the whole mind and soul to God. "To pray is a far more difficult and noble exercise than most [people] are aware of," Burgess says. "It's not running over a few words like a parrot." Burgess further explains heavenly minded prayer in the following points:

1) It is necessary that the Spirit of God enable and move the soul to this duty (Rom. 8). Without the fire of the Spirit, our prayers are like a body without a soul or birds without wings.

2) A heavenly prayer must come from a heavenly heart that delights in heavenly things. We should first seek God's glory and spiritual blessings.

---

54. Burgess, *Expository Sermons*, 141 (XXV).
55. Burgess, *Expository Sermons*, 5 (I).

3) Prayer is heavenly when it purifies and sanctifies the heart and affections for the enjoyment of God.

4) A heavenly prayer stirs the heart to delight in heavenly things. Prayer must not only be heavenly in nature but in its effects. True prayer is like exercise to the body, making us more strong and active. It is like the rich ship that brings in glorious returns from God.[56]

Prayer is communion with the great God as well as the divine worship of God, Burgess says. Thus it calls for a "heavenly, holy, fervent and undistracted disposition." Most prayers are more like the utterances of an ape rather than a human. In our prayers we must give diligent attention to:

1) What we pray for; that it be lawful, good, and agreeable to God's will. We should not pray like pagans in ignorance of what pleases God, for we have the Word of God to direct us and His Spirit to incline us.

2) The order of what we pray for; that we seek first the kingdom of God (Matt. 6:33), giving highest priority to God's glory and our salvation, then praying for temporal goods with submission and subordination, if these be God's will and will further our spiritual good.

3) The words we use in prayer; that they be grave, decent, and comely. Our prayers should be free of "vanity, affectation,[57] or irreverence." Prayer worships God.

4) The One to whom we pray, namely, to almighty God. Our majestic King deserves the attention of

56. Burgess, *Expository Sermons*, 5–6 (I).

57. "Affectation" is putting on a show of what is not real, here a show of spiritual desires which are not real in the heart.

an undivided heart. Who goes into the presence of
a king without preparing to please Him?

5) How we should pray; that we pray with the con-
comitant graces, such as faith which is "the life and
soul of all," as well as zeal, fervency, faith, heavenly
mindedness, and hatred of sin. Without those graces,
prayer is like a bird without wings or a rusty key.

6) Why we are praying; that we not lose sight of the
true purpose of prayer. James 4:3 tells us, "Ye ask,
and receive not, because ye ask amiss, that ye may
consume it upon your lusts." We must seek God's
kingdom before asking for temporal things.[58]

Since prayer engages the whole person, the character of the person who prays is crucial to the power of his prayers. Burgess says
our prayer must be like that of a righteous man who is washed of
sin, for sins "have a tongue, and they cry for vengeance, and will
quickly cry louder than our prayers." Burgess does not demand perfection in order to pray. He encourages sinners to pray, mourn, and
repent, as the publican does in Luke 18:13. But he warns that a
sinner who willfully continues in wickedness is an abomination to
God when he prays (Prov. 28:9). He writes, "Oh then look to thyself
and thy life when thou goest to pray. If the tongue that prayeth be
a cursing, swearing tongue, if the eyes lifted up to heaven be full of
wantonness and adultery, if the hands held out towards heaven be
full of violence, fraud, and injustice, God is of purer eyes than to
behold such."[59]

Though prayer begins in the heart, Burgess notes that Christ
prayed aloud. This too is a helpful model, for although God does
not need to hear our words to know our hearts, vocal prayer helps
to excite and stir up our affections, for the soul and body to mutually help each other. So we glorify God with both body and soul,

58. Burgess, *Expository Sermons*, 131–33 (XXIV). See also ibid., 8, (II).
59. Burgess, *Expository Sermons*, 141 (XXV).

expressing with the mouth what is strong in the heart.[60] Vocal
prayer is also important when a minister, elder, or the head of a
household publicly leads others in prayer. In public, the one who
prays must also consider what will edify listeners (1 Cor.
14:15–17). He must consider what they need and how to affect their hearts.[61]

Repetition can sometimes be helpful in prayer. Jesus prays,
"Glorify thy Son" (John 17:1), and shortly afterwards, "Glorify thou
me" (John 17:5). Burgess thus infers, "Repetition of the same matter
in a prayer is not always a sinful tautology, but is sometimes lawful, yea, useful and necessary."[62] Repetition is appropriate in prayer
when a matter is pressing upon the heart, such as a sinner's cry
for forgiveness (Ps. 51) or a person in great danger (Matt. 26:44).
The same request may be repeated if the matter is very important,
but the heart needs to be stirred to action. Fervent affections may
also rightly move us to repetition in prayer, as when the Spirit
moves God's children to pray, "Abba, Father," which means, "Father,
Father" (Gal. 4:6). Repetition may also seal upon us the certainty of
the truths we are praying.[63]

At the same time, Burgess recognizes the Lord's warning
against vain repetition in prayer (Matt. 6:7). Burgess says such vain
repetition includes babbling words without the understanding of
the mind, eloquent or long-winded speech to cover coldness of
heart, making prayers long to impress others, or repeating forms of
prayer such as the Lord's Prayer to appease God or the Ave Maria
to make amends for sins.[64]

*Intercession for the Saints and the World*
Our duty is to pray for ourselves as well as others, just as our Lord
did. Christ calls us to be intercessors. Burgess writes, "It's the duty of
godly men to pray for others. Our Saviour doth suppose that in his

60. Burgess, *Expository Sermons*, 7 (II).
61. Burgess, *Expository Sermons*, 133 (XXIV).
62. Burgess, *Expository Sermons*, 131 (XXIV).
63. Burgess, *Expository Sermons*, 133–35 (XXIV).
64. Burgess, *Expository Sermons*, 135–36 (XXIV).

form of prayer, *Our Father*, and he extends this, Matt. 5, even to our very enemies that are enemies for our godliness sake, persecuting and reviling us, and that though continuing in their wickedness.... Yea, the apostle, 1 Tim. 2:1, exhorts, *that supplications and prayers be put up for all men*, that is, for all sorts of men."[65]

The doctrine of election is no obstacle to praying for the conversion of sinners. Burgess says we are to pray for the conversion of a particular person no matter how wicked he may be, because we cannot tell who is given by the Father to Christ and who is not. "God's decree about events is not the rule of our prayer, but his Word is,"[66] Burgess says.

Christ's prayer in John 17 particularly encourages us to pray for those who belong to Christ. It is comforting to know that our prayers will more likely obtain powerful answers since Christ is praying for believers who are in the covenant, who desire to walk with God, and in whom God has already begun salvation. Burgess says, "Shall Christ regard the estate of such an one, and shall I forget him? It's to be feared that the godly do not look upon this as so necessary a duty, and certainly such are the dissensions and alienations from one another, that I doubt not this great duty of prayer for one another is greatly neglected."[67]

Burgess presses upon believers their responsibility to pray for one another, arguing:

1) God has made you part of the body of Christ. If a part of your own body is injured, how does it affect you? You should have the same empathy for the body of Christ as for your own body.

2) God instituted prayer as a means to help others. Instead, we are quick to criticize each other. Rather than finding fault, we should pray for fellow believers. That is our duty.

65. Burgess, *Expository Sermons*, 229 (XLI).
66. Burgess, *Expository Sermons*, 229–30 (XLI).
67. Burgess, *Expository Sermons*, 230–31 (XLI).

3) Praying for one another will ease differences, jealousies, and suspicions. It will make the godly of one heart and one mind. If you find yourself thinking how poorly a brother has treated you, pray for that man. It will immediately "quiet those winds and waves."[68]

Burgess imagines someone asking if we should pray only for the godly. If so, we may, like the priest and Levite in Christ's parable of the Good Samaritan, omit the needs of the wicked. Burgess forbids such a response, saying the only people God forbids us to pray for are those who are sinning unto death (1 John 5:16).[69] When preaching on Judas as "the son of perdition" (John 17:12), Burgess observes, "There are some men so resolvedly and obstinately given to damn themselves, that let what will come in the way, they will go on." But he also notes that it is not easy to tell who these people are and that Judas himself ministered for a long time as an apostle.[70] Therefore Burgess says, "It is our duty to pray for the wicked though wallowing in their sins, that they may be converted and brought home to God." Christ prayed for the salvation of the wicked men who crucified Him (Luke 23:34). Who knows what God may do for the sinner I pray for? Perhaps my prayer may serve to "the execution of God's election."[71]

*Engaging the God of Glory*

Burgess recommends bringing holy arguments to God, just as Christ did (John 17:1–4). The best prayer is argumentative, he says, for "many words without arguments is like a great body without nerves or sinews." By "argumentative," Burgess does not mean prayers that arise from a critical or contentious spirit towards God; he refers to prayers that are strengthened by faith and reasons why it is good

68. Burgess, *Expository Sermons*, 232, 225 (XLI). These pages are immediately sequential in the book.
69. Burgess, *Expository Sermons*, 229, 231 (XLI).
70. Burgess, *Expository Sermons*, 364 (LXVIII), 372 (LXX).
71. Burgess, *Expository Sermons*, 231–32 (XLI).

and right for God to grant your requests. Burgess notes that our Lord began His prayer with three strong arguments, namely, that God was His Father and He was God's Son, that this was the hour that God had appointed, and that Christ's purpose was to glorify the Father.[72]

The first argument in prayer is our relationship to God as our Father. Burgess carefully distinguishes Christ's sonship from our adoption, saying, "That which Christ hath by nature we have by grace. Christ therefore is Son to the Father, yet so that he is of the same nature with the Father, having all the properties of the Godhead with him, but we are sons only by grace and adoption." Yet, amazingly, Christ joined our sonship to His in John 20:17, when He called His disciples His "brethren" and said, "I ascend unto my Father, and your Father; and to my God, and your God." Therefore successful prayer is prayer poured out to God as our Father. Christ taught us to pray "our Father" in "that directory of prayer which he hath left"—that is, the Lord's Prayer. Burgess asserts that all people are by nature enemies of God, but Christ purchased "this sweet relation of sonship to God the Father" by His sorrows. To pray as adopted sons, we need the following:

> To be able to call God Father is so great a matter that there needeth the Spirit of adoption to move us thereunto. Gal. 4:6, *He hath sent the Spirit of his Son into our hearts, crying Abba Father.* Although it be easy for a presumptuous self-justifying man to call God Father, yet take the afflicted mourner for sin, who is sensible of the great dishonor he puts upon God, it's the hardest thing in the world to think God is a Father to him. Because therefore it is so great a work, God sends his Spirit into our hearts that enableth us to cry boldly, vehemently, and notwithstanding all opposition, Abba, Father. Where then we would use this compellation ["Father"][73] with power and life, with success and heavenly advantage, there the Spirit of God

---

72. Burgess, *Expository Sermons*, 13 (III).
73. A "compellation" is a manner of addressing or greeting a person. Here it refers to calling God "our Father."

must inflame the heart, there all our servile fears and torment-
ing doubts must be removed.[74]

Praying to God the Father in the Spirit of adoption stirs the
soul to much good. Approaching God as Father raises our confidence and hope, puts fervency and zeal in our prayers, quickens a
childlike reverence and humility, breeds a peaceful and quiet spirit,
makes us earnest to pursue a holy likeness to God, enflames our
zeal for God's glory and honor, and supports us in our afflictions by
trusting that our Father disciplines us for our good. Furthermore,
such prayer engages God's heart to answer us, for He is a Father
who loves His children more than any mother loves her baby (Isa.
49:15). It is for God's glory to hear His children when they pray, so
He will not neglect them in their cries and needs.[75]

The ultimate objective of all prayer is the glory of God. Christ
prayed, "Glorify thy Son, that thy Son may also glorify thee" (John
17:1). Burgess thus says, "As Christ so much more all men are to
pray for and desire any comfort or advantages, not so much for
themselves as that thereby God may be glorified." Christ does all
things for the glory of His Father, both in His humiliation and in
His exaltation. Burgess laments, "Oh but in all our religious duties
how much vain-glory doth infect and rotten them? That is the
pirate which doth intercept the golden fleet of our prayers that they
return not again freighted with good things for us." However, even
our spiritual and heavenly well-being serves the larger purpose of
God's glory. Certainly we should not seek earthly goods to advance
ourselves or to satisfy our appetites, but only to glorify God. Burgess does not deny the legitimacy of human desires and happiness,
if only our happiness serves the ultimate end of glorifying God.[76]

In heaven we will know that God's glorification and our happiness are one goal, not two. Burgess says in God we have "all
our happiness and glory." In this life we are forbidden to glory in

74. Burgess, *Expository Sermons*, 13–15 (III).
75. Burgess, *Expository Sermons*, 15–18 (III). See also ibid., 658 (CXXXV).
76. Burgess, *Expository Sermons*, 30–34 (VI).

riches, honors, and greatness, but we must glory in knowing God (1 Cor. 1:31). How much more, then, will we experience the glory of enjoying God in heaven. All the happiness, excellence, and glory in heaven can be reduced to knowing that we are made partakers of God. In God is glory, and seeing that glory and our utmost happiness will finally become one perfectly in heaven.[77]

Just as Christ prayed for His glorification in the presence of God, so Christians should pray for the eternal enjoyment of God's glory and seek it above all earthly glories. The Scriptures commend seeking after glory from God (Rom. 2:7) and praying for the coming of God's kingdom (Matt. 6:10). Praying for this glory will kindle our desires and strengthen our hope. As Burgess says, "This glory with God is an universal medicine for all our diseases. It's a full treasury for all our wants.... This is the ocean, other are but shells." Nothing else will fill and satisfy our hearts.[78] The ultimate goal of prayer is communion with the altogether lovely triune God.

## Concluding Comfort: Christ's Prayers Are Effectual

The Bible has a high view of prayer. Christ gave us the perfect model for praying, which ought to humble us. Yet who prays with the frequency, filial fear, faith, and fervor that he should? Burgess says,

> To pray is such a solemn worship of God, that it requireth the whole man, the intellectual part, all our judgment, invention, and memory is to be employed therein, as also the whole heart, the will and affections, yea, and body also; and besides this there is also required the Spirit of God to enlighten the mind, and to sanctify the heart for mere judgment and invention, without God's Spirit enlivening of them, is like a sacrifice without fire. Oh then if all these things go together, may we not cry out, "Who is sufficient to pray?"[79]

---

77. Burgess, *Expository Sermons*, 144 (XXVI).

78. Burgess, *Expository Sermons*, 146–47 (XXVI).

79. Burgess, *Expository Sermons*, 136 (XXIV).

In Christ, however, we need not despair. All honest attempts to pray will drive believers back to Christ, the perfect intercessor. His blood and prayers cover our sins, even the sins of our prayers. It is a great comfort to have a godly friend praying for you. Some have said Augustine thought it impossible the he should perish because of the way his mother, Monica, wept and prayed for him. Burgess did not put such confidence in the prayers and tears of mere men and women. But he did say, "It is impossible that a child of Christ's prayers and tears should perish."[80]

---

80. Burgess, *Expository Sermons*, 9 (II).

*Chapter 6*

# John Bunyan on Praying with the Holy Spirit

MICHAEL A. G. HAYKIN

> *[Scripture] doth not say the Common prayer-book teacheth us how to pray, but the Spirit.*
>
> —JOHN BUNYAN

Central to any expression of biblical spirituality is prayer. It is not surprising, therefore, that the Puritans, men and women who sought to complete the Reformation in the Church of England and who sought to frame their lives according to God's Word,[1] wrote a great deal about this subject and were themselves, in the words of John Geree (ca. 1601–1649), "much in prayer."[2] As the Congregationalist theologian Thomas Goodwin (1600–1680) remarked, "Our speak-

---

1. The words of the Calvinistic Baptist William Kiffin (1616–1701), writing about a fellow Puritan and Baptist, John Norcott (1621–1676), are typical of Puritanism in general: "He steered his whole course by the compass of the word, making Scripture precept or example his constant rule in matters of religion. Other men's opinions or interpretations were not the standard by which he went; but, through the assistance of the Holy Spirit, he laboured to find out what the Lord himself had said in his word" (cited by Joseph Ivimey, *A History of the English Baptists* [London: B. J. Holdsworth, 1823], 3:300).

2. John Geree, *The Character of an Old English Puritan or Non-Conformist* (London, 1646) in Lawrence A. Sasek, *Images of English Puritanism: A Collection of Contemporary Sources 1589–1646* (Baton Rouge: Louisiana State University Press, 1989), 209.

ing to God by prayers, and his speaking to us by answers thereunto, is one great part of our walking with God."[3]

Given their deep interest in the Holy Spirit, the Puritans invariably rooted their discussion and experience of prayer in Him and His work. A cluster of biblical texts—the description of the Spirit as "the spirit of grace and of supplications" (Zech. 12:10); the admonition to both "[pray] in the Holy Ghost" (Jude 20; cf. Eph. 6:18) and pray for the Spirit (Luke 11:13); the experience of calling upon God as "Abba, Father" (Rom. 8:15–16; Gal. 4:6); and that unique passage on the Spirit's intercessory work, Romans 8:26–27—were central in giving shape and substance to their reflections on this vital subject.[4] What follows is what one Puritan, the famous author of *Pilgrim's Progress,* John Bunyan (1628–1688), had to say about prayer and the Spirit.

### Historical Context

"Oft I was as if I was on the Ladder, with the Rope about my neck."[5] So John Bunyan reflected about his possible demise by hanging as he sat in a cold jail cell during the early 1660s. Bunyan's refusal to give up his God-given calling as an evangelist and preacher had led to his imprisonment in 1660, a possible death sentence by hanging, and his subsequent incarceration for twelve long years. When John Newton, famous evangelical leader of the eighteenth century and author of the well-known hymn "Amazing Grace," reflected on this difficult period in Bunyan's life, he noted that the "Lord has reasons, far beyond our ken, for opening a wide door, while he stops the mouth of a useful preacher. John Bunyan would not have done half the good he did had he remained preaching in Bedford, instead of

3. Thomas Goodwin, "The Return of Prayers," in *The Works of Thomas Goodwin* (reprint, Grand Rapids: Reformation Heritage Books, 2006), 3:362.

4. Roy Williams, "Lessons from the Prayer Habits of the Puritans" in D. A. Carson, ed., *Teach Us to Pray: Prayer in the Bible and the World* (Grand Rapids: Baker for the World Evangelical Fellowship, 1990), 279.

5. John Bunyan, *Grace Abounding to the Chief of Sinners,* ed. W. R. Owens (London: Penguin Books, 1987), 335.

being shut up in Bedford prison."[6] What Newton no doubt had in mind are the two evangelical classics that came from Bunyan's pen as a result of this imprisonment, namely, the account of his conversion which he entitled *Grace Abounding to the Chief of Sinners* (1666) and *The Pilgrim's Progress* (1678 and 1684). Down through the centuries, the vision contained in these two books has nourished believers and encouraged them in their pilgrimage. For instance, during the eighteenth-century Great Awakening, these two works of Bunyan were read with great spiritual relish. As N. H. Keeble notes:

> Leaders of the Evangelical Revival and of Methodism were inspired by him [i.e. Bunyan], returned to him often, and recommended him constantly. Howel Harris was a devoted reader. George Whitefield contributed a preface to the third edition of *The Works* (1767). John Wesley more than once read through *The Pilgrim's Progress* (and other Bunyan titles) on horseback, and himself abridged it in 1743.... Methodist preachers made frequent reference to Bunyan, who exerted a formative influence on their own autobiographies.[7]

However, Bunyan wrote other works during this long time of imprisonment, and though they are now not so well known, they are still deserving of consideration. One of the earliest of these works is *I Will Pray with the Spirit*, written around 1662.[8] It is a powerful plea to the religious authorities of his day to recognize the sovereignty of the Holy Spirit in the prayer life of the believer and

---

6. John Newton, *The Works of the Rev. John Newton* (London: George King, 1833), I, lxxxv. In 1776 Newton had contributed notes to one of the first annotated editions of Bunyan's *The Pilgrim's Progress*, Part I.

7. N. H. Keeble, "'Of Him Thousands Daily Sing and Talk': Bunyan and His Reputation" in *John Bunyan: Conventicle and Parnassus—Tercentenary Essays*, ed. Neil H. Keeble (Oxford: Clarendon Press, 1988), 249–50.

8. For the date, see Richard L. Greaves, introduction to his ed., John Bunyan, *The Doctrine of the Law and Grace Unfolded and I Will Pray with the Spirit* (Oxford: Clarendon Press, 1976), xl–xli. Subsequent quotations from *I Will Pray with the Spirit* will be taken from this text, which is the latest critical edition. For a recent modernization and abridgment of *I Will Pray with the Spirit*, see Louis Gifford Parkhurst, Jr., ed., *Pilgrim's Prayer Book* (Wheaton, Ill.: Tyndale, 1986).

in the worship of the church. In what follows, the theological and historical contexts of Bunyan's treatise on prayer are outlined, along with the heart of its argumentation, and its abiding significance.

## The Theological Context of *I Will Pray with the Spirit*

When Bunyan was put on trial in January 1661, he was accused of having broken the Elizabethan Conventicle Act of 1593, which specified that anyone "devilishly and perniciously abstained from coming to Church [i.e., the Church of England] to hear Divine Service" and of being "a common upholder of several unlawful meetings and conventicles" could be held without bail until he or she agreed to submit to the authorities of the national church.[9] In the eyes of the authorities Bunyan was an uneducated, unordained common mechanic. It was made clear to Bunyan that he would be released if he promised to desist from preaching.

Bunyan, though, had a higher loyalty than obedience to an earthly monarch—obedience to King Jesus. Like the majority of his fellow Puritans, he believed in obedience to the laws of the state, and he emphasized that he looked upon it as his duty to behave himself under the king's government both as becomes a man and a Christian. But Bunyan knew that the Spirit of God had given him a gift for preaching, a gift that had been confirmed by the congregation of which he was a member. In Bunyan's own words, "The Holy Ghost never intended that men who have gifts and abilities should bury them in the earth."[10] For Bunyan, those imbued with the gifts of the Holy Spirit to preach had no choice but to exercise the gifts that God had given them. During his trial, Bunyan defended his right to preach by quoting 1 Peter 4:10–11. Those judging his case maintained that only those ordained by the Church of England could lawfully preach. Bunyan's disagreement was rooted in the fact that for him the ultimate authority in religious matters was not human tradition or man-made laws but the Scriptures and their

---

9. Bunyan, *Grace Abounding to the Chief of Sinners*, 127, n.137.
10. Ibid., 270.

author, God. Bunyan had to obey his God; otherwise, on the day of judgment he would be counted a traitor to Christ.

At his trial, Bunyan had also been asked by Sir John Kelynge, one of the judges, to justify his absence from worship in the local parish church. Bunyan, true to his Puritan heritage, stated that "he did not find it commanded in the word of God."[11] Kelynge pointed out that prayer was a duty. Bunyan agreed, but he insisted that it was a duty to be performed with the Spirit's aid, not by means of the Book of Common Prayer, the prescribed liturgy of the Church of England. Bunyan proceeded to argue: "Those prayers in the Common Prayer-book, was such as was made by other men, and not by the motions of the Holy Ghost, within our hearts.... The scripture saith, that it is the Spirit as helpeth our infirmities; for we know not what we should pray for as we ought; but the Spirit itself maketh intercession for us, with sighs and groanings which cannot be uttered. Mark...it doth not say the Common prayer-book teacheth us how to pray, but the Spirit."[12]

Bunyan's outright rejection of the use of written prayers cannot be understood apart from the view of his Puritan contemporaries and forebears.[13] John Calvin (1509–1564), the spiritual father of English-speaking Puritanism, had defined prayer as essentially an "emotion of the heart..., which is poured out and laid open before

---

11. "A Relation of the Imprisonment of Mr. John Bunyan," in *Grace Abounding to the Chief of Sinners*, 95.

12. Ibid., 95, 96.

13. The following discussion of "prayer in the Spirit" is indebted to Geoffrey F. Nuttall, *The Holy Spirit in Puritan Faith and Experience*, 2nd ed. (Oxford: Basil Blackwell, 1947), 62–74; A. G. Matthews, "The Puritans at Prayer" in his *Mr. Pepys and Nonconformity* (London: Independent Press, 1954), 100–122; Horton Davies, *The Worship of the English Puritans* (1948; reprint, Morgan, Pa.: Soli Deo Gloria, 1997), 98–161; Garth B. Wilson, "The Puritan Doctrine of the Holy Spirit: A Critical Investigation of a Crucial Chapter in the History of Protestant Theology" (Th.D. diss., Knox College, Toronto, 1978), 208–223; Alan L. Hayes, "Spirit and Structure in Elizabethan Public Prayer," in E. J. Furcha, ed., *Spirit Within Structure: Essays in Honor of George Johnston on the Occasion of His Seventieth Birthday* (Allison Park, Pa.: Pickwick Publications, 1983), 117–32. The texts cited from Calvin, Cradock, and Owen are taken from these studies.

God." At the same time, Calvin was tolerant of written prayers. Some of his spiritual children among the English Puritans, like Richard Baxter, preserved both of these emphases. Many of the Puritans, however, took Calvin's view of prayer to its logical conclusion and saw little need for written prayers.

Walter Cradock (ca. 1610–1659), a Welsh Congregationalist preacher and author, stated forthrightly, "When it may be the (poor Minister)...would have rejoyced to have poured out his soule to the Lord, he was tied to an old Service Booke, and must read that till he grieved the Spirit of God, and dried up his own spirit as a chip, that he could not pray." John Owen (1616–1683), Bunyan's friend and admirer,[14] similarly maintained that "constant and unvaried use of set forms of prayer may become a great occasion of quenching the Spirit." Owen conceded that the use of written prayers is not intrinsically evil. But since the Spirit whom God had given to the believer is "the spirit of grace and of supplications" (Zech. 12:10), the believer has all the resources that he needs for prayer. Moreover, Owen affirmed that the "Holy Ghost, as a Spirit of grace and supplication, is nowhere, that I know of, promised unto any to help or assist them in composing prayers for others; and therefore we have no ground to pray for him or his assistance unto that end in particular."[15]

These criticisms of the Book of Common Prayer reflect Puritan dissatisfaction with both the manner and content of its prayers. Moreover, undergirding the approach to prayer of both Cradock and Owen was an intense interest in the work of the Spirit in general and the accompanying recognition that only with His empowering could God be rightly served and worshiped. Bunyan shared these perspectives on prayer and the Spirit but states them in his own expressive way.

---

14. Owen helped Bunyan publish *The Pilgrim's Progress.* It is also said that he told Charles II that he would willingly give up all of his learning if he could preach like Bunyan. See Neil H. Keeble, "Bunyan and His Reputation," in *John Bunyan: Conventicle and Parnassus—Tercentenary Essays,* ed. Neil H. Keeble (Oxford: Clarendon Press, 1988), 243.

15. Bunyan, *I Will Pray with the Spirit,* 293.

## The Heart of Bunyan's Treatise on Prayer

Bunyan's interest in extemporaneous prayer, quickened by his debate with Kelynge, found written form not long after his trial in *I Will Pray with the Spirit*. There are no surviving copies of the first edition. The second edition, dated 1663, appears without a bookseller's or publisher's name on the title page. The title page simply states "Printed for the author." The book was probably too hot for any publisher to handle![16] And no wonder when Bunyan declared near the end of the book: "Look into the Gaols in England, and into the Alehouses of the same: and I believe, you will find those that plead for the Spirit of Prayer in the Gaol, and them that look after the Form of men's Inventions only, in the Alehouse."[17]

Bunyan's tract on prayer opens with a definition of prayer that is reminiscent of Calvin's: "Prayer is a sincere, sensible, affectionate pouring out of the heart or soul to God through Christ, in the strength and assistance of the Holy Spirit, for such things as God hath promised, or according to the Word, for the good of the Church, with submission, in Faith, to the will of God."[18] The rest of the book takes up each individual item in this definition.

Understandably, it is his discussion of the phrase "in the strength and assistance of the Holy Spirit" that forms the heart of his treatise, for it was this very point that was in dispute. In discussing this phrase regarding the Spirit's role in prayer, Bunyan took his start from Ephesians 2:18 and Romans 8:26–27. On the basis of these Pauline texts, Bunyan asserted that "there is no man, nor Church in the world, that can come to God in Prayer but by the assistance of the Holy Spirit."[19]

Bunyan then proceeded to detail a number of reasons the Spirit's aid is so vital when it comes to prayer. A consideration of the more important of these reasons brings the reader to the center of

---

16. Roger Sharrock, "'When at the First I Took My Pen in Hand': Bunyan and the Book" in Keeble, ed., *John Bunyan*, 80.

17. Bunyan, *I Will Pray with the Spirit*, 294.

18. Ibid., 235.

19. Ibid., 246.

Bunyan's plea that the Spirit be allowed full freedom to work in the lives of men and women.

First, only by the Spirit can a person think rightly of the One to whom he prays: "They then, not being able to conceive aright of God to whom they pray, of Christ through whom they pray...how shall they be able to address themselves to God, without the Spirit help this infirmity?"[20] Bunyan is emphatic that the Book of Common Prayer is of absolutely no help when it comes to the imparting of such spiritual understanding. The Spirit, and He alone, can reveal the Father and the Son as the proper recipients of prayer.

Second, only the Spirit can "shew a man clearly his misery by nature, and so put a man into the posture of prayer."[21] But such sensibility of sin would cause a man to flee from God's presence were it not for the Spirit's encouragement to run to God for mercy. Moreover, Bunyan stressed that only the Spirit can enable the believer to persevere in prayer once he or she has begun.

> May I but speak my own experience, and from that tell you the difficulty of praying to God as I ought; it is enough to make your poor, blind, carnal men, to entertain strange thoughts of me. For, as for my heart, when I go to pray, I find it so loath to go to God, and when it is with him, so loath to stay with him, that many times I am forced in my prayers; *first* to beg God that he would take mine heart, and set it on himself in Christ, and when it is there, that he would keep it there (Psalm 86:11). Nay, many times I know not what to pray for, I am so blind, nor how to pray, I am so ignorant; only (blessed be grace) the *Spirit helps our infirmities* [Rom. 8:26].
>
> Oh the starting-holes that the heart hath in time of prayer! None knows how many by-ways the heart hath, and back-lanes, to slip away from the presence of God. How much pride also, if enabled with expressions? how much hypocrisy, if before others? and how little conscience is there made of

---

20. Ibid., 249.
21. Ibid., 251.

Prayer between God and the Soul in secret, unless the *Spirit of Supplication* [Zech. 12:10] be there to help?[22]

This passage displays a couple of the most attractive features of the Puritans: their transparent honesty and in-depth knowledge of the human heart. From personal experience, Bunyan well knew the allergic reaction of the old nature to the presence of God. So were it not for the Spirit, none would be able to persevere in prayer. Little wonder that Bunyan followed the preceding passage, which, it should be noted, concludes with an allusion to Zechariah 12:10, with this observation: "When the Spirit gets into the heart then there is prayer indeed, and not till then."[23]

Moreover, it is the Spirit who enables a man to know the right and only way to come to God, namely, through His beloved Son. "Men may easily say," Bunyan wrote, "they come to God in his Son: but it is the hardest thing of a thousand to come to God aright and in his own way, without the Spirit."[24] It is only the Spirit who can enable a person fully conscious of his sinful nature to address God as Father. Bunyan's discussion of this point is worth quoting in full:

O how great a task is it, for a poor soul that becomes sensible of sin, and the wrath of God, to say in faith, but this one word, *Father*! I tell you, how ever hypocrites think, yet the Christian, that is so indeed, finds all the difficulty in this very thing, it cannot say, God is its *Father*.

Oh! saith he, I dare not call him Father; and hence it is, that the Spirit must be sent into the hearts of God's people for this very thing, to cry, *Father*, Gal. 4.6, it being too great a work for any man to do *knowingly*, and *believingly*, without it. When I say, *knowingly*, I mean knowing what it is to be a child of God, and to be born again. And when I say, *believingly*, I mean, for the soul to believe, and that from good experience, that the work of grace is wrought in him: this is the right calling of God *Father*; and not as many do, say in a babbling way,

---

22. Ibid., 256–57 (italics mine).
23. Ibid., 257.
24. Ibid., 251.

the Lord's Prayer (so called) by heart, as it lyeth in the words
of the book. No, here is the life of prayer, when in, or with the
Spirit, a man being made sensible of sin, and how to come
to the Lord for mercy; he comes, I say, in the strength of the
Spirit, and cryeth, *Father.*

That one word spoken in faith, is better than a thousand
prayers, as men call them, written and read, in a formal, cold,
lukewarm way.[25]

Here Bunyan spoke from experience. Rightly calling God
"Father" comes not from the mere recitation of the Lord's Prayer
"in a babbling way," but from the inner work of the Spirit.[26] Bunyan
referred again to his own experience in prayer when he stressed that
only the Spirit can enable the believer to persevere in prayer once he
has begun.[27] The Puritans generally emphasized that were it not for
the Spirit, none would be able to persevere in prayer. Thus Bunyan
affirmed that a "man without the help of the Spirit cannot so much
as pray once; much less, continue...in a sweet praying frame."[28]

### The Significance of *I Will Pray with the Spirit*

Bunyan's treatise on prayer helped to secure what has become a
dominant attitude, at least among evangelical Christians, toward
written and read prayers: extreme wariness. More significantly,
Bunyan's treatise can also be seen as a declaration that without the
Spirit, not only our prayer life but also our entire Christian walk is
hollow, stale, and lifeless. It is often forgotten that Bunyan was a
vital participant in what Ronald Reeve has described as the Puritan
"rediscovery of the Holy Spirit as the mainspring of all Christian
activity."[29] The claim by some contemporary authors and theologians that no post-Reformation movement until this century has

25. Ibid., 252.
26. Greaves, introduction, xliii–xliv. See also Nuttall, *Holy Spirit*, 63–65.
27. Bunyan, *I Will Pray with the Spirit*, 256–66.
28. Ibid., 256. Cf. also ibid., 256–66.
29. Ronald Reeve, "John Wesley, Charles Simeon, and the Evangelical
Revival," *Canadian Journal of Theology*, 2 (1956):205.

really given the Spirit His due is shown to be quite false by the interest that the Puritans had in the person and work of the Spirit.

Bunyan, like most of his fellow Puritans, had an intense desire for the experience of the Spirit, for he knew that the Spirit of Christ alone could lead him to God. Thus, at the conclusion of the treatise, Bunyan expressed the hope that "Christians...pray for the Spirit, that is, for more of it, though God hath endued them with it already.... The Lord in mercy turn the hearts of the people to seek more after the Spirit of Prayer, and in the strength of that, pour out their souls before the Lord."[30]

When John Bunyan lay dying in August of 1688, a number of his deathbed sayings were recorded. Among them was one dealing with prayer. "The Spirit of Prayer," he told those gathered to hear his final words, "is more precious than treasure of gold and silver."[31] It was Bunyan's conviction of the work of the Spirit in prayer and preaching that led him in the first place to embrace an ecclesial position outside of the Church of England. Clearly, as this dying statement shows, it was this conviction that had sustained him to the end of his life.[32]

---

30. Bunyan, *I Will Pray with the Spirit*, 271, 285.

31. *Mr. John Bunyan's Dying Sayings* (*The Works of John Bunyan* [London: John Ball, 1850], 1:47).

32. Richard L. Greaves, "Conscience, Liberty, and the Spirit: Bunyan and Non-conformity," in Keeble, ed., *John Bunyan*, 43.

*Chapter 7*

# The Puritans on the Help
# of the Holy Spirit in Prayer

⸺∾⃝∾⸺

## JOHNNY C. SERAFINI

*[The Spirit] writes our petitions in the heart, we offer*
*them; he indites a good matter, we express it. That*
*prayer which we are to believe will be accepted, is the*
*work of the Holy Ghost; it is his voice, motion, opera-*
*tion, and so his prayer. Therefore, when we pray he is*
*said to pray, and our groans are called his.*

—David Clarkson

"Prayer, in the whole compass and extent of it, as comprising meditation, supplication, praise, and thanksgiving, is one of the most
signal duties of religion…. It is not only an important duty in religion, but…without it there neither is nor can be the exercise of any
religion in the world."[1] So wrote John Owen (1616–1683), who, like
his Puritan brethren, saw that prayer is essential to the Christian
life. Prayer must also be true, that is, acceptable to God and according to His will; for this, the believer needs the help of the Spirit.
The Puritans were keen on showing that Spirit-less prayer is as
good as "a little cold prattle and spiritless talk," as Thomas Manton
(1620–1677) wrote.[2] William Fenner (1600–1640) concurred and

---

1. John Owen, *The Works of John Owen* (Edinburgh: Banner of Truth Trust,
1999), 4:251.
2. Thomas Manton, *The Complete Works of Thomas Manton* (London: James
Nisbet & Co., 1873), 5:337.

described it as no better than "the lowing of oxen, or the grunting of hogs."[3] John Bunyan (1628–1688) said that prayer without the assistance of the Holy Spirit could not possibly be "according to the will of God."[4] On the other hand, the Puritans excelled in declaring the truth that those who have the indwelling Spirit will truly pray, as Matthew Henry (1662–1714) pointed out: "You may as soon find a living man without breath as a living saint without prayer."[5] "When the Spirit gets into the heart then there is prayer indeed, and not till then." said Bunyan.[6]

The indwelling Spirit is the author of prayer in the soul of the believer. There simply cannot be true prayer—heaven-bound prayer—without the Spirit's help. And all true Christians, being indwelt by the Spirit, have the gift of true prayer and will seek to grow in the exercise of that gift. The Puritans based most of their writing upon the Spirit's work in prayer upon the classic text, Romans 8:26–27.

Romans 8:26 declares that the Spirit "helpeth our infirmities." Thus, the Spirit's work of intercession is characterized as giving assistance and carrying the weight, both with and in one's stead, as the word in the original suggests. Robert Traill (1642–1716) defined the word "helpeth" (Greek, *sunantilambanomai*) as the Spirit's helping us "over-against us, as a powerful assistant to the weak, in carrying a heavy burden."[7] Manton showed the Spirit's help is necessary, first, due to the economy of the Trinity, for in prayer we come to the Father through Christ our Mediator with the Spirit as our guide; second, due to the spirituality of all Christian duties, for

---

3. William Fenner, "The Sacrifice of the Faithful," in *The Works of W. Fenner* (London: George neer Fleet-Bridge for E. Tyler, 1657), 267 (sermon 20).

4. John Bunyan, "I Will Pray with the Spirit," in *The Doctrine of the Law and Grace Unfolded and I Will Pray with the Spirit,* ed. Richard L. Greaves (Oxford: Clarendon Press, 1976), 243.

5. Matthew Henry, *Commentary on the Whole Bible* (Peabody, Mass.: Hendrickson, 2003), 4:1152.

6. Bunyan, *The Doctrine of the Law and Grace Unfolded,* 257.

7. Robert Traill, *The Works of the Late Reverend Robert Traill* (Edinburgh: The Banner of Truth Trust, 1975), 1:72.

"all the children of God are led by the Spirit of God, Rom. 8:14; as in their whole conversation, so especially in this act of prayer"; and third, due to our spiritual impotency, for, as Manton said, "We cannot speak of God without the Spirit, much less to God."[8]

James Ussher (1581–1656) listed the many infirmities that comprise our need for the Spirit's help in prayer: "Roving imaginations, inordinate affections, dullness of spirit, weakness of faith, coldness in feeling, faintness in asking, weariness in waiting, too much passion in our own matters, and too little compassion in other men's miseries."[9] Manton added "afflictions, and the perturbations occasioned thereby, as fretting or fainting; or more generally any sinful infirmities, as ignorance, distrust, etc."[10]

Although believers are regenerate, they still must deal with indwelling sin, which renders them to be of "little strength," as Thomas Boston (1676–1732) said, and "much bowed down with pressure."[11] Owen wrote of the blinding effect of sin: "Nature is so corrupted as not to understand its own depravation.... Nature is blind, and cannot see them; it is proud, and will not own them; stupid, and is senseless of them." Although this blindness renders man hopeless, the Spirit's work is exactly the remedy we need. Owen expressed this well: "It is the work of the Spirit of God alone to give us a due conviction of, a spiritual insight into, and a sense of the concernment of, these things." He concluded, "Without a sense of these things, I must profess I understand not how any man can pray."[12]

The apostle Paul shows in Romans 8:26 that these infirmities leave us in need of the Spirit's help in two particular aspects of prayer. The first is the matter or content of prayer or, as Paul says, "we know not what we should pray for." The second is the manner

---

8. Manton, *Complete Works*, 12:235–36.

9. James Ussher, *A Body of Divinity: or the Sum and Substance of Christian Religion* (London: J.D., 1677), 335.

10. Manton, *Complete Works*, 12:225.

11. Thomas Boston, *The Complete Works of Thomas Boston* (Stoke-on-Trent, England: Tentmaker Publications, 2002), 11:20.

12. Owen, *Works*, 4:279.

of prayer, or how we ought to pray: "We know not what we should pray for as we ought."

## The Spirit's Help in the Matter or Content of Our Prayers

"We know not what we should pray for" (Rom. 8:26). This ignorance extends to the words we should use, the petitions we should present, the petitions we should refrain from presenting—indeed, the thoughts we should think. Thus we need help, and divine help at that. The traditions of men and the wisdom of this world will never inform us sufficiently. We need the Spirit to give us the mind of Christ (1 Cor. 2:14–16). Traill wrote, "The voice of the Spirit is the best thing in our prayer; it is that God hears and regards."[13] David Clarkson (1622–1686) described the Spirit's help as simply this: "to pray in us, i.e., to make our prayers." He continued, "He, as it were, writes our petitions in the heart, we offer them; he indites [composes] a good matter, we express it. That prayer which we are to believe will be accepted, is the work of the Holy Ghost; it is his voice, motion, operation, and so his prayer. Therefore, when we pray he is said to pray, and our groans are called his."[14]

Our human condition renders us, Boston said, "apt, instead of bread, to ask a stone; instead of a fish, a scorpion; to pray for what would do us ill, and against what is for our good."[15] He elaborated that 1) we might pray against God's mercy; 2) we might pray for that which could hurt us; 3) we might pray for that which would feed our sinful desires; 4) we might not pray for what we truly need; 5) we might forget what we should pray for; and simply, 6) we might not pray according to God's will. Boston concluded, "There is so much remains of corruption in the best of us, that it is hard even in our prayers to keep within the compass of what is agreeable

---

13. Traill, *Works*, 1:73.
14. David Clarkson, *The Works of David Clarkson* (Edinburgh: The Banner of Truth Trust, 1988), 3:207.
15. Boston, *Works*, 11:21.

to his will."[16] And in the same vein, he said, "We are so weak, that in God's dispensations many times we take our friends for our foes, and call what is for our good, evil, as Jacob did when he said, 'All these things are against me.'"[17] Therefore we need the Holy Spirit to inform our minds so that we will know what to pray for.

*Informing Our Prayers with the Knowledge of God and Christ*
Bunyan spoke of our ignorance of the "*Object* to whom we pray," as well as the "*Medium* by, or through whom we pray," and said, "None of these things know we, but by the help of the Spirit."[18] He referred, of course, to our ignorance of God the Father as the object of prayer, the One to whom we pray, and Christ as the medium of prayer, the One by whom or through whom we pray. The Spirit reveals both the Father and the Son to us, so that we pray to the true God. Bunyan explained, "Without the Spirit, man is so infirm, that he cannot with all other means whatsoever, be enabled to think one right saving thought of God, of Christ, or of his blessed things; and therefore he saith of the wicked, *God is not in all their thoughts,* Ps. 10:4, Unless it be that they *imagine him altogether as one as themselves,* Ps. 50:20. *For every imagination of the thought of their heart, is only evil, and that continually,* Gen. 6:5; Gen. 8:21."[19]

Only with a right view of the One with whom we converse in prayer will the heart be in the right frame for prayer. Owen wrote that the "Holy Spirit gives the soul of a believer a *delight in God* as the *object of* prayer" and explained, "without it ordinarily the duty is not accepted with God, and is a barren, burdensome task unto them by whom it is performed."[20]

Boston wrote that a right view of God gives the soul "holy reverence" as well as "holy confidence" in prayer.[21] Regarding the

16. Ibid., 11:45.
17. Ibid., 11:44.
18. Bunyan, *The Doctrine of the Law and Grace Unfolded,* 247.
19. Ibid., 249.
20. Owen, *Works,* 4:291.
21. Boston, *Works,* 11:62.

Spirit's work of instilling reverence in the heart, Boston said, "By this view he strikes us with holy dread and awe of the majesty of God, whereby is banished that lightness and vanity of heart, that makes such flaunting in the prayers of some."[22] Although reverence is essential, faith or confidence in prayer is also necessary, for "without this there can be no acceptable prayer," said Boston, alluding to Hebrews 11:6 and James 1:6. And, as all else needful in prayer, the Spirit supplies this. The Spirit "helps the soul to approach with confidence, and yet with reverence," said Clarkson, "with filial fear, and yet with an emboldened faith; with zeal and importunity, and yet with humble submission; with lively hope, and yet with self denial."[23]

Manton spoke of the Spirit helping us approach God in prayer with childlike reverence and confidence.[24] He asserted, "Our familiarity with God must not mar our reverence, nor confidence and delight in him our humility."[25] The presence of this confidence in prayer is a proof of the Spirit's help. It reflects His "ability and willingness to help," said Boston, "the Spirit exciting in us holy confidence in God as Father."[26] And as Manton reminded us, "A great part of the life and comfort of prayer consisteth in coming to God as a reconciled father,"[27] which is the Spirit's work, as seen in passages like Romans 8:15 and Galatians 4:6. Richard Sibbes (1577–1635) said, "[The crying as a son] comes from the Spirit. If we be sons, then we have the Spirit, whereby we cry, Abba, Father. So, if we can go to God with a sweet familiarity, Father, have mercy upon me, forgive me;…this sweet boldness and familiarity, it comes from the spirit of liberty, and shews that we are sons, and not bastards."[28]

---

22. Ibid.
23. Clarkson, *Works*, 3:209–210.
24. Manton, *Works*, 12:234.
25. Ibid.,12:234–35.
26. Boston, *Works*, 11:62.
27. Manton, *Works*, 12:234.
28. Richard Sibbes, *The Works of Richard Sibbes* (Edinburgh: The Banner of Truth Trust, 2001), 4:233.

There are many things that we need to be reminded of in prayer, but surely the most essential thing is the promises of God found in Scripture. Prayer is dependent upon the promises, for by them we are assured that our prayer will be accepted. The promises are so foundational to prayer that without them, "the sinner, pressed with a sense of need, has nothing to support him, and therefore cannot pray in faith."[29] Owen stated that ignorance of the promises of God is one of the reasons why "men are so barren in their supplications."[30] Thankfully, this is one of the chief ways in which the Spirit helps us in prayer. Boston spoke of the Spirit as giving us a right view of the grace and promise of the covenant. Similarly, John Gill (1697–1771) said the Spirit helps "by bringing to remembrance, and applying the precious promises of the Gospel."[31] This help is essential if we would pray with understanding and faith, for, as Boston wrote, "The promises are the rule and encouragement of prayer"; they "regulate our prayers" and act as "God's bills and bonds to his people, and by them he shows what he allows us to ask of him."[32]

The promises of God are, as Owen wrote, "the measure of prayer." He affirmed, "What God hath promised, all that he hath promised, and nothing else, are we to pray for; for 'secret things belong unto the Lord our God' alone, but the declaration of his will and grace belongs unto us, and is our rule."[33] Owen described the help offered by the Spirit in making us comprehend the promised grace and mercy of God as "that which gives spiritual beauty and order unto the duty of prayer, namely, the suiting of wants and supplies, of a thankful disposition and praises, of love and admiration, unto the excellencies of God in Christ, all by the wisdom of the Holy Ghost."[34] Owen warned of the danger of thinking we do

---

29. Ibid., 4:65.

30. Owen, *Works*, 4:282.

31. John Gill, *An Exposition of the Old and New Testament* (Paris, Ark.: The Baptist Standard Bearer, 1989), 8:492.

32. Boston, *Works*, 11:65.

33. Owen, *Works*, 4:275.

34. Ibid., 4:284.

not need the Spirit's help in reminding us of the grace and promises of God: "To say that of ourselves we can perceive, understand,
and comprehend these things, without the especial assistance of the
Holy Ghost, is to overthrow the whole gospel and the grace of our
Lord Jesus Christ."[35]

The heart of all the promises is Christ our Mediator. If the
Spirit did not give us a view of Christ, He would be, as Boston said,
"a hidden beauty to us."[36] This help is to "point us to the only way of
acceptance of our prayers.... He teaches us to pray as we ought, and
so to pray in the name of Jesus Christ, depending on his merit and
intercession."[37] Boston argued that this is to lay before the believer a
"firm foundation of confidence before the Lord."[38] We must realize
that Christ, through whom our prayers are heard by God, is an advocate who never loses a case, "having an undisputable ground to go
upon, namely, the purchase of his own blood."[39] Boston wrote, "Are
we sinful and vile? The merit of Christ is of infinite value. Are we
unworthy for whom God should do such a thing? Yet the Mediator
is worthy. Can our prayers, smelling so rank of sinful imperfections,
not be accepted at our polluted hands? Yet being perfumed with his
merit, they can be accepted at his hand, Revelation 8:4."[40]

*Informing Our Prayers with the Knowledge of Our True Needs*
John Flavel (1628–1691) wrote that the Spirit within believers is
"teaching them what they should ask of God."[41] The Holy Spirit
"shows them their need, what their wants are; he stirs them up
to prayer, he supplies them with arguments, puts words into their
mouths," as Gill said.[42] The Spirit helps by "opening the eyes of the

35. Ibid., 4:275.
36. Boston, *Works,* 11:66.
37. Ibid.
38. Ibid.
39. Ibid.
40. Ibid., 67.
41. John Flavel, *The Works of John Flavel* (Edinburgh: The Banner of Truth
Trust, 1997), 2:339.
42. Gill, *Exposition,* 8:492.

mind to discern the wants and needs we are compassed with," wrote Boston.[43] He helps us remember matters to be prayed for but not merely to be mentioned in prayer, for the Spirit also "impresses us with a sense of need," said Boston, so that we also "pray feelingly, that the tongue does but express what the heart feels."[44] As a result, we become sincere in our prayers, importunate, and specific as to the requests, praises, and thanksgivings.[45] Clarkson wrote of this work of the Spirit:

> We know not what is proper and expedient for us, what is seasonable, what is best for us, or when it will be so. We of ourselves would be ready to ask that which is impertinent, or unseasonable, or hurtful to us; we would have ease, and liberty, and plenty, and deliverance out of troubles, or freedom from sufferings; we would have joy and assurance, yea, triumphs and raptures; we would have these or the like presently, and in full measure, at such a time, in such a degree as might be prejudicial to our souls; and so we would seek them if we were left to ourselves, if the Spirit did not better direct us, and lead us to what is most necessary, and proper, and advantageous.[46]

Here we see the utter inability we find in ourselves even to know what our true needs are. We need help to know what to pray for and how to pray for it. Clarkson explained how this help occurs: "That the soul may pray well, the Spirit goes before it, and guides it into the right way, that we may not seek what is carnal, nor things that are either too small or too great for us."[47] The Spirit then acts "as a remembrancer," wrote Boston, "seasonably suggesting to us our needs for ourselves or others. So he sets things before us in time of prayer."[48]

43. Boston, *Works*, 11:63.
44. Ibid., 64.
45. Ibid.
46. Clarkson, *Works*, 3:208.
47. Ibid.
48. Boston, *Works* 11:64.

We who address a holy God must remember our state of sin and lowliness. As Boston said, we easily "lose sight of our sinfulness,"[49] but the Spirit helps us by revealing our hearts to us. The Spirit works to "fill us with low thoughts of ourselves before him," said Boston, which "makes us see ourselves unworthy of the mercies, that either we have got, or desire to have." Such a view of ourselves "fits us for the receipt of mercies of free grace; and the want of it makes sinners to be in their prayers, as if they came to buy of God, and not to beg, and so to be sent empty away."[50]

Bunyan said it is the Spirit who works to "show the soul its misery, where it is, and what is like to become of it; also the intolerableness of that condition." He grounded this assertion in John 16:7–9 and said, "For it is the Spirit that doth effectually *convince of sin and misery, without the Lord Jesus*...and so puts the soul into a sweet, serious, sensible, affectionate way of praying to God according to His Word."[51] He argued that even if a man were to see his own sin, without the help of the Spirit, the result would be to flee from God as Cain and Judas instead of fleeing to Him through Christ. He wrote, "When a man is indeed sensible of his sin, and God's curse, then it is an hard thing to persuade him to pray. For saith his heart, *There is no hope, It is in vain to seek God,* Jer. 2:25, Jer. 18:12. I am so vile, so wretched, and so cursed a creature, that I shall never be regarded." But the Spirit "stayeth the soul, helpeth it to hold up its face to God, by letting into the heart some small sense of mercy, to encourage it to go to God; and hence it is called the *Comforter,* John 14:26."[52] Therefore, when the Spirit helps us have a right view of ourselves, He shows us both our misery and the hope to be found in Christ. This help enables true prayer, for Christ is the one through whom we can pray to God.

The Spirit's work to give us a right view of God, Christ, and ourselves is intertwined. Boston showed how a correct view of

---

49. Ibid., 11:62.
50. Ibid., 11:63.
51. Bunyan, *The Doctrine of the Law and Grace Unfolded,* 251.
52. Ibid.

God and of oneself inevitably lead to sincere confession of sin, true thanksgiving for God's mercies, and a high valuing of Christ.[53] We need humility to see the preciousness of Christ (Ps. 69:32), and "the higher the Mediator is [valued], the more fit one is to pray."[54] The right view of ourselves is always related to the right view of God, as Manton reminded us: "Serious dealing with God in prayer is wrought in us by the Spirit, in whose light we see both God and ourselves, his majesty and our vileness, his purity and our sinfulness, his greatness and our nothingness."[55] William Gurnall (1616–1679) wrote that the Spirit "excites the saint's fear, filling it with such a sense of God's greatness, his nothingness and baseness, as makes him with awful thoughts reverence the divine majesty he speaks unto, and deliver every petition with a holy trembling upon his spirit."[56]

So the Holy Spirit helps the Christian in regard to the matter or content of prayer. However, spiritual knowledge involves the motions of the heart as well as the notions of the mind. This leads us to consider the Spirit's help in the manner of prayer.

## The Spirit's Help in the Manner of Our Praying

We must also be concerned with having the right frame of heart in prayer, so that, as Paul says, we may pray "as we ought" to pray. As Boston said, "We cannot put our prayer in right shape, even when we are right as to the matter of them.... We cannot put our petitions in form, in the style of the court of heaven."[57] Among many examples of the ways that we fail to pray in the right manner, Boston mentioned the following:

---

53. Boston, *Works*, 11:63.

54. Ibid.

55. Manton, *Works*, 12:235.

56. William Gurnall, *The Christian in Complete Armour* (Edinburgh: The Banner of Truth Trust, 2002), 2:489.

57. Boston, *Works*, 11:21.

1) We may pray with an unfit spirit for prayer, "being either entangled with worldly cares, or discomposed with unruly passions."

2) We can be lifeless, formal, and cold in prayer. Boston added, "We are called to be fervent in spirit.... But even where the fire of grace is in the hearth, unless it be blown up by the influence of the Spirit of God, the prayers will be mismanaged."

3) We have wandering hearts. "Many a prayer is lost this way," wrote Boston, "while the heart steals away after some other thing than what it should then be on."

4) We may exercise the gift without the grace, that is, without giving due thought to the "exercise of praying graces, reverence, faith, love, humility, etc."

5) We pray disproportionately, for "how ready are we to be more concerned for our own interest, than for the honour of God; more fervent for temporal than for spiritual mercies." This lack of right proportion "makes the prayers like legs of the lame that are not equal, the affections being disproportioned to the matter."

6) We may be prone to faint, that is, to cease praying if a prayer is not answered, for "long trials are apt to run us out of breath."[58]

Left to ourselves, these failings would describe the best part of our prayers. Carnal, cold, wandering, graceless, and self-centered prayers are too common among us. It is encouraging to know that although we will always labor under these infirmities, the Spirit is ever to be trusted to help us fight against them, both in giving us new godliness and in taking away the old ungodliness.

58. Ibid., 11:48–50.

*Pouring Godly Affections into the Heart*

Before there are words or expressions, there has to be a sense of our obligation and need to pray, and the Spirit works this in us. Boston referred to this as the Spirit's work in exciting us to pray. He wrote that the Spirit "impresses our spirit with a sense of a divine call to it, and so binds it on our consciences as duty to God.... He disposes our hearts for it, inclines us to the duty, that we willingly comply with it."[59] Indeed, as Manton pointed out, the duty becomes a delight as He raises "our hearts to a desire after and a delight in God...and causeth the soul to follow hard after God."[60] "The Spirit's work," said Manton, "is to raise the heart to things eternal and heavenly, that our main business might be there."[61] There may be plenty of words without the Spirit's help, but, as Manton wrote, "these lively motions and strong desires [are] from the Spirit of God."[62]

Clarkson also spoke of the Spirit's work of giving us a heart for prayer: "He prepares and disposes, incites and inclines the heart to make requests.... He puts the heart into a praying frame, and sometimes excites us so powerfully, as we cannot withhold from pouring out our souls before him."[63] Owen wrote, "It is he alone who worketh us unto that frame wherein we pray continually...our hearts being kept ready and prepared for this duty on all occasions and opportunities, being in the meantime acted and steered under the conduct and influence of those graces which are to be exercised therein."[64] Among what Owen called "animating principles of prayer," which are all given us by the Spirit, are faith, love, trust, delight, desire, and self-abasement.[65] Clarkson wrote that while the Spirit stirs the heart to pray, He also gives the emotions that suit the

---

59. Ibid., 11:61.
60. Manton, *Works*, 1:351.
61. Ibid., 11:443.
62. Ibid., 12:234.
63. Clarkson, *Works*, 3:208.
64. Owen, *Works*, 4:259.
65. Ibid., 4:269.

matter to be prayed for: "He stirs up affections in prayer suitable to the subject thereof, joy or sorrow, and love and delight, with earnest desires.... [He] fills the heart with affections."[66] Gurnall wrote, "As the strings under the musician's hand stir and speak harmoniously, so doth the saint's affections at the secret touch of the Spirit."[67]

The Puritans demonstrated that this help of the Spirit translates, in our experience, into "praying aright."[68] For the Spirit to intercede is for Him to create in us "right" prayers. Boston explained that "right" is used not in a legal, moral, or rhetorical sense but in an evangelical sense—prayers containing "gospel graces" that Boston called "the soul and life of prayer."[69] Right prayers always have their origin in the Spirit, though much imperfection enters them from us. Boston said, "The water comes pure from the fountain, the Spirit; but running through a muddy channel, such as every saint here is, it cannot be accepted in heaven, but as purified and sweetened by the intercession of Christ."[70] "All that is right in our prayers is the Spirit's work," said Boston, "and all that is wrong in them from ourselves, either as to matter or manner." He concluded, "In the incense of our prayers there is smoke that goes up toward heaven, ashes that remain behind on earth; it is the fire from the altar that sends up smoke, it is the earthly nature of the incense that occasions the ashes."[71]

The Spirit stirs our hearts. He excites those "graces in us which incline us to God; he raiseth our minds in the vision and sight of God," wrote Manton.[72] The Spirit "stirreth up in us ardent groans in prayer, or worketh up our hearts to God with desires expressed by sighs and groans."[73] Elsewhere Manton said, "He quickeneth

---

66. Clarkson, *Works*, 3:209.
67. Gurnall, *The Christian in Complete Armour*, 2:488–89.
68. Boston, *Works*, 11:55.
69. Ibid., 11:55–56.
70. Ibid., 11:60.
71. Ibid., 11:59.
72. Manton, *Works*, 1:351.
73. Ibid., 12:226.

and enliveneth our desires in prayer."[74] The Spirit takes the knowledge of God and uses it to fill us with the love of God, confidence in Him as our Father, and the fear of the Lord. Owen wrote that the "Holy Spirit gives the soul of a believer a *delight in God* as the *object of* prayer" and explained, "Without it ordinarily the duty is not accepted with God, and is a barren, burdensome task unto them by whom it is performed."[75]

Romans 8:26 says that the Spirit helps with "groanings which cannot be uttered." What are these groanings? Whose groanings are they? The common Puritan interpretation of Romans 8:26 attributed such groanings to the person praying by the help of the Holy Spirit, and not immediately to the Holy Spirit[76] (compare Romans 8:15 and Galatians 4:6). Boston explained the groans as the natural expression of the believer's soul living under external and internal afflictions: "Such is the imperfection of our state in this life, that if there is life in a soul, it must groan, because there is no escaping of pressures, from an evil world without, and an evil heart within."[77] Sin is the greatest cause of groaning in the Christian. Boston said, "This is a light burden to the most part of mankind, but it is the heaviest burden to a child of God, and causes in him, through the Spirit, the heaviest groans. For it is of all things the most contrary and opposite to the new nature in him."[78] In such groaning we experience fellowship with the suffering Savior, as Boston observed: "True Christians…will be found to resound as an echo to a groaning Saviour."[79]

Audible groans or even the silent groans of the soul may not seem impressive as a prayer. But Gurnall said, "It is a voice well understood [in heaven], and more musical in God's ear than the

---

74. Ibid., 12:234.
75. Owen, *Works*, 4:291.
76. Traill, *Works*, 1:73; Boston, *Works*, 11:21; Gill, *Exposition*, 8:492.
77. Boston, *Works*, 11:73.
78. Ibid., 11:76.
79. Ibid., 11:74.

most ravishing music can be to ours."[80] Just as a child cries out as an
expression of his trust that his father will hear and care, so the Spirit
causes these groanings in our soul, mixed with trust that our heavenly Father will hear and understand them as our cries for His help.
Such groanings are, in essence, the living confession of the believer's
faith in a prayer-hearing God. Clarkson said that the Spirit "fills the
heart with affections and motions, as manifest themselves by sighs
and groans, and cannot otherwise be expressed…so full of affectionate workings as it cannot find vent by words."[81] So we can agree
with Traill, who said, "There is more of the Spirit in a sensible groan,
than in many formal words of prayer."[82]

William Perkins (1558–1602) expressed the comfort we should
have in such help:

> Men in extremities of danger confounded in themselves know
> not what in the world to say, or do. In his sickness, Hezekiah
> could not say anything, but chatter in his throat, and mourn
> like a dove, Isa. 38:14. Some lie under the sword of the enemy,
> others in a tempest are cast over shipboard into the sea. Now
> this must be their comfort, if they can lift up their heart unto
> God, if they can but sigh and groan for his presence and assis-
> tance, the Lord will hear the petitions and their hearts: for
> their inward sobs, groans, and sighs of repentant sinners, are
> loud and strong cries in the ears of God the Father.[83]

### Removing Ungodly Attitudes from the Heart
The Spirit removes what is present in the heart that is not conducive
to right praying. Thus Clarkson spoke of the Spirit's work in remov-
ing "that backwardness, averseness, indisposedness, that is in us
naturally unto this spiritual service."[84] "He removes," said Clarkson,

80. Gurnall, *The Christian in Complete Armour*, 2:489.
81. Clarkson, *Works*, 3:209.
82. Traill, *Works*, 1:73.
83. William Perkins, *The Works of William Perkins* (London: John Legatt, 1613), 3:279.
84. Clarkson, *Works*, 3:208.

"or helps the soul against distempers which are ready to seize on the soul in prayer, distractions, straitness of heart, indifferency, formality, lukewarmness, hypocrisy, weariness, pride, self-confidence."[85] Flavel wrote, "It is he that humbles the pride of their hearts, dissolves, and breaks the hardness of their hearts; out of deadness makes them lively; out of weakness makes them strong."[86]

The Scriptures speak to the need of committing to prayer the things that would make us anxious (Phil. 4:6), but these are the very things that quench a trusting, prayerful spirit in our hearts. Gratefully, the Spirit comes to the aid of the troubled heart. Boston spoke of this help during prayer: "He frames the heart, that is out of frame for it; commands a heavenly calm in the soul, whereby it may be fitted for divine communications; saying to the heart tossed with temptations, troubles and risings of corruption, 'Peace and be still'; and he blows up the fire of grace into a flame, 2 Tim. 1:7."[87] Thus, the Spirit helps by overcoming those "distempers of the soul" that might otherwise keep us from praying at all.

Another inward obstacle to prayer is wandering thoughts. We tend not to regard wandering thoughts as a serious sin. However, as Boston said, "The Spirit convinces and humbles the soul under the sense of that sin, and so makes it more serious than before, from thence shewing the corruption of nature."[88] The Spirit also manages the heart in prayer by keeping it from wanderings, "for the heart itself is apt to wander off from the serious purpose, and the powers of hell exert themselves to divert from it. But the supply of the Spirit in prayer keeps the heart fixed."[89] We must ourselves fight against this tendency to let our thoughts wander, but the Spirit helps us in that fight: "It will always cost a struggle to hedge in the heart in duty, and the help of the Spirit is necessary to maintain the struggle."[90]

---

85. Ibid., 3:210.
86. Flavel, *Works*, 2:339.
87. Boston, *Works*, 11:67.
88. Ibid., 11:68.
89. Ibid.
90. Ibid.

Yet another failing in prayer is giving up too quickly. We do not only need to prepare our hearts to pray, but we also need to persevere in praying. The Spirit helps us do this too. "He causes us to continue in prayer from time to time," wrote Boston, "till we obtain a gracious answer; and so makes us pray perseveringly." He continued, "The Lord may keep his people long hanging on for an answer ere they get it. The promise may be big with the mercy prayed for, and yet it be not only many months but years ere it bring forth, as in the case of Abraham and David. This is a sore trial, and there would be no keeping from fainting if the Spirit did not help our infirmity. But he helps to hang on."[91]

We all know perseverance is necessary in prayer, for often good requests, such as the salvation of loved ones, may go years unanswered. Boston presented three graces that the Spirit works in us during the time a prayer goes unanswered:

1) *Satisfaction.* The Spirit satisfies us in His delay by accounting for it in a consistent way with "God's honor and our good.... And so he keeps up in us kind thoughts of God's dispensations."

2) *Strength.* The Spirit strengthens faith and hope, "Hangers on at the throne of grace may get a long stand, but they will get their strength renewed, Psalm 27:13–14." Boston explained that the Spirit does this "by shining anew on the promise; adding other promises to it tending to the same scope;... whereby the soul is refreshed in the time; and helping to observe the signs of the approaching day while yet the night continues."

3) *Sensitivity.* The Spirit sensitizes our spirit to our continuing need, "which, pinching us anew, obliges to renew our suit for relief until the time we get it." We respond, as do our senses to other stimuli, to the Spirit's prodding, recognizing that prayer

---

91. Ibid.

must continue although unanswered. As the eye senses light, so the Spirit helps our soul sense the need for prayer.[92]

Without help from God, after a long time of prayer we would be tempted to seek help "from another quarter," wrote Boston, and "our sense of need would wear off, and we would drop our petition. But the Spirit perfects what he begins; Psalm 138:8, 'The Lord will perfect that which concerneth me.'"[93] Thus the Spirit helps by keeping us hopeful, trusting we do not plead in vain, keeping us sensing our need of that for which we pray so that we faint not in praying for it.

Therefore by imparting gracious affections to the heart and by overcoming our infirmities, the Holy Spirit helps us to pray "as we ought." In sum, it is His office as "the Giver of life" (John 6:63) to impart life to prayers that would otherwise be dead and barren. Boston wrote, "A prayer without life is as incense without fire, which sendeth forth no perfume or sweet savour."[94] With His assistance, our prayers become fragrant and acceptable to the Father, prayers He will both hear and answer.

## Conclusion: A Many-Sided Work

The help of the Spirit in prayer is all encompassing. Truly the Christian prays "in the Spirit" (Eph. 6:18), for when he prays he finds the Spirit's help on every side. Flavel wrote that the Holy Spirit helps us *before* prayer by working upon the desires and affections; He helps *during* prayer by providing the right requests, "teaching them what they should ask of God," as well as by instilling the right manner of prayer, "supplying them with suitable affections, and helping them to be sincere in all their desires to God"; and He helps *after* prayer, "helping them to faith and patience, to believe and wait for the returns and answers of their prayer."[95] This many-sided work of

---

92. Ibid.
93. Ibid., 11:68–69.
94. Ibid.,12:234.
95. Flavel, *Works*, 2:338–39.

the Spirit shows that true prayer is more than a matter of the words we might utter. True prayer is related to a whole way of life, for our prayer life is an extension of our life in Christ. It is not an isolated devotion we offer as a mere duty, but a breathing after God as we praise, thank, ask, and extol our great God. So we need the Spirit to breathe upon every aspect of our lives if we are to pray with understanding and faith, to pray according to God's will, to pray fervently and effectually, to pray always and not faint.

Praying in the Spirit is both an absolute necessity and one of the great privileges of the children of God. Owen said of prayer, "If we are left unto ourselves, without the especial guidance of the Spirit of God, our aims will never be suited unto the will of God."[96] Without the help of the Spirit, our attempts to pray would make us, as Boston put it, "like dumb [deaf-mute] people making a roar."[97] On the other hand, what a glorious thing it is to draw help in prayer from the resources of the Spirit of God, for if our prayers are Spirit wrought, they shall be heaven bound!

---

96. Owen, *Works*, 4:276.
97. Boston, *Works*, 11:20.

*Chapter 8*

# Matthew Henry on a Practical Method of Daily Prayer

———————————————cჿ⌒⌒ჿ———————————————

## JOEL R. BEEKE

*I love prayer. It is that which buckles on all the Christian's armour.*
　　　　　　　　　　　　 —Matthew Henry

Few Bible commentators are better known than Matthew Henry (1662–1714). The *Commentary on the Whole Bible* that bears Henry's name continues to be reprinted, although Henry himself died after finishing Genesis through Acts, and the remainder was written by his friends drawing on his notes. The great evangelist George Whitefield (1714–1770) repeatedly read through Henry's commentary during his devotions and found it rich food for his soul. For all the fame of his commentaries, few people know that Henry also wrote a book on prayer that has been a bestseller for a century and a half.[1] And though his commentaries are read today around the world, few people know much about Henry's life.

Matthew Henry was an English Puritan born in 1662, the same year that Puritan ministers were ejected from the Church of England for refusing to conform to prescribed forms of worship. His father, Philip Henry, had already lost his pulpit in 1661. The period

---

1. "Matthew Henry's *A Method for Prayer* was, by its sheer popularity, a classic which for a hundred and fifty years went through more than thirty editions" (Hughes Oliphant Old, "The Reformed Daily Office: A Puritan Perspective," *Reformed Liturgy and Music* 12, no. 4 [1978]: 9). Cf. idem, "Matthew Henry and the Puritan Discipline of Family Prayer," in *Calvin Studies* 7, ed. John H. Leith (Davidson, N.C.: Davidson College, 1994), 69–91.

of the 1660s to the 1680s was a dark time of persecution for the
Puritans. Though frail in health, Henry distinguished himself intel-
lectually early in life, reading the Bible to himself when he was only
three. He initially studied to be a lawyer, but the Lord had other
plans for him. From age twenty-four to fifty, Henry served as pastor
of a church in Chester, having been privately ordained by Presbyterian ministers such as Richard Steele (1672–1729). The church
began in private homes but over time grew to 350 communicant
members, with many more adherents. Henry spent eight hours a
day in study, sometimes rising at four o'clock in the morning. In
addition to serving his own church, he preached monthly in five
nearby villages and to prisoners. Henry's first wife died in child-
birth, and three children from his second wife died in infancy.

Henry began writing his Bible commentary at age forty-two,
drawing from the well of his years of expository preaching and
research in Hebrew, Greek, Latin, and French. He spent the last two
years of his life serving a prominent church in London. Henry died
after falling from his horse, leaving the task of completing his commentary on the New Testament to thirteen of his ministerial friends.[2]

In 1710, Henry published *A Method for Prayer with Scripture
Expressions Proper to Be Used under Each Head*.[3] In 1712, he preached
sermons that were published as *Directions for Daily Communion
with God*.[4] Those books reveal Henry's passion for biblical spirituality, for it must have been difficult for a busy pastor and author of

2. Joel R. Beeke and Randall J. Pederson, *Meet the Puritans: With a Guide
to Modern Reprints* (Grand Rapids: Reformation Heritage Books, 2006), 323–28;
J. Ligon Duncan III, "A Method for Prayer by Matthew Henry (1662–1714)," in
*The Devoted Life: An Invitation to the Puritan Classics*, ed. Kelly M. Kapic and Randall C. Gleason (Downers Grove, Ill.: InterVarsity, 2004), 239–40.

3. *The Complete Works of the Rev. Matthew Henry* (1855; reprint, Grand Rapids:
Baker, 1979), 2:1–95. These complete works do not include his commentaries or the
recently published *Matthew Henry's Unpublished Sermons on The Covenant of Grace*,
ed. Allan Harman (Ross-shire, Scotland: Christian Focus Publications, 2002).

4. Henry, *Works*, 1:198–247. Both *A Method for Prayer* and *Directions for Daily
Communion with God* have been republished as a single book: Matthew Henry, *A
Method for Prayer*, ed. J. Ligon Duncan III (Ross-shire, Scotland: Christian Focus
Publications, 1994).

a massive Bible commentary to find time to write about prayer as well. We will consider Henry's directions on prayer from his second book, then move on to his method of praying the Scriptures.

## Directions for Praying All Day

Henry wrote in his diary, "I love prayer. It is that which buckles on all the Christian's armour."[5] Since the Christian must wear God's armor at all times, he must pray without ceasing. According to Henry, the access that Christians have to God in Christ gives them

1) "a companion ready in all their solitudes, so that they are never less alone than when alone. Do we need better society than fellowship with the Father?"

2) "a counsellor ready in all their doubts,... a guide (Ps. 73:24), who has promised to direct with his eye, to lead us in the way wherein we should go."

3) "a comforter ready in all their sorrows... [to] support sinking spirits, and be the strength of a fainting heart."

4) "a supply ready in all their wants. They that have access to God have access to a full fountain, an inexhaustible treasure, a rich mine."

5) "a support ready under all their burdens. They have access to him as *Adonai* [my Lord], my stay and the strength of my heart (Ps. 73:26)."

6) "a shelter ready in all their dangers, a city of refuge near at hand. The name of the Lord is a strong tower (Prov. 18:10)."

7) "strength ready for all their performances in doing work, fighting work. He is their *arm every morning* (Isa. 33:2)."

---

5. J. B. Williams, *The Lives of Philip and Matthew Henry* (Edinburgh: Banner of Truth Trust, 1974), 2:210.

8) "salvation insured by a sweet and undeceiving earnest.... If he thus guides us by his counsel he will
   receive us to glory."[6]

Since God has made Himself available to us so fully, we should
go to Him throughout the day. Henry wrote, "David solemnly
addressed himself to the duty of prayer three times a-day, as Daniel
did; 'Morning and evening, and at noon, will I pray, and cry aloud,'
Ps. 55:17. Nay, he doth not think that enough, but 'seven times a
day will I praise thee, Ps. 119:164.'"[7] Accordingly, Henry wrote three
discourses of directions for prayer: beginning the day with God,
spending the day with God, and closing the day with God.

*Directive One: Begin Every Day with God*
David wrote in Psalm 5:3, "My voice shalt thou hear in the morning, O LORD; in the morning will I direct my prayer unto thee, and
will look up." Henry wrote, "It is our wisdom and duty to begin
every day with God." Much of his discourse is devoted to motivat-
ing us to pray. Henry reminded us that we can pray with assurance
that "wherever God finds a praying heart, he will be found a prayer-
hearing God." If we pray to God as our Father through Christ the
Mediator according to God's will as revealed in the Bible, then we
can know that He has heard us and will answer according to His
kindness.[8] God requires us to pray to remind us of His authority
over us and His love and compassion toward us. We always have
something to talk to God about. He is a dear friend, so it is a pleasure to know Him personally and to walk with Him intimately. He
is also the Lord of us and everything that touches our lives. Shall
a servant not talk to his Master? Shall a dependent not talk to his
Provider? Shall one in danger not converse with his Defender?[9]

---

6. Henry, *The Covenant of Grace*, 200.
7. Henry, *Works*, 1:199.
8. Henry, *Works*, 1:199–200.
9. Henry, *Works*, 1:201–202.

Let no obstacle hinder you from coming to God. Though God is in heaven, He will hear your cries, even from the depths (Ps. 130:1). Though God be fearsome, He grants believers the Spirit of adoption to have freedom to speak with Him (Rom. 8:15). Yes, God already knows what you need, but He requires your prayers for His glory and to fit you to receive mercy (Ezek. 36:37–38). Though you are busy with many things, only one thing is necessary: to walk with God in peace and love.[10]

In beginning a time of prayer, Henry advised directing prayers with "a fixedness of thought, and a close application of mind," like an archer shooting an arrow with a steady hand and an eye fixed on his target. The target of our prayers is always "God's glory, and our own true happiness," which, Henry cheerfully reminded us, God has been pleased to "twist" together into one indivisible object in the covenant of grace, "so that in seeking his glory, we really and effectually seek our own true interests." Just as a shooter aims with one eye while shutting the other, so in prayer we must "gather in our wandering thoughts." When you pray, close your eye to the glory and praise of men (Matt. 6:2) and the glitter and honors of this world (Hos. 7:14).[11] In light of the first three petitions of the Lord's Prayer, Henry wrote:

> Let not self, carnal self, be the spring and centre of your prayers, but God; let the eye of the soul be fixed upon him as your highest end in all your applications to him; let this be the habitual disposition of your souls, to be to your God for a name and a praise; and let this be your design in all your desires, that God may be glorified, and by this let them all be directed, determined, sanctified, and, when need is, overruled.[12]

Just as a letter must be properly addressed to reach its intended recipient, so our prayers must be addressed to God. Henry wrote, "Give him his titles, as you do, when you direct to a person of hon-

---

10. Henry, *Works*, 1:203–204.
11. Henry, *Works*, 1:204–205.
12. Henry, *Works*, 1:205.

our.... Direct your prayer to him as the God of glory with whom is terrible majesty, and whose greatness is unsearchable." Do not forget also that sweet name which Christ taught us to use in prayer, "Our Father who art in heaven." Then take your letter and put it in the hand of "the Lord Jesus, the only Mediator between God and man...and he will deliver it with care and speed, and will make our service acceptable."[13]

David testified in Psalm 5:3 that the morning hours are especially good for prayer. Likewise, Henry observed that the priests offered a sacrificial lamb and burned incense every morning (Ex. 29:39; 30:7), and singers thanked the Lord every morning (1 Chron. 23:30). He cited these examples to indicate that all Christians, who are spiritual priests in Christ, should offer spiritual sacrifices every morning to God. God, who is Alpha (Rev. 1:11), requires our first-fruits; therefore, we should give Him the first part of our day. God deserves our best, not just leftovers of the day when we are tired and worn out.[14] Henry wrote, "In the morning we are most free from company and business, and ordinarily have the best opportunity for solitude."[15] God gives us fresh mercies every morning, so we should give Him fresh thanksgivings and fresh meditations on His beauties. In the morning, as we prepare for the work of the day, let us commit it all to God.[16] Begin every day with God.

*Directive Two: Spend Every Day with God*
David wrote, "On thee do I wait all the day" (Ps. 25:5). Henry said this waiting involves "a patient expectation" of God to come in mercy at His time, and "a constant attendance" upon the Lord in the duties of personal worship. The saints need patient expectation, for they often wait through long, dark, stormy days for God to

---

13. Henry, *Works*, 1:205–206.
14. Henry, *Works*, 1:207–208.
15. Henry, *Works*, 1:208.
16. Henry, *Works*, 1:208–211.

answer their prayers. But they wait in hope.[17] Henry quoted Anglican priest and poet George Herbert (1593–1633):

> Away despair! my gracious God doth hear;
>     When winds and waves assault my keel,
> He doth preserve it: he doth steer
>     Ev'n when the boat seems most to reel.
> Storms are the triumph of his art,
> Well may he close his eyes, but not his heart.[18]

The Christian's attendance upon God throughout the day is captured in the phrase *to wait upon the Lord*. "To wait on God, is to live a life of desire towards him, delight in him, dependence on him, and devotedness to him," Henry wrote. We should spend our days desiring God, like a beggar constantly looking to his benefactor, hungering not only for His gifts but for the One who is the Bread of Life. We should live in delight of God, like a lover with his beloved. "Do we love to love God?" Henry asked. Constant dependence is the attitude of a child towards his Father whom he trusts and on whom he casts all his cares. A life of devotedness is that of a servant towards his Master, "ready to observe his will, and to do his work, and in every thing to consult his honour and interest." It is "to make the will of his precept the rule of our practice," and "to make the will of his providence the rule of our patience."[19] Henry thus argued that to pray without ceasing is a disposition of the heart waiting upon the Lord all through the day.

We must wait on God *every day*, both in public worship on the Lord's Day and in the work of our callings on weekdays. We must wait on Him in the days of prosperity when the world smiles on us and in the days of adversity when the world frowns on us. We must lean on Him in the days of youth and in the days of old age. We must wait on God *all the day*.

---

17. Henry, *Works*, 1:213–15.
18. Henry, *Works*, 1:215. The quotation is from "The Bag" in George Herbert, *The Temple* (1633), http://www.ccel.org/h/herbert/temple/Bag.html (accessed December 3, 2010).
19. Henry, *Works*, 1:216–18.

Are you burdened with cares? Cast them on the Lord. Do you have responsibilities to fulfill? In your business do you know that God assigned you this "calling and employment" and requires that you work according to the precepts of His Word? God alone can bless your efforts, and the glory of God should be the ultimate goal of all your work. Are you tempted to follow another way? Shelter yourself under His grace. Are you suffering? Submit to His will, and trust the love behind His fatherly corrections. Is your mind caught up in hopes or fears about the future? Wait on God, who rules over life and death, good and evil.[20] Henry's writings show us that every minute of every day contains ample reasons to look to the Lord.

We put into practice this constant attendance upon God by exercising private prayer with God repeatedly. Henry called men to secret prayer lest their prayers prove to be temptations to spiritual pride and self-display. He wrote, "Shut the door lest the wind of hypocrisy blow in at it."[21]

In addition, Henry calls us to family worship in which we train our household in godliness. Henry strongly advocated family devotions in *Family Hymns* (1694) and *A Church in the House: Family Devotions* (1704). He promoted such devotions, not to withdraw from the local church, but to strengthen the church by promoting godliness in the home. Henry practiced in his home what he preached. Every morning, he reviewed a portion of the previous Sunday's sermon with his family and prayed with them. He catechized his children in the afternoon and taught the older children after the little ones went to bed.[22] He considered family worship as a time for the whole family to come to God in prayer, seeking His blessing, thanking Him for His mercies, and bringing Him fractures in our relationships so He might heal them. Pray for your children to grow in wisdom and to "wait upon God for his grace to make the means of their education successful," Henry said. He

---

20. Henry, *Works*, 1:219–24.
21. Williams, *Lives of Philip and Matthew Henry*, 2:211. See Matt. 6:5–6.
22. Beeke and Pederson, *Meet the Puritans*, 327.

reminded parents that prayer begets patience, saying, "If they are but slow, and do not come on as you could wish, yet wait on God to bring them forward, and to give them his grace in his own time; and while you are patiently waiting on him, that will encourage you to take pains [make diligent efforts] with them, and will likewise make you patient and gentle towards them."[23]

When you go to work, Henry wrote, your job "calls for your constant attendance every day, and all the day." But do not neglect God in your work. Work in the presence of God. Open the doors of your shop with the thought that you are on God's appointed road of obedience and you depend on God to bless you in it. See every customer or client as a person sent by divine providence. Perform every transaction in justice as if God's holy eye were upon you. Look to God for the skill to make an honest profit by honest diligence.[24]

If you take a book into your hands, be it "God's book, or any other useful good book," rely on God to make it profitable to you. Do not waste time reading unprofitable books. When you read, do so not out of vain curiosity but with love for God's kingdom, compassion for human beings, and the intent to turn what you learn into prayers and praises. When you sit down for lunch, remember that the Creator gave us the right to eat of His created provisions, but we must eat and drink for the glory of God. When you visit friends, be thankful to God that you have friends — and clothing, houses, and furniture to enjoy with them. If you go on a trip, put yourselves under God's protection. "See how much you are indebted to the goodness of his providence for all the comforts and conveniences you are surrounded with in your travels," said Henry.[25]

Wherever you go, whatever you do each day, search for abundant reasons for prayer and praise, Henry said. As James wrote, if you are sad, then pray to God; if you are happy, then sing praises to God (James 5:13). That covers all of life.

---

23. Henry, *Works*, 1:224–25.
24. Henry, *Works*, 1:225.
25. Henry, *Works*, 1:225–27.

*Directive Three: Close Every Day with God*

David declared, "I will both lay me down in peace, and sleep: for thou, LORD, only makest me dwell in safety" (Ps. 4:8). Henry said we may end our days in contentment if we have the Lord as our God. He wrote, "Let this still every storm, command and create a calm in thy soul. Having God to be our God in covenant, we have enough; we have all. And though the gracious soul still desires more of God, it never desires more than God; in him it reposeth itself with a perfect complacency; in him it is at home, it is at rest."[26]

Henry advised us to lie down with thanksgiving to God when we go to bed at night. We should review His mercies and deliverances at the end of each day. "Every bite we eat, and every drop we drink, is mercy; every step we take, and every breath we draw, mercy." We should be thankful for nighttime as God's provision for our rest, for a place to lay our heads, and for the health of body and peace of mind which allows us to sleep.[27]

Bedtime also offers an opportunity to reflect upon both our mortality and our Christian hope. Henry encouraged us to think that just as we retire from work for a time when we go to bed, so we shall retire for a time in death until the day of resurrection. Just as we take off our clothes at night, so we will put off this body until we receive a new one the morning of Christ's return. Just as we lie down in our beds to rest, so we will lie down in death to rest in Christ's presence where no nightmares can trouble us.[28] Henry's focus on death was not unhealthy morbidity but a realistic consideration in a fallen world where many people die each day with or without the Christian hope that extends beyond this life to eternal glory.

As the light of eternity breaks upon us even after the sun has set, we should reflect upon our sins with repentant hearts, remembering our corrupt natures and examining our conscience for particular transgressions of the law. Henry taught us continually to

26. Henry, *Works*, 1:231.
27. Henry, *Works*, 1:235–36.
28. Henry, *Works*, 1:237.

plead for repentance with godly sorrow, making fresh application of the blood of Christ to our souls for forgiveness and drawing near to the throne of grace for peace and pardon each night. Let us commit our bodies to the care of God's angels, and our souls to the influence of His Holy Spirit who works mysteriously in the night (Job 33:15–16; Ps. 17:3; 16:7). Then we may lie down in peace, resting upon the intercession of Christ to grant us peace with God and forgiving our fellow men all their offenses against us, so that our hearts may be at peace with God and man.[29]

Henry suggested we might fall asleep with thoughts such as these:

> To thy glory, O God, I now go to sleep. Whether we eat or drink, yea, or sleep, for this is included in whatever we do, — we must do it to the glory of God....To thy grace, O God, and to the word of thy grace I now commend myself. It is good to fall asleep, with a fresh surrender of our whole selves, body, soul, and spirit, to God; now, 'return to God as thy rest, O my soul; for he has dealt bountifully with thee.'... O that when I awake I may be still with God; that the parenthesis of sleep, though long, may not break off the thread of my communion with God, but that as soon as I awake I may resume it![30]

So it was that Henry directed the Christian to the wonderful experience of walking with God in prayer. From morning, throughout the day, and until our eyes close at night, we are invited to enjoy the access to God granted to us in Jesus Christ. Ephesians 2:18 says, "For through him [Christ Jesus] we both have access by one Spirit unto the Father." Henry wrote, "Prayer is our approach to God and we have access in it. We may come boldly...to speak all our mind. We may come with freedom.... We have access to his ear, 'tis always open to the voice of our supplications. We have access in all places, at all times." We need not wait until heaven to enjoy God. "What's heaven but an everlasting access to God, and present access is a

---

29. Henry, *Works*, 1:238–40.
30. Henry, *Works*, 1:243.

pledge of it," Henry said.[31] "This life of communion with God, and constant attendance upon him, is a heaven upon earth."[32]

## A Method for Praying the Scriptures

When a Christian devotes himself to prayer, whether privately or publicly, his prayers should be many because his burdens, concerns, needs, desires, and sins are many, and God's mercies are great, Henry said. This commends the use of some method in prayer. To be sure, there are times when a Christian's heart is so lifted up in prayer that a method is a hindrance. But those times are rare; ordinarily our prayers require method, for we do not want to speak rashly before "the glorious Majesty of heaven and earth." The Bible shows us that our prayers should consist of short, clear, potent sentences, such as those found in the Lord's Prayer, rather than a rambling stream of consciousness (or semi-consciousness) in which you forget what you are saying before your prayer is ended.

To help us form prayers that are better focused, Henry directs us to the source that is sufficient for every good work: the Holy Scriptures.[33] He said, "Hear [God] speaking to you, and have an eye to that in every thing you say to him; as when you write an answer to a letter of business, you lay it before you. God's word must be the guide of your desires and the ground of your expectations in prayer."[34]

At the heart of Henry's method is praying in the words of Scripture—that is, praying God's Word back to God. O. Palmer Robertson wrote that "prayer in this form is nothing more and nothing less than what the old Puritans called 'pleading the promises.' God has made promises to his people. His people respond by redirecting those promises to the Lord in the form of prayer."[35] Henry

---

31. Henry, *The Covenant of Grace*, 185, 200.
32. Henry, *Works*, 1:228.
33. Henry, *Works*, 2:2–3.
34. Henry, *Works*, 1:204.
35. O. Palmer Robertson, introduction to Matthew Henry, *A Way to Pray: A Biblical Method for Enriching Your Prayer Life and Language by Shaping Your*

did not restrict himself entirely to Bible promises, however. Ligon Duncan notes of Henry, "He ransacks the Scriptures for references to God's attributes and turns them into matters of adoration."[36] In every respect, Henry sought to fill the mouth of God's people with God's own words, although he acknowledged that "it is convenient, and often necessary, to use other expressions in prayer besides those that are purely Scriptural."[37]

Henry's method included adoration, confession, petition for ourselves, thanksgiving, intercession for others, and a conclusion. This pattern generally follows the Westminster Directory for Public Worship (1645).[38] In each section, Henry briefly introduced the focus and gave an outline of its parts. Each point of the outline includes Scripture after Scripture woven together as possible expressions of prayer. Henry guarded readers against merely reading these prayers aloud without meditation, saying, "After all, the intention and close application of the mind, the lively exercises of faith and love, and the outgoings of holy desire toward God, are so essentially necessary to prayer, that without these in sincerity, the best and most proper language is but a lifeless image [i.e., a dead

---

*Words with Scripture*, ed. O. Palmer Robertson (Edinburgh: Banner of Truth Trust, 2010), xii. Robertson writes of this republication of Henry's *Method for Prayer*, "This current edition does not represent simply an effort to modernize the language of Matthew Henry's original. Instead it is an effort to provide a respectful but thorough reworking of the text of Matthew Henry in light of careful exegetical considerations." Robertson has removed some of Henry's materials, added some of his own, and presented a fresh translation of the Scriptures (ibid., xvii).

36. Duncan, "A Method for Prayer," in *The Devoted Life*, 241.

37. Henry, *Works*, 2:2–3.

38. Duncan, "A Method for Prayer," in *The Devoted Life*, 240. The Westminster Directory set forth this order of worship: 1) a call to worship, 2) a prayer acknowledging God's greatness, 3) Scripture reading, 4) singing a psalm, 5) a prayer of confession and petition for grace through the Mediator for the church, worldwide missions, and the governing authorities, 6) preaching the Word, 7) a prayer of thanksgiving and petition for grace, 8) the Lord's Prayer, 9) singing a psalm, and 10) dismissal. See *The Westminster Directory of Public Worship*, discussed by Mark Dever and Sinclair Ferguson (Ross-shire, Scotland: Christian Focus Publications, 2008).

idol]."[39] Henry clearly believed that our prayers should be expressed in words and phrases from the Bible that have penetrated our hearts.

Let us consider a small sample of Henry's method. He was first concerned that we pray in the fear of the Lord, saying, "In every prayer remember you are speaking to God, and make it to appear you have an awe of him upon your spirits. Let us not be 'rash with our mouth; and let not our heart be hasty to utter any thing before God;' but let every word be well weighed, because 'God is in heaven, and we upon earth,' Eccl. 5:2."[40] Henry introduced the reader to the adoration of God:

> Our spirits being composed into a very reverent serious frame, our thoughts gathered in, and all that is within us charged, in the name of the great God, carefully to attend the solemn and aweful [awe-inspiring] service that lies before us, and to keep close to it; we must—with a fixed intention and application of mind, and an active lively faith—set the Lord before us, see his eye upon us, and set ourselves in his special presence; presenting ourselves to him as living sacrifices, which we desire may be holy and acceptable, and a reasonable service; and then bind those sacrifices with cords to the horns of the altar, with such thoughts as these....
>
> Let us now with humble boldness enter into the holiest by the blood of Jesus, in the new and living way, which he hath consecrated for us through the veil.[41]

Henry then offered page after page of suggested prayers of adoration in scriptural language, arranged by topics. It is a study of the biblical doctrine of God turned into prayer. To appreciate the fullness of Henry's method, consider his outline of biblical materials to direct our adoration:

  I. Address the Infinitely Great and Glorious Being
   A. With Holy Awe and Reverence
   B. Distinguishing Him from False Gods

---

39. Henry, *Works*, 2:3.
40. Henry, *Works*, 1:204.
41. Henry, *Works*, 2:4.

II. Reverently Adore God as Transcendently Bright and Blessed
   A. The Self-Existent, Self-Sufficient, Infinite Spirit
   B. His Existence Indisputable
   C. His Nature Beyond Our Comprehension
   D. His Perfection Matchless
   E. Infinitely Above Us and All Others

   *In particular, adore the Lord as:*
   1. Eternal, Immutable
   2. Present in All Places
   3. Perfect in His Knowledge of All
   4. Unsearchable in Wisdom
   5. Sovereign, Owner, and Lord of All
   6. Irresistible in Power
   7. Unspotted in Purity and Righteousness
   8. Always Just in His Government
   9. Always True, Inexhaustibly Good
   10. Infinitely Greater Than Our Best Praises

III. Give God the Praise of His Glory in Heaven
IV. Give Him Glory as Our Creator, Protector, Benefactor, and Ruler
V. Give Honor to the Three Distinct Persons of the Godhead
VI. Acknowledge Our Dependence on Him and Obligation to Our Creator
VII. Declare God to Be Our Covenant God Who Owns Us
VIII. Acknowledge the Inestimable Favor of Being Invited to Draw Near to Him
IX. Express Our Unworthiness to Draw Near to God
X. Profess Our Desire for Him as Our Happiness
XI. Profess Our Hope and Trust in His All-Sufficiency
XII. Ask God to Graciously Accept Us and Our Poor Prayers
XIII. Pray for the Assistance of the Holy Spirit in Our Prayers

XIV. Make the Glory of God as the Highest Goal of
Our Prayers
XV. Profess Our Reliance on the Lord Jesus Christ
Alone.[42]

Each point of the outline includes several prayers drawn from
the Scriptures. For example, one prayer under the topic of God's
matchless perfection is, "Who is a God like unto thee, glorious in
holiness, fearful in praises, doing wonders?"[43] In the section on pro-
fessing hope in God's sufficiency, Henry wrote, "In thee, O God,
do we put our trust, let us never be ashamed; yea, let none that
wait on thee be ashamed. Truly our souls wait upon God, from
him cometh our salvation; he only is our rock and our salvation! In
him is our glory, our strength, and our refuge, and from him is our
expectation."[44]

In adoration of God's power, he wrote, "We know, O God, that
thou canst do every thing.... Power belongs to thee; and with thee
nothing is impossible. All power is thine, both in heaven and on
earth. Thou killest and thou makest alive, thou woundest and thou
healest, neither is there any that can deliver out of thy hand. What
thou hast promised thou art able also to perform."[45]

Other sections such as confession and petition also have
detailed outlines. Henry's method would give remarkable depth and
variety to our prayers if we consulted his book regularly for guidance. His method would deliver our prayers from bland repetition
and thoughtless irreverence. It would help us become more specific
as well as more brokenhearted in our confession of sin, leading us
to pray: "We have not had the rule we ought to have over our own
spirits, which have therefore been as a city that is broken down and
has no walls. We have been too soon angry, and anger hath rested in
our bosoms: and when our spirits have been provoked, we have spo-

42. Henry, *Works,* 2:4–12.
43. Henry, *Works,* 2:5. See Ex. 15:11.
44. Henry, *Works,* 2:10–11. See Ps. 31:1; 25:3; 62:1, 2, 5–7.
45. Henry, *Works,* 2:6. See Job 42:2; Ps. 62:11; Luke 1:37; Matt. 28:18; Deut.
32:39; Rom. 4:21.

ken unadvisedly with our lips, and have been guilty of that clamour and bitterness which should have been put far from us."[46] Henry's words of confession are humbling. In our glib and frivolous day, we might hesitate to give such careful thought to confessing our sins. But Duncan writes, "Henry understood that without the inclusion of sufficient confession of sin in our prayers, we will never attain a real and right sense of divine forgiveness and reconciliation.... We will be burdened by unresolved guilt—or else cope with that nagging guilt through denial, delusion, and self-deception."[47]

Our intercessions for the church would likewise be more pointed and powerful if we used words such as these: "Let pure religion, and undefiled before God and the Father, flourish and prevail everywhere; that kingdom of God among men, which is not meat and drink but righteousness and peace, and joy in the Holy Ghost. O revive this work in the midst of the years, in the midst of the years make it known, and let our times be times of reformation."[48] We might then cry out with scriptural boldness, "Let no weapon formed against thy church prosper, and let every tongue that riseth against it in judgment be condemned."[49]

Henry also marshaled Scriptures for our intercession for the lost world and the propagation of the gospel to all nations. He called us to pray for all men, to cry out that the nations would praise the Lord and sing for joy, to pray for the conversion of the Jewish people, for the suffering churches in Islamic nations, and for the conversion of atheists and deists. He instructed his readers to pray, "O give thy Son the heathen for his inheritance, and the uttermost parts of the earth for his possession; for thou hast said, It is a light thing for him to raise up the tribes of Jacob, and to restore the preserved of Israel, but thou wilt give him for a light to the Gentiles. Let all the kingdoms of this world become the kingdoms of the

---

46. Henry, *Works*, 2:15. See Prov. 25:28; 14:17; Eccl. 7:9; Ps. 106:33; Eph. 4:31.
47. Duncan, "A Method for Prayer," in *The Devoted Life*, 244.
48. Henry, *Works*, 2:50. See James 1:27; Rom. 14:17; Hab. 3:2; Heb. 9:10.
49. Henry, *Works*, 2:51. See Isa. 54:17.

Lord, and of his Christ."[50] Praying the Scriptures back to God will certainly lead us to pray for missions.

## Conclusion: Pray the Scriptures

We have only scratched the surface of Henry's book. In addition to many more scriptural prayers of adoration, confession, petition for ourselves, thanksgiving, and intercession for others, Henry also assembled Scriptures into a multi-page paraphrase of the Lord's Prayer, a set of simple Bible prayers for children, prayers for children based on catechism answers, scriptural prayers for family devotions in the morning and evening and on the Lord's Day, a parent's prayers for children, prayers to prepare for the Lord's Supper, and prayers to say at mealtimes. Henry's *Family Hymns* (1694), a collection of selections from the Psalms and passages from the New Testament in poetic form, can also enrich family worship with biblical truth.[51] Duncan says of the *Method for Prayer*, "Reading and rereading Henry's book will train us in the use of biblical truth and language in prayer, and thus assist and encourage modern Christians in both public and private prayer." Praying the Scriptures will "engrave in our minds biblical patterns of thought" and move us to a "God-centered way of praying."[52]

We should learn from Henry's great maxim: pray the Scriptures. In this assertion, Henry stood with Reformed writers through the ages. William Gurnall (1616–1679) wrote, "The mightier any is in the Word, the more mighty he will be in prayer." Later, Robert M'Cheyne (1813–1843) said, "Turn the Bible into prayer."[53] Nothing is surer or more helpful as a rule or guide in prayer than the whole Word of God. All this echoes the magisterial words of Christ, "If ye abide in me, and my words abide in you, ye shall ask what ye will, and it shall be done unto you" (John 15:7).

50. Henry, *Works*, 2:48–49. See Ps. 2:8; Isa. 49:6. See also chapter 11, "Puritan Prayers for World Missions."

51. Henry, *Works*, 1:413–43.

52. Duncan, "A Method for Prayer," in *The Devoted Life*, 249.

53. Cited in John Blanchard, comp., *The Complete Gathered Gold* (Darlington, England: Evangelical Press, 2006), 473.

*Chapter 9*

# Thomas Boston on Praying to Our Father

─────────co೦ೲ೦ೀ─────────

## JOEL R. BEEKE

*The Spirit of Christ presses forward the elect, and determines them to seek to be received into the family of God.*

— THOMAS BOSTON

Thomas Boston (1676–1732) rose to prominence as a minister of the Church of Scotland and a prolific theological writer.[1] Converted under the preaching of Henry Erskine, father of Ebenezer and Ralph Erskine, Boston served two congregations, first in the parish of Simprin (1699–1707), then in the parish of Ettrick (1707–1732). Boston mastered the classical languages as well as French and Dutch.

Though he was an able linguist, theologian, and author, Boston did not seek the limelight. He did not teach in a university, but his books and published sermons were great commentaries on Christian theology. *An Illustration of the Doctrines of the Christian Religion*

─────────────────

1. For Boston's biography see Jean Watson, *The Pastor of Ettrick: Thomas Boston* (Edinburgh: James Gemmell, 1883), 34–45; William Addison, *The Life and Writings of Thomas Boston of Ettrick* (Edinburgh: Oliver and Boyd, 1936); D. J. Innes, "Thomas Boston of Ettrick," in *Faith and a Good Conscience* (London: Puritan and Reformed Conference, 1962), 32–46; Stephen Albert Woodruff III, "The Pastoral Ministry in the Church of Scotland in the Eighteenth Century, with Special Reference to Thomas Boston, John Willison, and John Erskine" (Ph.D. diss., University of Edinburgh, 1966); Joel R. Beeke, introduction to *The Complete Works of Thomas Boston*, ed. Samuel M'Millan, 12 vols. (Stoke-on-Trent, England: Tentmaker Publications, 2002), 1:1–16 [hereafter, *Works*].

is one of the best expositions of the Westminster Shorter Catechism ever published. His *Human Nature and Its Fourfold State*, published in Edinburgh in 1720, is a classic that traces the human condition through four states: man's original state of righteousness or innocence, man as a fallen creature, man as a redeemed and regenerated being, and man in the eternal state of heaven or hell.[2]

Boston experienced many sorrows in life. He lost his mother when he was fifteen and his father a decade later, shortly after Boston settled in Simprin. He discovered that people there were ignorant of spiritual truths and negligent in family worship. In Simprin, Boston married Catherine Brown, fifth daughter of Robert Brown of Barhill, Clackmannan. Boston saw "sparkles of grace" in her.[3] He considered marriage a gift of the Lord, even though his wife suffered frequent bouts of acute depression and insanity; from 1720 on, she was often confined to an apartment, "the inner prison," where Boston says she was "an easy target for Satan's onslaughts, both concerning her assurance of salvation and her peace with God."[4] He buried six of their ten children, two in Simprin and four at Ettrick. His first ten years of ministry at Ettrick were a long season of plowing with little yield. His advocacy of the free grace of God put him at the center of a grievous controversy in his denomination.[5] Then, too, Boston often suffered acute physical pain and

2. Phil Ryken, *Thomas Boston (1676–1732) as Preacher of the Fourfold State* (Carlisle, England: Paternoster Press, 1999).

3. George H. Morrison, biographical introduction in Thomas Boston, *Human Nature in Its Fourfold State* (London: Banner of Truth Trust, 1964), 14–15.

4. For Catherine Boston's trials, see Faith Cook's *Singing in the Fire* (Edinburgh: Banner of Truth Trust, 1995), 122–31; Maureen Bradley, "A Brief Memorial of Thomas Boston," in Thomas Boston, *The Crook in the Lot* (Morgan, Pa.: Soli Deo Gloria, 2000), viii–ix.

5. See especially Donald J. Bruggink, "The Theology of Thomas Boston, 1676–1732" (Ph.D. diss., University of Edinburgh, 1958); David C. Lachman, *The Marrow Controversy, 1718–1723: An Historical and Theological Analysis* (Edinburgh: Rutherford House, 1988); A. T. B. McGowan, *The Federal Theology of Thomas Boston* (Carlisle, U.K.: Paternoster, 1997); William VanDoodewaard, "The Marrow Controversy and Seceder Tradition: Marrow Theology in the Associate Presbytery and

weakness. Yet he endured such trials cheerfully in submission to a loving heavenly Father.

Spiritual discipline was essential to the ministry, Boston believed, so he rose early each Monday and devoted hours to prayer and reflection. He also devoted time to prayer throughout the week. On nearly every page of his autobiography, Boston says he laid one matter or another before the Lord in prayer. He also established regular times for fasting and communion with God. "When his congregation saw him enter the pulpit on the morning of the Lord's Day, they knew they were looking into the face of one who had just come forth from intimate communion with God, and who at once was God's ambassador and their friend," wrote Andrew Thomson.[6] By the time Boston died, his name was a virtual synonym in Scotland for holiness of life. D. D. F. MacDonald said Boston's preaching "did more to fan the flame of true piety in Scotland than any other single minister in his generation."[7]

Central to Thomas Boston's view of prayer is the doctrine of adoption. The Puritans in England and Scotland made much of adoption; they were the first group to incorporate an article on adoption into a Reformed confession of faith (Westminster Confession of Faith, chapter 12).[8] Boston traced the development of the doctrine of our adoption by God as His children into the doctrine of prayer to God as our Father. He taught that adoption is the foundation of prayer, and prayer is the fruition of adoption.

### Adoption as the Foundation of Prayer

The Lord Jesus taught His disciples to pray, "Our Father, which art in heaven" (Matt. 6:9), to which Boston comments, "The children of

---

Associate Synod Secession Churches of Scotland (1733–1799)" (Ph.D. diss., University of Aberdeen, 2009).

6. Andrew Thomson, *Thomas Boston of Ettrick: His Life and Times* (London: T. Nelson and Sons, 1895), 173.

7. McGowan, *The Federal Theology of Thomas Boston*, xiii–xiv.

8. See Joel R. Beeke, *Heirs with Christ: The Puritans on Adoption* (Grand Rapids: Reformation Heritage Books, 2008).

God [are] those who only can or are capable to pray acceptably: for they only can indeed call God *Father*. We cannot pray acceptably unless he be our Father, and we his children, namely, by regeneration and adoption."[9] This does not excuse prayerlessness. "Prayer is a duty of natural religion," Boston says, and thus is obligatory for everyone.[10] Though unconverted sinners cannot please God in their performance of prayer, God still may answer their prayers because He ordained prayer as a means of grace.[11] But only a child of God can pray rightly. To get at the heart of Boston's theology on prayer, we must understand two major emphases: first, the status of adoption is necessary if one is to pray acceptably; second, the Spirit of adoption enables the child of God to pray spiritually.

*The Status of Adoption as the Key to Prayer*
"There are but two families in the world, and to one of the two every man and woman belongs," Boston writes. "One is Satan's family, the other God's."[12] All humans are born into the family of Satan because we are all born as sinners. God's effectual calling draws sinners out of Satan's family and brings them into God's family. Participating in the "external and federal" adoption "which is common to the members of the visible church" is not enough, Boston says. One must receive "an internal and saving adoption" by effectual calling, or regeneration by the Spirit, and conversion.

Boston distinguishes between regeneration and adoption. Regeneration changes our nature. Boston writes, "Adoption is not a real change of the sinner's nature; but, as [with] justification, is a relative change of status." Adoption brings us "out of the state of alienation from God." He says, "Our names are enrolled among those of the family; and though a new nature accompanies it, yet adoption itself is a new name, not a new nature, Rev. 2:17, though it

---

9. *Works*, 2:561.
10. *Works*, 2:526.
11. *Works*, 2:562.
12. *Works*, 1:612.

is not an empty title, but has vast privileges attending it."[13] Simply put, true spiritual adoption operates much like legal adoption in today's world. When a child is legally adopted, he or she is declared the child of new parents. But legal adoption does nothing to change the cellular makeup, genes, or blood of the adopted child. Nevertheless, adoption places a child into a household where he may learn from his father's love, example, instruction, and discipline to become more like his father. Similarly, when children of Satan are adopted by God, they are no longer children of Satan but are *counted* as children of God, even though remnants of sin remain in them. Yet the privileges of adoption change their lives.

Boston views divine adoption as the work of the Trinity. First, the Adopter is God the Father who, in His great love, eternally predestines sinners to be brought back into His family (Eph. 1:3, 5; 1 John 3:1). Boston writes, "The Adopter can be no higher, for he is the Sovereign King of the world, the adopted no lower, for they are not only the children of base men, but of the devil, the most miserable creature in the universe." This magnifies the Father's love but also requires the satisfaction of His law "that forbids the staining of the Adopter's honor by the meanness of the party adopted."

Second, divine wisdom requires that these children be adopted in Jesus Christ (Eph. 1:5–6; Gal. 3:26–27). He is the Son of God who became incarnate as "the Elder Brother in the repaired family of heaven." Christ is the elder brother to whom supremely belongs the kingdom, priesthood, blessing, and inheritance of sonship. Boston writes, "By his obedience and satisfaction he purchased their adoption, with all other privileges to them, Gal. 4:4, 5. And this natural bond with them gives Him the direct interest to redeem them as their near Kinsman. So law and justice can have nothing to object against the adoption."[14]

---

13. *Works*, 1:615. Boston's Scripture references have been modernized to use Arabic, not Roman, numerals.
14. *Works*, 1:616, 618–19, 622–23.

Finally, Christ sends forth His messengers to preach the gospel offer of adoption, and the Father sends His Spirit to open the ears and hearts of people to seek adoption. Boston says, "Whosoever will comply with the gospel call, shall be adopted into God's family; God will be their Father, and they shall be his sons and daughters." Though Satan fights to retain his children, "the Spirit of Christ presses forward the elect, and determines them to seek to be received into the family of God." The elect soul comes to Christ and joins himself to Christ by faith, as in a marriage covenant. Christ then presents the believer to His Father as one with the Son so that the Devil is forced to renounce his former child. God then receives the believer into the family of His children, which is a privilege beyond justification.[15] Their new status as adopted children flows out of their union with Christ. Boston says, "By their union with him, who is the Son of God by nature, they become the sons of God by grace…sinners, being engrafted into Jesus Christ, whose name is the Branch, his Father is their Father, his God their God, John 20:17. And thus they, who are by nature children of the devil, become the children of God."[16]

Adoption offers distinct privileges to the sons of God, which Boston says are as follows:

1) "A new name, Rev. 2:17 and 3:12…. They are called of God sons and daughters, Heb. 12:5."

2) "The Spirit of adoption, Rom. 8:15." We will discuss this privilege later in the chapter.

3) "Access to God and communion with him. They may come farther in than others and come forward with holy boldness, when others must stand back, Eph. 3:12. God as a Father is familiar with his children, allows them a holy confidence with him, as children to pour their complaints into his bosom and tell him all their wants. Never did a father take

---

15. *Works*, 1:614, 619–21.
16. *Works*, 8:209.

so much delight in his child's talking to him, as God, in the prayer of his people poured out, by virtue of the Spirit of adoption, Prov. 15:8. Song. 2:14."

4) "Special immunities and freedoms...from the law as a covenant of works...from the curse...from the hurt of everything...Rom. 8:35, 38, 39 [being] bettered by the worse things that befall them, ver. 28."

5) "God's fatherly love and pity.... No mother [is] so tender of the fruit of her womb as God is of his children, Isa. 49:15."

6) "Protection, Prov. 14:26.... In all cases they have a Father to run to, both able and willing to protect them, Ps. 90:1.... And at length he will set them beyond all danger, Rev. 21:25."

7) "Provision, 1 Pet. 5:7.... Come what will, God's children shall be provided for; for he that feeds his birds, the ravens that cry, will not starve his children."

8) "Seasonable and sanctified correction.... It is a special benefit of the covenant of grace, proceeding from God's fatherly love, Ps. 89:30–32."

9) "Lastly, an inheritance and portion, according to their Father's quality. They are heirs of God, and joint-heirs with Christ, Rom. 8:17. So all is theirs, grace and glory."[17]

Adoption privileges have remarkable implications for the prayers of the children of God. It is no wonder that a man with this view of divine adoption would spend much time in communion with God. However, these privileges belong only to those adopted by the Father, in the Son, through the Spirit. Unbelievers may cry out to God for mercy, but access to the Father is a benefit reserved for the children of God. Prayer is the duty of all, but acceptance with God is a privilege. Boston writes, "It is a privilege that God

---

17. *Works*, 1:624–26.

will allow us to come so near him, and to pour out our hearts before him, a privilege bought by the blood of Christ."[18]

Therefore the children of God must enjoy their privileges in prayer in conscious dependence upon Jesus Christ. Believers must pray in Jesus' name (John 16:23). Boston understands the meaning of praying in Jesus' name as far more than "a bare mentioning his name, in prayer, and concluding our prayers therewith." Rather, praying in Jesus' name means

1) Praying because Jesus commanded us to do so and thus authorized us to do so.

2) Praying because we have seen the glory of God in Jesus and so we love Him.

3) Praying in the strength that Jesus Christ supplies us to do our spiritual duty.

4) Praying with reliance upon Jesus as the only basis for God to hear and answer us.[19] This last point Boston elaborates in more detail, saying it means,

- "Renouncing all merit and worth in ourselves... Gen. 32:10."

- "Believing that however great the mercies are, and however unworthy we are, yet we may obtain them from God through Jesus Christ; Heb. 4:15–16."

- "Seeking in prayer the mercies we need of God, for Christ's sake accordingly." This means praying with both shame and confidence: "Our holy shame respects our unworthiness; but Christ's merit and intercession are set before us, as a ground of confidence."

- "Pleading on his merit and intercession.... Faith founding its plea on Christ's merit, urges

---

18. *Works*, 11:15.
19. *Works*, 11:82–90.

God's covenant and promise made thereupon;
Ps. 74:20."

- "Lastly, trusting that we shall obtain a gracious
answer for his sake; Mark. 11:24."[20]

Because prayer is a benefit of grace given through Christ, our
prayers are to be Christ-centered. Our adoption and all its benefits
are in Him. So Boston writes, "Going to God in prayer, we must
as it were put off our own persons, as not worth noticing in the
sight of God, and put on the Lord Jesus Christ; come and receive
the blessing in the elder Brother's clothes, having all our hope from
the Lord's looking on the face of his Anointed."[21] If we attempt to
approach God outside of or apart from Christ and seek God by any
other way, "the glory of God [will] fright the sinner away from him,
as from a consuming fire. So we must behold God in Christ, and go
to him as the object of our love and adoration."[22]

Adoption comes from the Trinity, so prayer depends on the
Trinity. Boston writes, "For thus the whole Trinity is glorified by
the praying [of] believers, the Father as the Hearer of prayer, the
Son as the Advocate and Intercessor presenting their prayers to the
Father, and the Spirit as the Author of their prayers; Eph. 2:18, 'For
through him we both have access by one Spirit unto the Father.'"[23]
This leads to how the Holy Spirit helps God's children pray.

### The Spirit of Adoption as the Life of Prayer

The Scriptures link together divine adoption, prayer, and the ministry of the Holy Spirit in the lives of believers. In Romans 8:15,
Paul writes, "For ye have not received the spirit of bondage again
to fear; but ye have received the Spirit of adoption, whereby we
cry, Abba, Father." Thus Thomas Boston says the second benefit of
adoption is "the Spirit of adoption," explaining, "That is the spirit of

---

20. *Works*, 11:91.
21. *Works*, 11:88.
22. *Works*, 11:84.
23. *Works*, 11:83.

the family of heaven, a noble and generous spirit, a spirit of love to God, and confidence in him as a Father. Hereby they are enabled to call God Father, and this is more worth than a thousand worlds."[24] Though some conforming Puritans held, with the Reformers, that written prayers could be used rightly if used in faith, most Puritans disdained the heartless reciting of form prayers.[25] They preferred prayers prompted by the Holy Spirit, who engages the believer's heart to cry to God as a child to his father.

Prayer is not just a privilege of adoption; it is a sign of the adoption, for it is a fruit of the Spirit of adoption. The Spirit of adoption is "a Spirit of prayer," says Boston. "This casts all prayerless persons that are come to years of discretion, as none of God's children. It also casts all those, who though they have a gift of prayer, and use it too, are strangers to the spirit of prayer."[26] "The children of God are all praying persons," Boston says. "There is no child so unnatural as to be still in his father's presence, and never to converse with him."[27]

Paul illuminates the ministry of the Holy Spirit in prayer in Romans 8:26–27: "Likewise the Spirit also helpeth our infirmities: for we know not what we should pray for as we ought: but the Spirit itself maketh intercession for us with groanings which cannot be uttered. And he that searcheth the hearts knoweth what is the mind of the Spirit, because he maketh intercession for the saints according to the will of God." Boston explains,

> Among praying people there is a twofold cry that goes to heaven, (1.) The cry of strangers, not known and approved there. That is prayer wrought out by ourselves, in virtue of a natural sense of want, by a gift of knowledge and utterance. (2.) The cry of children; that is prayer wrought in us by the help of

24. *Works*, 1:624.
25. Leland Ryken, *Worldly Saints: The Puritans as They Really Were* (Grand Rapids: Zondervan, 1986), 127.
26. *Works*, 1:635.
27. *Works*, 11:43; cf. 11:51.

the Holy Spirit dwelling and acting in us, and is accepted of God. Of this our text speaks.[28]

God's children need spiritual help, especially in prayer. Boston writes, "Whenever the grace of God touches their hearts, they are set a-praying; however, they are in it but like children beginning to speak." They babble like toddlers. They know neither what to pray nor how to ask for it in a way fit for the court of heaven. Boston says, "We are apt, instead of bread, to ask a stone; instead of a fish, a scorpion; to pray for what do us ill, and against what is our good."[29] We tend to pray against the very things God intends for us in His mercy. We seek things that are hurtful to us and chase after the objects of our sinful lusts. We fail to pray for what we really need and forget to pray for good things. We do not know ourselves, and we do not know the Scriptures. Believers enter into prayer with minds entangled with the world, hearts disturbed by passions, spirits lifeless and cold in devotion, thoughts wandering from spiritual duties, and priorities out of order. They are too easily impressed with people's words and give up too quickly on God's answers.[30] Believers need help in prayer!

Yet, Boston says, believers have "the best of help, the help of God himself, the eternal Spirit of the Father and the Son, the third person of the glorious Trinity, by whom the Father and the Son do act in them."[31] "The Spirit's intercession is the fruit of Christ's intercession, and what is done by the sinner through the Spirit's intercession is accepted of God through the intercession of Christ. Christ by his death purchased the Spirit for his people, and through his intercession the Spirit is sent into their hearts, where he helps them to pray."[32] The Son and the Spirit of the Son cooperate to

---

28. *Works*, 11:19. On gifts of eloquence in prayer, Boston writes, "If the best gift without the Spirit were bestowed on a man, he could not make a prayer that would be acceptable to God, though it might be much admired of men" (*Works*, 11:21).

29. *Works*, 11:20–21.

30. *Works*, 11:44–50.

31. *Works*, 11:20.

32. *Works*, 11:60.

bring people in prayer to the Father. The Spirit is the friend who helps a poor man to write up his petition to the king; the Son is the friend who brings the petition into the king's presence, and gets it granted.[33] The Holy Spirit enables believers to pray by giving them abilities to think, speak, and serve God. More significantly, He empowers their grace, or the spiritual life activated in them by regeneration. The Spirit acts as the Spirit of Christ. Boston says, "The quickening spirit of Christ being communicated to the dead elect in the time of loves [or conversion],[34] they are made to live and believe in Christ, and so are united to him; upon which union the same Spirit takes of the treasure of grace in Christ, and plants in the believer grace for grace in Christ Jesus."[35]

Despite the mutability of our wills, the corruption of our nature, the animosity of Satan, and the weakness of the new creation in us, the Spirit preserves grace in the believer. He also excites grace into activity (Phil. 2:13). He blows upon the coals to stir up the soul to flaming love. He brings truth to our minds and awakens our affections. He strengthens and increases grace within us (Eph. 3:16). He supplies grace for our immediate needs, like oil added to a lamp in danger of going out (Phil. 1:19). The Spirit has various tools to empower grace, including both happy and hard providences and the ordinances of worship such as the sacraments and especially the Word.[36]

The Spirit of God uses the gospel to lift up our hearts to God as our Father. Boston writes, "He gives us a view of God as a gracious and merciful Father in Christ; Gal. 4:6… by the Spirit viewing Him

---

33. *Works*, 11:60–61.

34. The "time of loves" alludes to Ezek. 16:8, when in a parable the Lord describes His taking Israel like an outcast girl into a marriage covenant with Himself. Boston used it here of personal entry into the covenant of grace.

35. *Works*, 11:30–32. On the inseparability of the Spirit from Christ, see also ibid., 70. The quotes at the beginning of this paragraph remind us again of how Trinitarian Puritan theology was.

36. *Works*, 11:32–38.

in Christ, we have at once the sight of majesty and mercy." This works in us the following:

1) "A holy reverence of God, to whom we pray, which is necessary in acceptable prayer, Heb. 12:28. By this he strikes us with a holy dread and awe of the majesty of God, whereby is banished that lightness and vanity of heart, that makes such flaunting in the prayers of some, as if they were set down on their knees to shew their gift, and commend themselves."

2) "A holy confidence in him, Eph. 3:12, 'Abba Father,' speaks both reverence and confidence, whereof the Spirit is the Author, Rom. 8:15. This confidence respects both his ability and willingness to help us, Matt. 7:11. Without this there can be no acceptable prayer, Heb. 11:6; James 1:6.... Hereby is cut off that unbelieving formality, whereby some expect nothing by prayer, and get as little; as also the despondency, wherewith others are struck, from the sense of God's justice, and their own sinfulness."[37]

The Holy Spirit does not act upon the praying believer as an external agent but "as a Spirit of life, dwelling in the man as a member of Christ." Boston says Galatians 4:6 depicts the Holy Spirit "crying, Abba, Father." Even though God is the Father of the Son, not of the Spirit, the Spirit is so directly involved in moving believers to pray that their cries of "Father!" are the cries of the Holy Spirit within them (cf. Rom. 8:15). The Spirit is the fire that sends the smoke of the incense of our prayers to heaven. He is the Spirit of the Head who animates all the members of the body.

However, Boston guards against attributing our imperfections to the Spirit.[38] He does not confuse God's Spirit with the human spirit, but he does identify the Holy Spirit as the principle of spiritual life in the regenerated human spirit. He ascribes any good in

---

37. *Works*, 11:62.
38. *Works*, 11:57, 59.

our prayers to the Spirit of the Lord. He says prayers are "spiritual desires...which the saints breathe out unto God, having them first breathed into them by the Spirit."[39] He adds,

> We are spiritually dead without the Spirit indwelling, and spiritually asleep without the Spirit influencing.... The former, praying, is like a ghost walking and talking; the latter, like a man speaking through his sleep.... To praying aright is required light and warmth, a light of the mind and warmth of affections; the former for the matter, the latter for the manner. And it is a false light and warmth that makes some natural men think that sometimes they pray aright, Isa. 58:2. But all genuine light, and vital warmth comes from the Spirit, Eph. 1:17, 18; 2 Tim. 1:7.[40]

Boston thus says, "Resist not the Spirit, Acts 7:51.... Quench not the Spirit, 1 Thess. 5:19.... Grieve not the Spirit, Eph. 4:30.... Vex not the Spirit; Isa. 63:10.... When ye go to prayer, be convinced of your absolute need of the Spirit."[41] The Holy Spirit is the Spirit of adoption, who makes the invisible reality of adoption real in the believer. How precious is the ministry of the Holy Spirit in the prayers of God's children!

Boston paints a picture of prayer that is far from either a religious poetry recital or stream-of-consciousness babbling. Prayer is man's response to the Father's grace as authorized by the Son's grace and energized by the Spirit's grace. In prayer, the believer experiences the glorious Trinity at work before him, for him, and in him within the intimacy of family. Boston rejoices in this, saying, "Hence see the happiness of the saints in the love of the Father, who is their Father; of the Son, who has made them children of God, and of the Holy Spirit, who teaches them to call God their Father. How happy must those be who are so nearly related to all the three persons of

---

39. *Works*, 11:11.
40. *Works*, 11:58.
41. *Works*, 11:70–71.

the adorable Trinity, and are loved by, and have communion with each of them!"[42] Therefore adoption is the foundation of prayer.

## Prayer: The Fruition of Adoption

Prayer is built upon adoption, and adoption bears fruit in prayer. Boston expresses this concept in discourses on the Lord's Prayer from a series of sermons on the Westminster Shorter Catechism. Though Boston views all of Scripture as a guide for prayer, he especially treasures the Lord's Prayer both as an example of prayer and as a directory for the prayers of God's children.[43] Boston divides the Lord's Prayer into three sections: the preface, the petitions, and the conclusion.[44] Each section illustrates the heart of adopted children for their Father.

*The Preface: "Our Father which art in heaven"*
After establishing that acceptable prayer requires adoption into God's family through faith in Jesus Christ, Boston goes on to say, "We should draw near to God in prayer with child-like dispositions and affections towards him." This includes the following responses:

1) "Though he be very kind and admit us into familiarity with him, yet we must come with a holy reverence, Mal. 1:6, 'If then I be a Father, where is mine honor?' Familiarity must not breed contempt. The character of a Father bears not only kindness, but reverence and fear in it. It is a mixture of love and awful authority; and the ingenuous child will regard both. Slavish fear is to be laid aside, but child-like reverence is necessary [Heb. 12:28]."[45]

---

42. *Works*, 565.
43. *Works*, 2:557–58.
44. *Works*, 2:561.
45. Note Boston's allusion to Rom. 8:15. "Slavish fear" was a subject frequently explored by the Puritans in their attempt to distinguish the fear of God commended in Scripture from the terror of rejection and punishment by God.

2) "Though we have offended God...we must come
with confidence, whatever we want, whatever we
need, Eph. 3:12. While he bids us call him *Father*,
he requires us confidence in him for the supply of
all our wants. For fatherly affection is tender...Ps.
103:13."

3) "God is ready and willing to help us, and we should
come to him in that confidence, Matt. 7:11, 'If ye
then, being evil, know how to give good gifts to
your children, how much more shall your Father
which is in heaven give good things to them that
ask him?' If the mother's tenderness towards the
child be ordinarily greater than that of the father's,
yet the Lord is still more, Isa. 49:15, 16, 'Can a
woman forget her sucking child, that she should
not have compassion on the son of her womb? yea,
they may forget, yet I will not forget thee. Behold, I
have graven thee upon the palms of my hands; thy
walls are continually before me.'"[46]

Boston also says "our Father *in heaven*" encourages us "to eye
his sovereign power and dominion over all, in our address to him,
believing that he is able to help us in our greatest straits, and that
nothing is too hard for him but he can do whatsoever he will, Ps.
115:3. This is a noble ground for faith. Our fathers on earth may be
unable to help; but our Father in heaven is almighty, and has power
to help in every case."[47]

The fruit of adoption thus flourishes in the prayer life of a child
of God. So Boston asks his believing readers to shape their prayers
with faith in a reconciled Father who is the sovereign Lord of all.

*First Petition: "Hallowed be thy name"*
Boston divided the petitions of the Lord's Prayer into two groups:
first, three petitions for God's glory; and second, three for our good.

---

46. *Works*, 2:562–63.
47. *Works*, 2:564.

The first petition concerns the glory of God's name, and Boston explains, "because of all things it should be nearest our hearts."[48] Boston says we do not pray for God to be made holy; rather, we pray for God's holiness to be manifested, declared, shown, and acknowledged. So this first petition is a prayer for God to be glorified and His beauty to shine.[49] It is a prayer for providential victories for His church, but also a prayer for powerful grace to "cause the sons of men, ourselves and others, to glorify and hallow His name," both "internally, by knowing, acknowledging, and highly esteeming him" and "externally, in our words and actions, speaking and living to his praise."[50]

Again, Boston connects prayer with the heart of a child for his divine Father. He writes,

> Why truly, if thou belongest to God, it will be a matter of thy hearty consent and prayer, that God may be honoured by others as well as by thyself. Without this concern a man cannot be a Christian; he is not a child of God; for every true believer ardently wishes and prays that God may be glorified; and as far as his power, authority, influence, and example, can reach, he will use his utmost endeavors to induce others to glorify the name of his God....
>
> It is the disposition of a child of God, to submit his lot and condition in the world to the Lord, to be cut and carved as may serve his glory. Without this one cannot be a child of God.[51]

The adopting love of the Father and glorious loveliness of God move His adopted children to love Him and long to see Him honored as God. With this emphasis Boston reflects the heart of the Son, who trembled in anticipation of Calvary and yet cried out, "Father, glorify thy name" (John 12:28).

---

48. *Works*, 2:565.
49. *Works*, 2:566–67.
50. *Works*, 2:568–69.
51. *Works*, 2:570.

*Second Petition: "Thy kingdom come"*

Boston says the coming of the kingdom of our Father in heaven "that is the advancement thereof, is desired by all the children of God. And that is the great means of glorifying his name; for then is his name hallowed, when his kingdom comes, is advanced and carried on till it come to perfection."[52] Boston distinguishes a fourfold kingdom of God:

1) "The kingdom of his power," the universal reign of God over all His creation by divine providence whether they are willing or unwilling (Ps. 103:19).

2) "The kingdom of his gospel," the visible church over which Christ reigns by His Word and the officers of the church (Matt. 21:43).

3) "The kingdom of his grace," a subset of the visible church consisting of those hearts where Christ dwells and reigns in saving, spiritual power (Luke 17:21; Rom. 14:17).

4) "The kingdom of his glory," the blessed, eternal state that will arrive when Jesus Christ comes (1 Cor. 15:50).[53]

Boston says these kingdoms all serve one kingdom purpose: "Here it is to be observed concerning this fourfold kingdom, that they are sweetly linked together, and stand in a line of subordination, the end of which is the kingdom of glory, the kingdom of grace being subordinated to it, the gospel-kingdom to that of grace, and the kingdom of power to the kingdom of the gospel."[54] All of these kingdoms are moving or progressing towards the kingdom of glory, of which Boston says, "The ordinances of it are perpetual praises and hallelujahs, never-ceasing songs to God and the Lamb. There is no temple there, for God and the Lamb are the temple thereof. There

---

52. *Works*, 2:571.
53. *Works*, 2:571–74.
54. *Works*, 2:575.

is no need of preaching or prayer; for perfect knowledge takes place, and every saint is made perfect and full, so as to seek no more. Faith is swallowed up in vision, and hope in fruition."[55] Boston views the coming of the kingdom of glory as inevitable. It is impossible that it should not come, because, he says, "The Father's truth, the Son's blood, and the Spirit's seal, are pledges of its erection. The Father has promised it, the Son purchased it, and the Spirit sealed it on the souls of all the saints."[56]

God works progressively through other kingdoms to bring about His final end, however. Therefore saints must pray for the destruction of sin and Satan in the hearts and lives of men, the conversion of sinners to God, the perfecting of the saints in grace, the overcoming of obstacles to the gospel, and the propagation of the gospel to all nations.[57]

Boston applies this truth by telling his readers,

Shew yourselves of the family of heaven, by your concern that the Lord's kingdom may come, even that of glory, grace, the gospel, and power. For this is the language of those who cry unto God, 'Abba, Father.'… It is their Father's kingdom. How then can the children not be concerned for it? Matt. 6:9, 10. Their Father's honour must be dear to them, Mal. 1:6…. Their brethren's interest lies in it too, Ps. 122:8. All the saints are born brethren…. Try by this whether ye be of the family of God or not. Have ye a kindly concern for the coming of his kingdom? Do your hearts say within you, *Thy kingdom come?* If it be not so, God is not your Father; but if so, he is.[58]

So, for Boston, a life of God-centered prayer is the necessary consequence of the adoption of a sinner into God's family.

---

55. *Works*, 2:574.
56. *Works*, 2:576.
57. *Works*, 2:578–80. Note the heart of the Puritans for worldwide missions.
58. *Works*, 2:581, 583.

*Third Petition: "Thy will be done"*

Boston notes the essential unity of the first three petitions by say-ing, "As by the coming of his kingdom his name is hallowed, so by doing his will his kingdom comes, or is advanced, and we own him to be King, Heb 13:21. So these three petitions meet to advance the glory of God."[59] The will of God may be seen as "the will of God's commands," that is, God's commands for faith in His Son (1 John 3:23) and holiness of life (1 Thess. 4:3). The will of God may also be seen as "the will of God's providence" in ruling over all things (Ps. 135:6).[60]

With respect to the will of God's commands, this petition compels us to confess that we have disobeyed God's will and are completely unfit to obey Him. It calls us to profess our grief over the sins of mankind and to trust that God has the power to reform our will to match His. The petition leads Christians to pray "that he would by his grace remove from themselves and others all spiritual blindness and cause them to know his will, Eph. 1:17, 18," and "that God by his grace would remove from themselves and others all weakness, indisposition, and perverseness, and cause them to obey and do his will, as it is done in heaven, Ps. 119:35." Boston specifies this means praying that we would do God's will consistently, ener-getically, universally, humbly, cheerfully, quickly, and constantly.[61]

With respect to the will of God's providence, Boston says this petition directs us to confess that people by nature are apt to com-plain and quarrel with God over His management of their lives. It summons us to profess our sorrow for not cheerfully submitting to God's ways and our confidence that God's grace can subdue our will to His providences. It requires us to pray for God to work in us "a submission to the will of God in afflicting providences...Ps. 39:9," "a thankful acceptance of merciful and kind providences, Luke 1:38,"

59. *Works*, 2:586–87.
60. *Works*, 2:587–89.
61. *Works*, 2:592–96.

and "a compliance with the design of providences of all sorts" by using our talents, position, and opportunities to serve Him well.[62]

Though Boston did not mention adoption in his treatment of this petition in the Lord's Prayer, his earlier treatment of adoption emphasizes that a son must submit wholeheartedly to his father's will: "God must command, and ye must obey without disputing your Father's orders…. Your Father's will must be yours…. Ye must give him internal as well as external obedience. Filial [son-like] affections are due to a father; love, reverence, delight in him, and fear to offend him…. Ye and your lot must be at God's disposal, Ps. 47:4. Ye must take what place, and act what part, in the family the Father shall think meet to dispose you to."[63]

*Fourth Petition: "Give us this day our daily bread"*
Boston now examines the second triad of petitions, which concern our own good. He deduces from the order of the petitions "that it is the duty of all, and the disposition of God's children, to prefer God's honour to all their personal and private interests." He says, "If the chariot of God's honour cannot drive forward, but it must drive over their table, they bid it welcome to drive on, though it cast down their table, making its way over it, Luke 14:26."[64] The reason for this is that "God is man's chief end, and the chief good. All things are from him, and so must be for him, Prov. 16:4; Rev. 4:11. And to alter this order, is for men to make God's honour the means, and their own welfare the end; which is to lift themselves very proudly above God."[65]

Boston says that this petition implies, "Men depend wholly and entirely on God's bounty, for all the means and comforts of life." God is the creator of all things and is their preserver, owner,

---

62. *Works*, 2:597–98.
63. *Works*, 1:639.
64. *Works*, 2:601.
65. *Works*, 2:602–603.

and life-giver. He is sovereign over all usefulness and comfort, and holder of veto-power over all our efforts.[66]

Boston says, "Our Lord teaches all his people to come unto God, and say, *Our Father—give us bread.*" This means "we are allowed to lay our temporal concerns and wants before the Lord in prayer, as well as our spiritual concerns.... The praying Christian is a trader with heaven, and he may trade in small things as well as in great things; nay, he ought to do it." It also means:

> Our bread is God's free gift of mercy, without any merit of ours, Gen. 32:10. The least rag for our clothing, crumb for our food, breathing in God's air, etc. is what we deserve not at the hand of God, Luke 17:10. In Adam we forfeited our right to God's creatures, Gen. 2:17; and by that sin of breaking the first covenant, and many other rebellions against the sovereign God, we have deserved to be stript of our comforts: so that all we get is God's free undeserved gift.[67]

Because of God's grace, the children of God have "a covenant-right to them, through Jesus Christ, by whom the lost right to the creatures is restored to believers, 1 Cor. 3:22," Boston says. "For if one be in Christ, he enjoys his bread by a new tenor, the tenor of the covenant, Isa. 33:16. And that makes dry bread sweet."[68] Even prayer for our daily needs is framed within the covenant of grace, for we have communion with the Father, whose love is like honey and butter spread across all our bread.

*Fifth Petition: "And forgive us our debts, as we forgive our debtors"*
This petition seeks blessings for the soul, for, as Boston says, "the removal of guilt is the opening of the spring of spiritual blessings, to run abundantly; it is the taking the stone off the mouth of the well." Justification precedes sanctification and spiritual comforts. Sin must

---

66. *Works*, 2:604–606.
67. *Works*, 2:608–609.
68. *Works*, 2:609.

be pardoned because sin "is a drowning debt, a debt so great as no mortal is able to pay, Matt. 18:24, 25."[69]

Boston says there are three kinds of pardon.

1) "Pardon of the guilt of eternal wrath." This frees sinners from vindictive justice that threatens to send them to the prison of hell. This pardon should be sought by those outside of Christ but is already possessed by the saints of God, for whom there is no condemnation (Rom. 8:1). Saints fearful of falling under eternal wrath may pray for this pardon, but Christ did not command them to do so, for they are under grace.

2) "Pardon of the guilt of temporary strokes and fatherly anger." God's covenant promises both fatherly discipline for sin and everlasting love which cannot fail (Ps. 89:30–33). Boston writes, "The children of God, who are beyond the reach of eternal wrath, are oft-times liable to temporary fatherly wrath, which they need a pardon for, as the child needs the father's pardon. Upon their fresh application to the Lord Jesus Christ they obtain it."

3) "A declarative pardon, which is the pardon manifested to the soul, a sense of pardon." Believers are forgiven, but they still need to be delivered from doubts and fears by the experiential shining of God's face upon them.[70]

This petition directs believers to confess the debt of their sins (Dan. 9:5), to plead their inability to pay the debt themselves (Ps. 130:3–4), and to seek God's forgiveness through the merits of Christ (Dan. 9:17; Rom. 3:24).[71] It also teaches believers to come to God believing He will forgive them just as they have sincerely (though imperfectly) forgiven those who sinned against them. Bos-

---

69. *Works*, 2:613–14.
70. *Works*, 2:615–17.
71. *Works*, 2:616–17.

ton sees evidence in the addendum to this petition, in which Jesus teaches His disciples to pray for fatherly forgiveness, not release from eternal wrath. He explains,

> And this is a demonstrative proof, that the forgiveness the saints here ask for themselves is only the pardon of the guilt of fatherly anger, and the manifestation of pardon, and not the pardon of the guilt of eternal wrath, which concerns their state. For till this last be obtained, one cannot sincerely forgive others, Matt. 18:32, 33.... No man can sincerely forgive his brother, who does not so love him; and none can love his brother, but he who loves God; and none loves God, but he who is forgiven by God, Luke 7:47.[72]

So Boston interprets the petition for forgiveness according to his covenant theology of atonement by Christ, adoption by God, and assurance by the Holy Spirit.

*Sixth Petition: "And lead us not into temptation, but deliver us from evil"*
The first petition for soul blessings asks for deliverance from the *guilt* of sin, and the second now asks for deliverance from the *power* of sin. Boston notes that, unless he is a hypocrite, the Christian is "equally concerned for justification and sanctification." The petition first asks for preventing grace ("Lead us not..."), then asks for assisting grace ("Deliver us from...").[73]

The request for preventing grace recognizes that pardoned sinners are still in danger from temptations from the Devil (Matt. 4:3), from men and women (Acts 26:11; Gen. 39:7), and from the lusts of their own hearts (James 1:14). Therefore the children of God must ask God not to place them in circumstances where their hearts will be tempted to sin. God tempts no one to sin, but He may lead people into situations to test them.[74] Boston concludes, "It is the duty of all, and the disposition of the people of God, to desire they

---

72. *Works*, 2:618.
73. *Works*, 2:619–20.
74. *Works*, 2:620–35.

may be kept from engaging with temptations, as with an enemy too strong for them."[75] He interprets the Lord's Prayer both as a revelation of the *duty* of God's children and as their *disposition* flowing from the grace they have received as sons of the holy Father.

The request for assisting grace seeks "deliverance from evil," that is, from sin and temptations to sin (Rom. 7:24). This part of the sixth petition therefore teaches believers to pray for these deliverances:

1) "Deliverance in temptation, that God would powerfully support and enable them to stand in the hour of temptation, 2 Cor. 12:8; that when they are engaged in the battle with Satan, the world, and the flesh, the Lord himself would come in for their rescue."

2) "Deliverance under temptation, Ps. 51:8. Sometimes believers are trod under foot by their lusts and passions: they are lying in the mire, and cannot get out. But they look again towards the Lord, as Jonah out of the whale's belly, that he would afford them his helping hand, and so sanctify their lot to them, as all may work for their good."

3) "Deliverance completely from all sin, and temptation to it.... Thus the petitions of this prayer end with a longing cry for perfect freedom from sin in another world."[76]

At the end of his treatment of the sixth petition, Boston returns to the theme of the nature of the children of God. He writes,

Sinning is more terrible than suffering, in the eyes of the children of God. They pray to be delivered from sin absolutely, at any rate, cost what it will.... It is a black mark of one that belongs not to God, when there is no parting betwixt him and his lusts.... It is not a spot of God's children.... It is in the nature of all God's children, to desire to be home. *Our Father which art in heaven — deliver us from evil.* They know that this

---

75. *Works*, 2:635.
76. *Works*, 2:636–37.

will never be completely and fully answered till they be beyond
the clouds: but from their hearts they desire it. Let us evidence
ourselves to be the children of God, by our ardent desires for
this complete deliverance from sins.[77]

Boston views the Lord's Prayer not just as a rule of duty but
as the natural expression of the heart of a child of God. In this he
closely links prayer with adoption. Prayer is the fruition of adoption.

*Conclusion: "For thine is the kingdom, and the power,
and the glory, for ever. Amen."*
We say these words, not to persuade God to hear us but rather "to
exercise and strengthen our own praying graces," Boston says. We
use such words to remind ourselves that the Father is the sovereign, almighty God whose glory shines forever through His works
as king. Boston illustrates the effect of these words:

> It is as if a hungry child should apply to his father for bread
> and the father should say, 'Child, wherefore should I give you
> bread?' and thereupon the child should say, 'Alas! I am pained
> with hunger, and who will give it me if you refuse? will it not
> be a reflection on your name, to say your children faint for lack
> of bread?' While the child pleads thus, the tear strikes in his
> eye, and his earnestness increases: whereupon he is answered.
> Here is it evident, that the effect of the pleading is not on the
> father.... The effect of it is plainly on the child himself.[78]

Prayer brings to fruition the effect of divine adoption, but it
also ripens the fruit of adoption. In prayer, Boston teaches the child
of God to reflect more deeply upon the One he is privileged to call
"our Father" and to seek to know Him more intimately.

## Concluding Comfort: Happy Children with the Best Father
Adoption is the foundation of prayer, for it is the key that opens
heaven's doors to receive our prayers as God's beloved children.

---

77. *Works*, 2:638.
78. *Works*, 2:640.

The Spirit of adoption is the life of our prayers, for He indwells our hearts as the Spirit of the Son and enlivens our hearts with childlike petitions. Prayer is the fruition of adoption, for it brings to full expression the desire of adopted children for the honor of their Father's name, their longing for the expansion of His kingdom among men, and their holy resolve to submit to His will. Prayer draws out and deepens their dependence upon His grace for the needs of their bodies, the forgiveness of their sins, and the sanctification of their souls. Prayer teaches the adopted children of God that "no children are so happy as God's children are," for they have "the most honourable Father...the most loving and compassionate Father...the most helpful Father...the richest Father...[and] the wisest Father" of all.[79]

---

79. *Works*, 1:640–41.

*Chapter 10*

# Jonathan Edwards on Prayer
# and the Triune God

## PETER BECK

*Our communion with God the Father and God the Son*
*consists in our partaking of the Holy Ghost.*
—JONATHAN EDWARDS

The revival of scholarly interest in the works of Jonathan Edwards that began in the twentieth century stands nearly complete. The last one hundred years have seen Edwards resurrected from the historical graveyard of America's selective memory. Once seen as the by-product of an obsolete and discarded Calvinism, regarded by some as the theology of "stern fanatical farmers" who had, "with tight-lipped intolerant mouths and the light of religious madness flickering in their eyes,"[1] established their faith in New England, Edwards has come to be seen again as the extraordinary man that he truly was. Along the way, scholars and ordinary Christians alike have discovered what Edwards's earliest admirers already knew.

In the esteem of all the judicious who were well acquainted with him, either personally or by his writings, President Edwards was one of the greatest, best, and most useful of men who have lived in this world. Sereno Dwight wrote, "Yet here and there an individual can be found, who, by his mere mental energy, has changed the

---

1. Henry B. Parkes, *Jonathan Edwards: The Fiery Puritan* (New York: Minton, Balch & Company, 1930), 175.

course of human thought and feeling, and led mankind onward in that new and better path which he had opened to their view. Such an individual was JONATHAN EDWARDS."[2]

He showed himself to be one of the greatest of divines by his conversation, preaching, and writings—a man of remarkable strength of mind, clearness of thought, and depth of penetration who well understood and was able, above most others, to vindicate the great doctrines of Christianity.[3] Today, over 250 years after his death, Jonathan Edwards is once again rightly recognized for his genius and passion.

Amid Edwards's more than twelve hundred extant sermons and thousands of pages of notes and published material lies a rich theological treasure. In his time, Jonathan Edwards influenced a generation of Christians on both sides of the Atlantic as to the reality of true revival. Within a half century of his death, Edwards was influencing a new generation of Baptists in England. Their reading of his *Freedom of the Will* resulted in the launch of what is today called the Modern Missionary Movement; subsequent centuries have seen Edwards impassion other generations of missionaries with his *Life of David Brainerd*, enlighten thinkers as to the marks of true religion with *Religious Affections*, and challenge scores of pious Christians with his *Resolutions*. Today, the wide and lasting influence of "America's theologian" cannot be denied.[4]

Edwards's value, however, is not to be found in his profundity or his popularity but in his synthesis of theology and piety, of preaching and practice, of thought and action. For Edwards, orthodoxy must always issue in orthopraxy—that is, right thinking always leads to right doing. Without the former, the latter is impossible; and without the latter, the former is immaterial. In Edwards, the

2. Sereno E. Dwight, *The Life of President Edwards* (New York: G. & C. & H. Carvill, 1830), 2.

3. Samuel Hopkins, *The Life and Character of the Late Reverend Mr. Jonathan Edwards* (1765; reprint, Northampton: S. & E. Butler, 1804), iii.

4. Robert W. Jenson, *America's Theologian: A Recommendation of Jonathan Edwards* (New York: Oxford University Press, 1988).

two are never far apart. In fact, they are inextricably intertwined. Thus, when his life and thought are seen and read together, Edwards challenges the mind and moves the heart. Martyn Lloyd-Jones observed, "Edwards takes you out into the depths where you begin to see man face to face with his Maker."[5]

For all the ink that has been spilled and all the kudos pronounced over the years, Edwards has yet another vein of theological gold to offer the church. Long overlooked, ignored by some, missed by others, Edwards's theology of prayer demands to be studied, not because the thoughts are his, but because the duty and privilege of prayer belong to all Christians. As Edwards said, "[Prayer] is one of the greatest and most excellent means of nourishing the new nature, and of causing the soul to flourish and prosper. It is an excellent means of keeping up an acquaintance with God, and of growing in knowledge of God. It is a way to a life of communion with God."[6]

To that end, though he never wrote a single treatise on the subject, prayer was never far from the center of Edwards's thought. Even a brief survey, such as what follows, should rightly establish Edwards as the "theologian of prayer." More importantly, rightly understood and applied, Jonathan Edwards's theology of prayer can and should change the way the present generation prays. After all, that's the way Edwards would have wanted it to be.

## God-Centered Prayer

Edwards wrote, "While they [believers] are praying, he gives them sweet views of his glorious grace, purity, sufficiency, and sovereignty; and enables them with great quietness, to rest in him, to leave themselves and their prayers with him, submitting to his will, and trusting in his grace and faithfulness."[7]

---

5. D. Martyn Lloyd-Jones, *The Puritans: Their Origins and Successors* (Edinburgh: Banner of Truth, 1997), 361.

6. Jonathan Edwards, "Hypocrites Deficient in the Duty of Prayer," in *Seeking God: Jonathan Edwards's Evangelism Contrasted with Modern Methodologies*, ed. William C. Nichols (Ames, Iowa: International Outreach, 2001), 371–72.

7. "The Most High a Prayer-Hearing God," in vol. 2 of *The Works of Jonathan Edwards*, 2 vols. (Peabody, Mass.: Hendrickson, 1998), 2:114. Hereafter, *Works*.

Noted Edwards scholar George Claghorn correctly identified the end for which Edwards strove in all areas of life and thought: "Personal communion with the Almighty."[8] The same holds true for his theology of prayer. Proper prayer, prayer which edifies us in God and satisfies us in God, finds its value in God alone. A proper knowledge of God in His Trinitarian glory is essential to understanding the nature of prayer and enjoying its spiritual blessings.

*God the Father*

Key to Edwards's theology of prayer was the nature of God. It is not enough to pray, he would argue. One must pray to the true God. "Herein," Edwards preached, "the most high God is distinguished from false gods. The true God is the only one of this character; there is no other of whom it may be said, that he heareth prayer."[9] To that end, Edwards devoted no small amount of energy to the study of God. For, as he told the congregation in Northampton, prayer begins and ends with God. "There is no other way that the heart can look to God, but only looking by faith, by faith seeking the blessing of God, and by faith depending on God for the mercy sought."[10]

As Edwards understood the Bible to teach, God desires to be known and worshiped. Thus, God reveals Himself in all His glory. He reveals Himself in nature. He reveals Himself in Scripture. He reveals Himself in His attributes, His divine character traits, those things that describe His very being. These attributes, Edwards maintained, relate not merely to what God does but who God is. Moreover, these attributes, he contended, relate to prayer. For that reason, "it would be greatly to the advantage of our souls," Edwards

---

8. George Claghorn, introduction to "Personal Writings," in *The Works of Jonathan Edwards, Volume 16, Letters and Personal Writings*, ed. George S. Claghorn, (New Haven: Yale University Press, 1998),745. Hereafter *WJE* 16.

9. "The Most High a Prayer-Hearing God," in *Works*, 2:115.

10. "Terms of Prayer," in *The Works of Jonathan Edwards, Volume 19, Sermons and Discourses: 1734–1738*, ed. M. X. Lesser (New Haven: Yale University Press, 2001), 787. Hereafter *WJE* 19.

told his congregation, "if we understood more of the excellency and gloriousness of God."[11]

The God to whom the Christian prays possesses infinite holiness. This holiness, Edwards held, is the "most lovely" of all His perfect attributes.[12] In this moral perfection, God can do no wrong. He cannot sin; He cannot fall; He cannot fail. Everything God does is right for He can do no other. For the Christian who prays, God's holiness ensures that his prayer will be answered not according to his worldly wants but according to God's heavenly perfection.

Just as God's holiness displays His character and impacts man's prayer, so too does God's loving nature. This attribute finds infinite expression in God. It "is a living spring, a spring that never fails," Edwards exulted.[13] God's love knows no bounds. No dam of sin can hold it back; no gulf of despair can quench its fire. The one whom God loves, He loves beyond measure. Moreover, all that God does relates intimately to that loving nature. This is so, Edwards noted, not because God is loving, but because God is love. From the doctrine of election to the answer of prayer, God's love drives His every act. He wrote, "And therefore nothing that [Christians] need, nothing that they ask of God, nothing that their desires can extend themselves to, nothing that their capacity can contain, no good that can be enjoyed by them, is so great, so excellent that God begrutches it to them."[14] The answers God gives are sure to bless as they are blessed by God's love for His people.

---

11. "God's Excellencies," in *The Works of Jonathan Edwards, Volume 10, Sermons and Discourses, 1720–1723*, ed. Wilson H. Kimnach (New Haven: Yale University Press, 1992), 417. Hereafter *WJE* 10.

12. "Yield to God's Word, or Be Broken by His Hand," in *The Works of Jonathan Edwards, Volume 25, Sermons and Discourses, 1743–1758*, ed. Wilson H. Kimnach (New Haven: Yale University Press, 2006), 215. Hereafter *WJE* 25.

13. "God's Care for His Servants in Time of Public Commotion," in *The Works of Jonathan Edwards, Volume 22, Sermons and Discourses 1739–1742*, ed. Harry S. Stout and Nathan O. Hatch with Kyle P. Farley (New Haven: Yale University Press, 2003), 351. Hereafter *WJE* 22.

14. "The Terms of Prayer," *WJE* 19:781.

God's knowledge, like His holiness and love, wrote Edwards, is "unsearchable and boundless."[15] Simply put, God knows everything.

[God] sees all over this world: every man, woman, and child; every beast on earth, every bird in the air, [every] fish in the sea. There is not so much [as] a fly or worm or gnat [that is unknown to God]. [He] knows every tree, every leaf, every spire of grass; every drop of rain or dew; every single dust [mote] in the whole world. [God] sees in darkness [and] under ground. [A] thousand miles under ground [is] not hid [from his view]. [God] sees all that men [do] or say, sees their hearts [and] thoughts.

[God] knows everything past, [even] things a thousand years ago. [He also knows] everything to come, [even] a thousand years to come. [He knows] all the men that will be, [and] all that they will do, say, or think.[16]

As with God's other attributes, His omniscience plays a vital role in a proper understanding of prayer. "The true God," Edwards preached, "perfectly knows the circumstances of everyone that prays to him throughout the world."[17] Because His knowledge is perfect, the Father knows what the children need before they ever ask. Better yet, God knows the perfect answer to those prayers. God's answers are always right and therefore to be sought with all urgency.

Knowledge alone, however, is insufficient. God must possess the ability to do as He sees fit as well. Thus, the two, omniscience and omnipotence, meet in prayer with divine wisdom. "'Tis the glory and greatness of the divine sovereignty," Edwards wrote, "that God's will is determined by his own infinite all-sufficient wisdom in everything."[18] "He is able to do everything that we need."[19] He

---

15. *The Works of Jonathan Edwards, Volume 3, Original Sin*, ed. Clyde A. Holbrook (New Haven: Yale University Press, 1970), 188. Hereafter *WJE* 3.

16. "God Is Infinitely Strong," in *WJE* 25:643.

17. "The Most High a Prayer-Hearing God," *Works*, 2:115.

18. *The Works of Jonathan Edwards, Volume 1, Freedom of the Will*, ed. Paul Ramsey (New Haven: Yale University Press, 1957), 380. Hereafter *WJE*, 1.

19. "God's All-Sufficiency for the Supply of Our Wants," in *The Works of*

can accomplish His perfect will because He exercises perfect power, a power shaped by love and informed by knowledge. To this end, God's absolute sovereignty upholds Edwards's theology of prayer for the Christian prays to a God who can answer.

While God's absolute perfection heightens the degree of man's separation from his Creator, those same attributes bridge that divide. The sovereign and holy God who exercises dominion over the creation has answered man's greatest need in the cross, and He answers man's ongoing needs through prayer. To that God, the true God, the Christian prays, for he knows with all confidence that God hears and answers prayer out of the well of His own riches. Because God is God, Edwards reasoned, His people should pray. He wrote,

> It is not in order that God may be informed of our wants or desires. He is omniscient, and with respect to his knowledge unchangeable. God never gains any knowledge by information. He knows what we want, a thousand times more perfectly than we do ourselves, before we ask him…yet it is not to be thought that God is properly moved or made willing by our prayers; for it is no more possible that there should be any new inclination or will in God, than new knowledge. The mercy of God is not moved or drawn by any thing in the creature; but the spring of God's beneficence is within himself only; he is self-moved; and whatsoever mercy he bestows, the reason and the ground of it is not to be sought for in the creature, but in God's own pleasure.[20]

Praying Christians need to rediscover Edwards's passion for God's greatness. They must seek God according to His nature and on His terms if they are to experience the glory of God for themselves.

### God the Son
In Edwards's theology of prayer, Christ stands central. In thoughts of salvation and of prayer, Edwards often marveled at the "excellency of

*Jonathan Edwards, Volume 14, Sermons and Discourses, 1723–1729*, ed. Kenneth P. Minkema (New Haven: Yale University Press, 1997), 474–75. Hereafter *WJE* 14.

20. "The Most High a Prayer-Hearing God," in *Works*, 2:115–16.

Christ" and His inestimable worth.[21] As Edwards saw it, the Christian faith begins in Christ and continues in Christ. Without Him, there is no restored relationship with God. Without Him, therefore, there is no prayer. Because of Christ, salvation is possible and prayer is acceptable. "The smoke of [Christ's] sacrifice has perfumed the souls of believers and has made them and their prayers and praises sweet in the nostrils of God, so that now he smells a sweet savor in their prayers which were most offensive to him before."[22] Edwards's theology of prayer stands or falls with his Christology.

According to Edwards, God desires to communicate His glory to His creation. That is, God wants man to know and enjoy His greatness. Man, however, reeks of his own sinfulness and cannot truly know God or appreciate His attributes. Therefore, God chose to reveal Himself in a new way, a way that displays His divine nature and spans the gap between Him and humanity. It is at this point that God's attributes and Christ's incarnation meet. As Edwards expressed this grand truth, "Jesus Christ, and that as God-man, is the grand medium by which God attains his end, both in communicating himself to the creatures and [in] glorifying himself by the creation."[23] In the incarnation, God through Christ made human relationship with the divine possible once again.

Jesus possesses all the attributes of God in their perfection, Edwards argued. In Him "there is an admirable conjunction of diverse excellencies."[24] That is, Christ is all that God is. God is holy. Jesus is holy. God is love. Jesus is love. God knows all. Jesus knows all. God is all-powerful. Jesus is all-powerful. As Edwards reasoned, "All the attributes of God, do illustriously shine forth in the face of Jesus Christ."[25] Such is true because Christ is truly divine. He is God.

---

21. "Diary," in *WJE* 16:760–61.

22. "Christ's Sacrifice," in *WJE* 10:600.

23. "Approaching the End of God's Grand Design," in *WJE* 25:116–17.

24. "The Excellency of Christ," in *WJE* 19:565.

25. "Glorious Grace," in *WJE* 10:395. See also "The Excellency of Christ," in *WJE* 19:565.

Desirous of a renewed relationship with man, the second Person of the Trinity became man. "[Jesus'] condescension is great enough to become their friend: 'tis great enough to become their companion, to unite their souls to him in spiritual marriage: 'tis great enough to take their nature upon him, to become one of them, that he may be one with them."[26] In keeping with the decisions of the early ecumenical councils, Edwards held to a strong view of Jesus' humanity. The divine took on flesh, and in flesh rose to heaven. "Everything that is lovely in God is in him, and everything that is or can be lovely in man is in him," Edwards proclaimed, "for he is man as well as God, and he is the holiest, meekest, most humble, and every way the most excellent man that ever was."[27] All that God is, all that humanity should have been, Jesus was and is.

As the perfect God-man, Christ was both the expression and communication of God's glory. He revealed God's glorious character and enabled mankind to bask in it. Edwards remarked in one of his personal theological journals,

> For Christ being united to the human nature, we have advantage for a far more intimate union and conversation with him, than we could possibly have had if he had remained only in the divine nature. So we, being united to a divine person, can in him have more intimate union and conversation with God the Father, who is only in the divine nature, than otherwise possibly could be. Christ, who is a divine person, by taking on him our nature, descends from the infinite distance between God and us, and is brought nigh to us, to give us advantage to converse with him.[28]

Christ embodied and revealed God's greatness so that man might revel in it. Still, Edwards argued, man's reunion with God remained incomplete. Christ must do more than simply live as a

---

26. "The Excellency of Christ," in *WJE* 19:566.

27. "Children Ought to Love the Lord Jesus Christ," in *WJE* 22:172.

28. "Miscellanies" no. 571, in *The Works of Jonathan Edwards, Volume 18, The "Miscellanies" 501–832*, ed. Ava Chamberlain (New Haven: Yale University Press, 2000), 110. Hereafter *WJE* 18.

man — He must die for man. He must fulfill His foreordained role of mediator. Since we could not and would not reach out to God, God reached out to us. In Christ, He reconciled man to Himself. As Edwards stated, Christ "takes upon him the work of a mediator between God and man, he puts himself in man's stead, he becomes man's representative."[29] By dying man's just death on the cross, the sinless Christ appeased God's wrath, atoned for man's sin, and restored fellowship between the Creator and the creature.

Being united to Christ by faith, accepting what He has done and who He is, the believer has eternal access to God. Faith, as Edwards defined it, implies a resting in and a leaning upon Christ as Savior. It is an ongoing experience of relationship that lasts longer than one moment in time. Faith is a present reality, not a past event; it endures a lifetime. He who has such faith and enjoys union with the Savior has discovered the majesty of his Maker and experiences profound joy. Edwards wrote, "He takes full contentment in Christ as a Savior. Having found Christ, he desires no other: having found the fountain, he sits down by it: having found Christ, his hungry and thirsty soul is satisfied in him. His burdened soul is eased in him: his fearful soul is confident: his weary soul is at rest."[30]

Christ becomes the believer's all. "It is He who clothes them with robes of glory and satisfies the soul with rivers of pleasure."[31] Having tasted of the divine, the Christian seeks satisfaction nowhere else and finds happiness in Christ alone.

The believer's joyous relationship with God begins with faith and continues with prayer. The Mediator's role extends to this as well. Christ prays for His people as their intercessor, and His people pray through Him as their Mediator. It was His meritorious works and the ineffable value of His life that puts power in their prayers.

---

29. "Even As I Have Kept My Father's Commandments," in *The Glory and Honor of God: Volume 2 of the Previously Unpublished Sermons of Jonathan Edwards*, ed. Michael D. McMullen (Nashville: Broadman & Holman, 2004), 212.

30. "The Sweet Harmony of Christ," in *WJE* 19:441–42.

31. "Christ Is the Christian's All," in *The Puritan Pulpit: The American Puritans, Jonathan Edwards*, ed. Don Kistler (Morgan, Pa.: Soli Deo Gloria, 2004), 201.

Edwards said, "There is probably a special respect to the speech of the saints in prayer, which is dyed in the blood of Christ, and by this means becomes pleasant, and acceptable, and of an attractive influence, like a scarlet cord, to draw down blessings. The prayers of the saints are lovely and prevalent only through the incense of Christ's merits."[32]

According to Edwards's theology of prayer, praying in Jesus' name is more than simply a spiritual sign-off for one's prayers. Edwards wrote,

> Seeing Christ is our only priest and sacrifice, let us offer up all our prayers, petitions, confessions, and praises in his name. He is our Mediator; wherefore, let us always come unto God by him. We are sure that we shall be accepted when we come in his name. Our prayers are loathsome till they are presented by him in his intercession for us, till they ascend up before God with this incense. When we ask mercy, let us hope for receiving only upon the account of an intercessor. Let us plead with his blood, for our prayers must be purified thereby before God will receive them. Christ has promised that we shall receive whatever we ask in his name.[33]

Praying in Christ's name is the means by which the believers' prayers are heard and answered.

Without Christ, fully God and fully man, there could be no reconciliation. In Christ, because of His work on the wondrous cross, salvation is accomplished; the impossible becomes possible, the unavailing becomes effectual. "He hath entered for us into the holy of holies, with the incense which he hath provided," Edwards rejoiced, "and there he makes continual intercession for all that come to God in his name; so that their prayers come to God the Father through his hands."[34]

---

32. *The Works of Jonathan Edwards, Volume 15, Notes on Scripture*, ed. Stephen J. Stein (New Haven: Yale University Press, 1998), 582–83. Hereafter *WJE* 15.

33. "Christ's Sacrifice," in *WJE* 10:602.

34. "The Most High a Prayer-Hearing God," in *Works*, 2:116.

*God the Holy Spirit*

The Holy Spirit stands between God and man, communicating love and changing hearts. As with Christ, so with the Spirit: apart from the work of the Spirit there would be no salvation and could be no prayer.

All that God is, Edwards explained, the Spirit is. The third Person of the Trinity, the Holy Spirit, is coexistent, coeternal, and coequal with the Father and the Son. "They are all the same God, and it is impossible there should be any inferiority," Edwards argued. "They all are the same substance, the same divine essence; and therefore whatsoever perfection, dignity or excellency belongs to the divine essence, belongs to every one of them."[35] Therefore, equal honor is due to the Spirit as well.

Given that the Father and the Spirit share the same essence, they share the same attributes. For example, just as God is holy, His Spirit must be. As Edwards said, "God's holiness consists in him." He is, after all, "the Spirit of God's holiness."[36] As with Christ and His possession of God's attributes, so, too, the Holy Spirit possesses them all.

Of direct import to Edwards's theology of prayer is the matter of God's love and the Spirit's relationship to it. God's omnibenevolence, His infinitely loving nature, Edwards held, belongs to the Spirit. Not only is the Spirit all-loving, he reasoned, the Spirit is the love of God.[37] As God loves, He must express His love. The expression or communication of that love is the Spirit. Such an interchange takes place within the Trinity as God's love overflows from the Father toward the Son, the Holy Spirit being the expression of that love within the Godhead.

---

35. "The Threefold Work of the Holy Ghost," in *WJE* 14:379.

36. "Miscellanies" no. 1047, in *The Works of Jonathan Edwards, Volume 20, The "Miscellanies" 833–1152*, ed. Amy P. Pauw (New Haven: Yale University Press, 2002), 389. Hereafter *WJE* 20.

37. "Miscellanies" no. 146, in *The Works of Jonathan Edwards, Volume 13, The "Miscellanies" a–500*, ed. Thomas A. Schaefer (New Haven: Yale University Press, 1994), 300. Hereafter *WJE* 13.

The same is true, Edwards contended, within divine-human relationships. As God must love because He is love, He loves His creation. The expression of that love is, again, the Holy Spirit. As God loves Himself and desires to be magnified and enjoyed, He draws humans to Himself through overtures of love by the work of the Holy Spirit. In love, the Spirit convicts man of his fallen condition. In love, He convinces man of the truth of the gospel. In love, He regenerates the soul that man might accept of God's loving grace. And, as an outcome of God's love for Himself and His people, the Spirit binds believers to the Father in love never to lose that relationship again.

For that reason, Edwards encouraged people to seek the operations of the Holy Spirit in their own lives. While the work of the Spirit includes acts of common grace, conviction of sin for example, it was special grace, the saving operations of the Spirit that they were to seek most urgently. For this even the unregenerate were called to pray.

> Let them pray that God would give them his Spirit to awaken them; this is proper for them, whether they have any true grace or not. And so let them pray that God would enable to strive for salvation, and that he would help them to enter in at the straight gate. Let them pray earnestly that God would show them their own hearts; [that God would] bring them off their own righteousness, that God would convert them; that God would give a true sight of Christ, and enable them sincerely to close with him and trust in him alone for salvation. Let them pray that God would open their blind eye; that God would cause light to shine out of darkness; and that he [would] raise their dead souls to life.[38]

When God does apply the work of His Spirit to the elect, their souls are revived and their spirits enlivened. This takes place as the Spirit takes up residence within them.

---

38. "Subjects of a First Work of Grace," in WJE 22:201. I have changed Edwards's shorthand "em" to "them" throughout this quotation.

God meets them in his mercy and gives them grace in their hearts. He gives them his holiness. He cleanses them from their filth and puts his own beauty upon them. He infuses a principle of spiritual life into them. He opens their blind eyes and calls them out of their darkness and causes them to see the refreshing light of his glory, so that they no longer are in a land of darkness and the shadow of death. By his grace he reunites them to himself, fills them with his Holy Spirit.[39]

In salvation, God gives man what was lost in the Fall and more. He gives them Himself in the Person of the Holy Spirit.

Thus renewed and restored, man enjoys the resident blessing of the Spirit. When the Spirit gives life, He maintains it for He is life itself, "the sum of salvation and of those saving benefits that are purchased by Christ."[40] The Spirit, then, is the source of the believer's ongoing relationship with God. "Hence our communion with God the Father and God the Son consists in our partaking of the Holy Ghost, which is their Spirit: for to have communion or fellowship with another, is to partake with them of their good in their fullness, in union and society with them," Edwards stated.[41] The recipient of the saving grace of God, indwelt by God Himself, enters into the inter-trinitarian relationship, sharing the love of God for Himself by expressing love toward God as it lives within and flows from Himself.

Now in a lasting, intimate relationship with God, the believer can pray—and pray he must. Here, too, Edwards said the Spirit plays a vital role. "The Spirit of God, the chief subject matter of prayer, [is] the great purchase and promise of Christ. [We have]

---

39. "Honey from the Rock," in *The Works of Jonathan Edwards, Volume 17, Sermons and Discourses 1730–1733*, ed. Mark Valeri (New Haven: Yale University Press, 1999), 127. Hereafter *WJE* 17.

40. "Miscellanies" no. 1164, in *The Works of Jonathan Edwards, Volume 23, "Miscellanies" 1153–1360*, ed. Douglas A. Sweeney (New Haven: Yale University Press, 2004), 86. Hereafter *WJE* 23.

41. "Treatise on Grace," in *The Works of Jonathan Edwards, Volume 21, Writings on the Trinity, Grace and Faith*, ed. Sang Hyun Lee (New Haven: Yale University Press, 2003), 188. Hereafter *WJE* 21.

more encouragement to pray for this than any other [thing]."[42] The Spirit, the greatest blessing acquired in salvation, the ongoing indwelling presence of God Himself, is to be both the source and the object of prayer in the believer's life. The Spirit is "the sum of all that Christ purchased."[43] He is the blessing to be sought, "the sum of the blessings that Christians have to pray for."[44] As Edwards said on another occasion, "The good that shall be sought by prayer is God himself." He continued,

> But certainly that expression of "seeking the Lord," is very commonly used to signify something more than merely, in general, to seek some mercy of God: it implies, that God himself is the great good desired and sought after; that the blessings pursued are God's gracious presence, the blessed manifestations of him, union and intercourse with him; or, in short, God's manifestations and communications of himself by his Holy Spirit.[45]

This prayer, Edwards declared, is one which God always answers. The Spirit, he said, is the "choicest gift," the one "that God delights to bestow in answer to prayer."[46] In fact, "God is more ready to bestow this than any other blessing."[47] Echoing Psalm 37:4, Edwards believed that if the believer would find his sole prayerful delight in the Lord, God would give him the desires of his heart.

Theocentric to the end, Edwards maintained that the Spirit of God lies at the heart of all true prayer. The Spirit gives the believer a new heart. With that new heart come new desires, desires fueled by God, and ultimately to be satisfied only in God. He wrote, "The true spirit of prayer is no other than God's own Spirit dwelling in

---

42. "Suitableness of Union in Extraordinary Prayer," in *WJE* 25:203.

43. "Miscellanies" no. 402, in *WJE* 13:402.

44. "An Humble Attempt," in *The Works of Jonathan Edwards, Volume 5, Apocalyptic Writings*, ed. Stephen J. Stein (New Haven: Yale University Press, 1977), 347. Hereafter *WJE* 5.

45. Ibid., 315.

46. "The Dangers of Decline," in *WJE* 17:97.

47. "The Terms of Prayer," in *WJE* 19:785.

the hearts of the saints. And as this spirit comes from God, so doth it naturally tend to God in holy breathings and pantings. It naturally leads to God, to converse with him by prayer."[48]

## The Human Experience of Prayer

Edwards said, "Therefore let the godly take encouragement from hence in their prayers to come boldly to the throne of grace, and to come frequently."[49]

According to Edwards's estimation, mankind was created for communion with God. In the beginning God created man in His image, the *imago Dei*, in order to facilitate and foster that relationship. Created in the image of God the first man had the capacity and the desire to love the Creator. He wrote,

'Tis evident, that man was made to behold and be delighted with the excellency of God in his works, or in short, to be made happy by beholding God's excellency; as it has been shown that intelligent beings, the consciousness of the creation, must be. But if man was made to delight in God's excellency, he was made to love God; and God being infinitely excellent, he ought to love [him] incomparably more than any man is capable of loving a fellow creature; and every power, and all that is in man, ought to be exercised as attendants on this love.[50]

Thus endowed, Adam had sweet fellowship with God in the Garden. "Man enjoyed the favor of God and smiles of heaven; there were smiles without any frowns," Edwards explained. "He had communion with God; God was wont to come to him and converse as a friend and father. How sweet was it thus to have the smiles and fellowship of the glorious Creator!"[51]

All that changed, however, when Adam rebelled, loved himself more than God, and ate of the forbidden fruit in an effort to

48. "Hypocrites Deficient in the Duty of Prayer," in *Seeking God*, 359.
49. Ibid.
50. "Miscellanies" no. 99, in *WJE* 13:265–66.
51. "East of Eden," in *WJE* 17:334.

become more like God. With a gain in knowledge came a loss in relationship. As Edwards said, "And his communion with God was lost; he lost God's favor and smiles. God ascended and forsook the earth, and instead of smiling and blessing, as he was wont to, now pronounces a curse on man. Instead of delighting in God's love and friendship, he had now the anger of the great God to think of, and his own folly in procuring it."[52]

Separated from God by a bottomless pit of sin and misery, man can no longer breach the divine-human divide. He is unfit to approach the Creator, even in prayer.[53] Fallen man does pray, however. The problem is that God does not hear the prayers of the lost. Or, as Edwards clarified, God hears the prayers of the lost, but He does not respond. Therefore, at its root, the inability to communicate via prayer lies not in God but man. Edwards wrote, "'Tis no real prayer in the sight of God, because it is not made with a humble sense of their unworthiness of what is prayed for, and a submissive sense of its being something that is in God's free disposal. If a prayer be not made with such a frame as this, 'tis no real prayer."[54]

Man now prays not to glorify God but to satisfy himself. He comes to God with a haughty heart and selfish desires. "That prayer which is not of faith, is insincere; for prayer is a show or manifestation of dependence on God, and trust in his sufficiency and mercy. Therefore, where this trust or faith is wanting, there is no prayer in the sight of God."[55] The prayer that is not God-centered is no prayer at all.

Yet, prayer remains a duty for all mankind, not just Christians. To ignore this duty, said Edwards, would only compound fallen man's sinfulness and impending doom. Thus, Edwards encouraged all who heard him to pray, for praying even for the wrong reason is

---

52. "East of Eden," in *WJE* 17:335.
53. Jonathan Edwards, "Cases of Difficulty for God's Church Occasions for Extraordinary Prayer to God" (1750), Beinecke Rare Book and Manuscript Library, Yale University, New Haven.
54. "Terms of Prayer," in *WJE* 19:787.
55. "The Most High a Prayer-Hearing God," in *Works*, 2:117.

better than not praying at all. At the least, prayer forces the unbeliever to come to God as God and submit himself to God's sphere of influence. As Edwards acknowledged, God occasionally seems to honor the prayer requests of the lost. When He does so, however, it is for His own reasons, not because of any alleged value in the one who prays or in his prayer.

Given man's depraved and deprived situation, God's plan of redemption becomes vital as God repairs what man destroyed. Through the saving work of Christ and its application by the Spirit, the believer once again enjoys "a more intimate union and communion with God."[56] In salvation, all things are made new. God is once again on His rightful throne in the life of the individual. "One design of God in the gospel, is to bring us to make God the object of our undivided respect, that he may engross our regard every way, that whatever natural inclination there is in us, he may be the center of it, and that God may be all in all."[57] That being the case, man's relationship with God is finally as it ought to be.

As faith in the person and work of Christ is the source of man's renewed fellowship with God, "prayer is only the voice of faith."[58] That is, those who have faith pray. Prayer, according to Edwards, proves the reality of one's faith.[59] It proves the depth of one's faith. More than that, prayer improves or strengthens one's faith. "They want to know more of God, and to know as much of God, and have as much of him in their hearts, and enjoy as much of God as their natures are capable," Edwards claimed.[60] For those reasons, faith exercises itself in prayer. Prayer is not an option for the believer but a divinely ordained duty, a duty done in obedience, rooted in love for God:

> All the pleasure of love consists in pleasing the beloved. 'Tis the nature of love to rouse and stir to an earnest desire to

---

56. "Miscellanies" no. 702, in *WJE* 18:298.
57. "Miscellanies" no. 510, in *WJE* 18:54.
58. "Justification by Faith Alone," in *WJE* 19:204.
59. "The Things That Belong to True Religion," in *WJE* 25:573.
60. "The Terms of Prayer," in *WJE* 19:784.

please, and certainly it must be a great pleasure to have earnest desires satisfied. Now the love of God causes those in whose heart it is implanted more earnestly to desire to please God than anything in the world, causes them heartily to embrace opportunities of pleasing him and sweetly to reflect on it when he knows they have pleased him.[61]

Such love drives the believer to the Father, leaning upon the Son, and depending upon the Spirit in prayer. The true believer prays because he has been loved and because he loves in return.

Edwards's conviction was that true believers enjoy regular converse with the greatest love of their life. The necessary implication of this is that those who don't pray are not Christians at all.

But how is a life, in a great measure prayerless, consistent with an holy life? To lead an holy life is to lead a life devoted to God; a life of worshipping and serving God; a life consecrated to the service of God. But how doth he lead such a life who doth not so much as maintain the duty of prayer? How can such a man be said to walk by the Spirit and to be a servant of the Most High God?[62]

Such people are the worst kind of hypocrites. They have taken unto themselves the name of Christ in vain. They claim to know the love of God and to love Him in return. Yet, their prayer life, or lack thereof, proves otherwise. As Edwards argued, those who don't pray live as if there were no God at all.[63] They are not believers. They are atheists.

## Conclusion

For Jonathan Edwards prayer was more than a mere duty, a Christian labor. Instead, he firmly believed it to be a great privilege and the evidence of true faith. That faith and the joy it should produce, Edwards believed, must be grounded in a right understanding of

---

61. "True Love to God," in *WJE* 10:637.
62. "Hypocrites Deficient in the Duty of Prayer," in *Seeking God*, 365.
63. Ibid.

God and man, of the Trinity, of man's needs, of divine grace, and of human faith. Ultimately, Edwards's theology of prayer begins and ends with God. As he argued over and over again, God is, in all of His trinitarian glory, the source and the sum of all grace. In saving fallen men through faith, God resumes communion with them that they might glorify and enjoy Him forever—that they might seek Him, find Him, and savor Him. In the present life, prayer is the vehicle that conveys the believer to spiritual heights untold.

If Edwards is right and if his theology is soundly grounded in biblical truth, one thing remains for the reader to do, namely, to pray: "Therefore let the godly take encouragement from hence in their prayers to come boldly to the throne of grace, and to come frequently. It may well be your delight to you to come to a God that is so ready at all times to hear and to grant whatever you desire that tends to your happiness."[64]

---

64. "The Terms of Prayer," in *WJE* 19:785.

*Chapter 11*

# Puritan Prayers for
# World Missions
———————— ᴄᴏᴐᴄᴏᴐ ————————

## JOEL R. BEEKE

*We glorify God by laboring to draw others to God; by
seeking to convert others, and so make them instruments of glorifying God.*

—Thomas Watson

Reformed, experiential Christianity birthed the pioneer missionary efforts of men such as John Eliot (1604–1690), David
Brainerd (1718–1747), William Carey (1761–1834), Adoniram
Judson (1788–1850), and John G. Paton (1824–1907). This mission
effort was small and struggling until it exploded into the modern
missionary movement begun by Carey at the end of the eighteenth
century. Persecution from Roman Catholic authorities in Europe,
numerous wars, the need to first evangelize homelands in Europe
and North America, the deaths of missionaries by disease and mar-
tyrdom, and the slowness of the church to respond to the Great
Commission all hindered the development of Reformed missions.
However, from the start, Reformed and Puritan Christians fervently
prayed for worldwide evangelization and revival. In some respects,
the Great Awakening and today's missionary movement may be
regarded as an answer to centuries of persevering prayer.

John Calvin (1509–1564) wrote with regard to prayer, "We
must daily desire that God gather churches unto himself from all
parts of the earth; that he spread and increase them in number; that
he adorn them with gifts; that he establish a lawful order among

them; on the other hand, that he cast down all enemies of pure teaching and religion; that he scatter their counsels and crush their efforts."[1] Calvin saw prayer as a weapon of missionary effort for the sake of lost souls and the glory of God on earth.

This mission perspective in prayer continued in the Puritans, the heirs of Calvin's theology. Walter Smith, a Scottish martyr (d. 1681), wrote some guidelines for prayer meetings in southwest Scotland two years before his death. Among them, he wrote:

> As it is the undoubted duty of all to pray for the coming of Christ's kingdom, so all that love our Lord Jesus Christ in sincerity, and know what it is to bow a knee in good earnest, will long and pray for the out-making of the gospel promises to his Church in the latter days, that King Christ would go out upon the white horse of the gospel, conquering and to conquer.... That the Lord's written and preached word [may be sent] with power, to enlighten the poor pagan world, living in black perishing darkness without Christ and the knowledge of his name.[2]

What motivated the Reformed and the Puritans to pray for the world? What guided their prayers for missions? To answer these questions, we turn to the writings of Calvin and the Puritan leaders of the sixteenth, seventeenth, and eighteenth centuries.

### The Puritan Motivation for Missionary Prayer

Both the Reformation and Puritanism sought to strip away human ideas accumulated in the church over centuries and restore the divine Word to its authoritative place, directing and energizing God's people. Since the Bible is a missionary book written by the God who sent His Son into the world to save sinners, it provided

---

1. John Calvin, *Institutes of the Christian Religion*, ed. John T. McNeill, trans. Ford Lewis Battles (Philadelphia: Westminster Press, 1960), 3.20.42.

2. Quoted in Iain H. Murray, *The Puritan Hope: A Study in Revival and the Interpretation of Prophecy* (Edinburgh: Banner of Truth Trust, 1971), 101–102.

the Reformers and the Puritans with compelling reasons to pray for
the lost world.

### The Destiny of the Human Soul

Christians of all times have been deeply affected by Christ's words
in Matthew 16:26, "For what is a man profited, if he shall gain the
whole world, and lose his own soul? or what shall a man give in
exchange for his soul?" Calvin commented,

> Christ reminds us that the soul of man was not created merely
> to enjoy the world for a few days, but to obtain at length its
> immortality in heaven. What carelessness and what brutal stu-
> pidity is this, that men are so strongly attached to the world,
> and so much occupied with its affairs, as not to consider why
> they were born, and that God gave them an immortal soul, in
> order that, when the course of the earthly life was finished,
> they might live eternally in heaven! And, indeed, it is univer-
> sally acknowledged, that the soul is of higher value than all the
> riches and enjoyments of the world.[3]

John Flavel (1628–1691) observed that the human soul was
specially created by God and thus has intrinsic worth and excellence,
including the capacity for divine grace and glory. God prepared a
place in heaven for souls that He purchased with the blood of His
own Son. The actions of the soul have eternity stamped upon them,
for every obedient action is a seed of joy and every sinful action a
seed of sorrow.[4] Flavel said, "The soul of man is the prize about
which heaven and hell contend: the great design of heaven is to
save it, and all the plots of hell to ruin it."[5] But though the soul is so
precious, it may be lost forever in hell.[6]

---

3. John Calvin, *Commentary* on Matt. 16:26 in *Calvin's Commentaries* (Grand
Rapids: Baker, 1996).

4. John Flavel, *The Works of John Flavel* (1820; reprint, Edinburgh: Banner of
Truth Trust, 1997), 3:153–61.

5. Flavel, *Works*, 3:161.

6. Flavel, *Works*, 3:180–81.

The value of a human soul remains the same, regardless of one's nationality or social status. Matthew Henry (1662–1714) noted of Christ's preaching in Matthew 9:35–38, "He visited not only the great and wealthy cities, but the poor, obscure villages; there he preached, there he healed. The souls of those that are meanest [least] in this world are as precious to Christ, and should be to us, as the souls of those that make the greatest figure.... Jesus Christ is a very compassionate friend to precious souls."[7] Such considerations led Reformed Christians to value the souls of all their fellow human beings and to pray for the extension of gospel preaching to the entire world.

### *The Efficiency of the Holy Spirit*

The Reformation rediscovered the work of the Holy Spirit as opposed to that of human religious activity, such as the priestly administration of the rites of the church. Zechariah 4:6 says God's temple will be built "not by might, nor by power, but by my spirit, saith the LORD of hosts." Calvin said, "We ought to be so dependent on God alone, as to be fully persuaded that his grace is sufficient for us."[8] This belief led men and women to rely upon God in prayer and to resist their innate tendency to rely upon human ability. John Howe (1630–1705) wrote, "There is as great an aptness to trust in other means and let out our hearts to them. An arm of flesh signifies a great deal, when the power of an almighty Spirit is reckoned as nothing. And persons are apt to be very contriving, and prone to forecast, how such and such external forms would do our business and make the church and the Christian interest hugely prosperous."[9]

Scripture and experience also awakened Reformers to the reality of large-scale outpourings of the Holy Spirit for the conversion of many sinners, lifting up the church to new degrees of holiness.

---

7. Matthew Henry, *Matthew Henry's Commentary* (Peabody, Mass.: Hendrickson, 1991), 5:104.

8. Calvin, *Commentary* on Zech. 4:1–6.

9. Murray, *The Puritan Hope*, 243.

John Knox (ca. 1510–1572) wrote of a remarkable work of God in Scotland in 1559, saying, "God did so multiply our number that it appeared as if men had rained from the clouds."[10] The Holy Spirit can do great things, far beyond our limited aspirations.

Confidence in the promises of God and the power of the Holy Spirit should thus lead us, in the words of Howe, "to wait patiently and pray earnestly" for a worldwide spiritual harvest. We can be sure as well that "he will give his Spirit to them that ask him."[11]

*The Instrumentality of the Gospel*
John Calvin and the Puritans taught the doctrine of sovereign or unconditional election: that God has chosen certain individuals and ordained them to eternal life, to glorify His grace in their salvation (Eph. 1:4–6). At the same time, they said that God brings His elect to faith and salvation through the preaching of the gospel (Eph. 1:13). Therefore, the Reformers and Puritans labored to spread the gospel.[12] They trained and sent out gospel preachers and prayed for the propagation of the gospel in the lost world.

William Perkins (1558–1602), a patriarch of English Puritanism, said a fundamental principle of Christianity is that Christ and His benefits must be applied to the soul by faith, and faith comes only by the hearing of the Word.[13] The gospel is "the instrument, and, as it were, the conduit pipe of the Holy Ghost, to fashion and derive faith into the soul: by which faith, they which believe, do, as with a hand, apprehend Christ's righteousness."[14] Perkins taught people to pray for God to send gospel preachers into the world. He wrote in his exposition of the Lord's Prayer, "When we shall see a people without knowledge, and without good guides & teachers,

---

10. Murray, *The Puritan Hope*, 5.

11. Murray, *The Puritan Hope*, 254–55.

12. Joel R. Beeke, *Puritan Reformed Spirituality* (Darlington, England: Evangelical Press, 2004), 54–72, 143–69.

13. *The Workes of that Famovs and VVorthy Minister of Christ in the Vniuersitie of Cambridge, Mr. William Perkins* (London: John Legatt, 1612), 1:2.

14. Perkins, *Works*, 1:70.

or when we see one stand up in the congregation not able to teach, here is matter for mourning.... It is time to say, *Lord, let thy kingdom come.*" Perkins said Christians must pray for gospel ministers and "pray that their hearts may be set for the building of God's kingdom, for the beating down of the kingdom of sin and Satan, and for the saving of the souls of his people."[15]

Christ has given His church the commission to make disciples of all nations (Matt. 28:18–20). So Henry wrote, "Salvation by Christ should be offered to all, and none excluded that did not by their unbelief and impenitence exclude themselves."[16] In light of Christ's compassion and command to pray for laborers (Matt. 9:35–38), Henry said, "All that love Christ and souls, should show it in their earnest prayers to God...that he would send forth more skillful, faithful, wise, and industrious labourers into his harvest; that he would raise up such as he would own in the conversion of sinners and the edification of saints; would give them a spirit for the work, call them to it, and succeed them in it."[17] God's appointment and use of this great means of grace for the salvation of men encourages us to pray for the calling, training, and sending forth of men who will preach the gospel to the very ends of the earth.

### *The Victory of Our Lord Jesus Christ*

Missionary work finds its foundation in Christ's mediatorial triumph over sin, death, and the world. Nonetheless, massive obstacles stand in the way of mission endeavors, such as distance; expense; language; culture; the sinful hostility and hardened hearts of fallen human beings; the sins and infirmities of Christians; coldness of heart, strife, and error in the church; and the wide-ranging opposition and destructive activity of Satan. Missionary work and missionary prayer must be fueled by confidence in the power of

---

15. Perkins, *Works*, 1:336, 339. These pages are consecutive in the book; the latter should read 337.

16. Henry, *Commentaries*, 5:361–62.

17. Henry, *Commentaries*, 5:105.

Christ enthroned as Head of the church and Lord of all to overcome these obstacles.

Though the government in Calvin's homeland of France harshly suppressed evangelical preaching, Calvin wrote to the king: "Indeed, we are quite aware of what…lowly little men we are…. But our doctrine must tower unvanquished above all the glory and above all the might of the world, for it is not of us, but of the living God and his Christ whom the Father has appointed to 'rule from sea to sea, and from the rivers even to the ends of the earth' [Ps. 72:8]."[18] The missionary prayers of the Reformers and Puritans sprang from a biblical vision of the sovereign Christ whose kingdom must fill the earth (Ps. 72; Dan. 2:34–35, 44).[19]

Jonathan Edwards (1703–1758) wrote *An Humble Attempt to promote Explicit Agreement and Visible Union of God's People in Extraordinary Prayer for the Revival of Religion and the Advancement of Christ's Kingdom on Earth, pursuant to Scripture-Promises and Prophecies concerning the last Time* (1748). In this book he called for regular prayer meetings for revival and world evangelization. The motivation for this prayer, he explained, was that "it is natural and reasonable to suppose, that the whole world should finally be given to Christ, as one whose right it is to reign, as the proper heir of him who is originally the King of all nations, and the possessor of heaven and earth." God the Father has made His Son the mediator of His kingdom and heir of all the nations (Ps. 2:6–8; Heb. 1:2; 2:8).[20]

In *An Humble Attempt*, Edwards argued for the great advance of the kingdom of God on earth. He cited as evidence the promises that all families of the earth would be blessed (Gen. 12:3; 18:18; 22:18; 26:4; 28:14), all nations would serve the Messiah (Ps. 72:11, 17), all nations would come to the Lord (Isa. 2:2; Jer. 3:17), true religion would prevail throughout the world (Pss. 22:27; 65:5, 8;

---

18. Calvin, *Institutes*, 12 [Prefatory Address to King Francis].

19. The subject of Iain Murray's book, *The Puritan Hope*, is this vision and the eschatology connected with it.

20. *The Works of Jonathan Edwards, Volume 5, Apocalyptic Writings*, ed. Stephen J. Stein (New Haven: Yale University Press, 1977), 330.

67:7; 98:3; 113:3; Isa. 11:9; 54:1, 2, 5; Mal. 1:11), idols and idola-
trous nations would perish from the earth (Isa. 60:12; Jer. 10:11, 15),
and the full number of Jews and Gentiles would be saved (Rom.
11:12, 25).[21] In typical Puritan fashion, Edwards urged believers to
turn these promises into prayers, calling upon the Lord to extend
the kingdom of His Son. Christ's victorious position at God's right
hand should move us to pray for God to establish Christ's royal
dominion ("the rod of thy strength") in the very midst of His enemies (Ps. 110).

## *The Glory of the Living God*

The very marrow of the Reformed movement was its God-
centeredness. The Reformers and Puritans were enamored with
the sovereign God and overwhelmed with His majestic beauty.[22]
The Puritans who composed the words of the Westminster Shorter
Catechism (1647) wrote, "Man's chief end is to glorify God and to
enjoy him for ever." Thomas Watson (ca. 1620–1686) wrote, "Glory
is the sparkling of the Deity."[23] He said glorifying God consists of
the following:

1) "Appreciation. To glorify God is to set God highest in our thoughts.... There is in God all that may
   draw forth both wonder and delight; there is a con-
   stellation of all beauties.... We glorify God, when
   we are God-admirers."

2) "Glorifying God consists in adoration, or worship....
   Divine worship must be such as God himself has
   appointed, else it is offering strange fire (Lev. 10:1)."

3) "Affection.... It is intense and ardent. True saints
   are...burning in holy love to God."

---

21. Edwards, *Works*, 5:329–34.
22. Joel R. Beeke, *Living for God's Glory: An Introduction to Calvinism*
(Orlando: Reformation Trust, 2008), 39–42.
23. Thomas Watson, *A Body of Divinity* (1692; reprint, Edinburgh: Banner of
Truth Trust, 2000), 6.

4) "Subjection. This is when we dedicate ourselves to
God, and stand ready dressed for his service."[24]

Watson also said, "We glorify God by laboring to draw others to
God; by seeking to convert others, and so make them instruments
of glorifying God."[25] The Great Commission is a further expression of the Great Commandment, for missions must be driven by
love of God and longing for His name to be glorified by all nations
in the earth. Calvin said God's attributes "should captivate us with
wonderment for him, and impel us to celebrate his praise." He
said further, "We should wish God to have the honor he deserves."
According to Christ's command, Calvin urged us "to request not
only that God vindicate his sacred name from all contempt and
dishonor but also that he subdue the whole race of mankind to
reverence for it."[26]

Experiencing God's overflowing glory causes one's heart to
overflow in prayers for others. David Brainerd (1718–1747), missionary to Native Americans, wrote in his journal, "I saw that God
is the only soul-satisfying portion, and I really found satisfaction in
him: My soul was much enlarged in sweet intercession for my fellow men everywhere, and for many Christian friends in particular,
in distant places."[27] Brainerd suffered from depression and severe
hardships in his work. He died in his twenties after a long bout with
tuberculosis. In all of that difficulty, he was sustained in missionary
labor by his love for the glory of God. He wrote, "I felt my soul
rejoice, that God is unchangeably happy and glorious; and that he
will be glorified, whatever becomes of his creatures."[28] By the end
of 1646, Brainerd's illness was so severe that he could do little more

---

24. Watson, *Body of Divinity*, 7–8.
25. Watson, *Body of Divinity*, 16.
26. Calvin, *Institutes*, 3.20.41.
27. *The Works of Jonathan Edwards, Volume 7, The Life of David Brainerd*, ed.
Norman Pettit (New Haven: Yale University Press, 1984), 177. See Tom Wells, *A
Vision for Missions* (Edinburgh: Banner of Truth Trust, 1985), 121–29.
28. Edwards, *Works*, 7:275–76.

than pray. But he had seen God work among the Native Americans he served, and he testified:

> Prayer was now wholly turned into praise; and I could do little else but try to adore and bless the living God: The wonders of his grace displayed in gathering to himself a church among the poor Indians here were the subject matter of my meditation and the occasion of exciting my soul to praise and bless his Name.... I could only rejoice that God had done the work himself; and that none in heaven or earth might pretend to share the honor of it with him; I could only be glad that God's declarative glory was advanced by the conversion of these souls, and that it was to the enlargement of his kingdom in the world.... Oh, that he might be adored and praised by all his intelligent creatures to the utmost of their powers and capacities.[29]

This vision for the glory of God in all nations also propelled William Carey to "expect great things from God and attempt great things for God." The rising flame of prayer for world missions thus bursts forth from burning coals in a heart in love with God. The essence of all true missionary prayer is found in Christ's words, "Hallowed be thy name!"

## The Puritan Method of Missionary Praying

In all their ways, the Puritans were orderly, that is, they governed their lives by principles. This was so even in their prayers for the spread of the gospel in the world. While the Puritans resisted prescribed forms and relied on the Holy Spirit's help for prayer, they also embraced methods of promoting and guiding such prayer.

### A Passionate Missionary Tradition: The Westminster Standards

The first Puritan method was to build missionary prayer into the public worship of the local church. The Westminster Assembly, famous for its Confession of Faith and two catechisms, also

---

29. Edwards, *Works*, 7:404.

produced the *Directory for the Public Worship of God* (1644). The *Directory* instructed that the minister, prior to delivering his sermon, was to lead the people in prayer to confess sins and to pray for grace through Christ Jesus. He was also instructed

> to pray for the propagation of the gospel and kingdom of Christ to all nations, for the conversion of the Jews, the fullness of the Gentiles, the fall of Antichrist [the Roman Catholic papacy], and the hastening of the coming of our Lord; for the deliverance of the distressed churches abroad, from the tyranny of the Antichristian faction, and from the cruel oppositions and blasphemies of the Turk [the Muslim power]; for the blessing of God upon all the Reformed churches, especially upon the Churches and Kingdoms of England, Scotland, and Ireland...and for our plantations [colonies] in the remote parts of the world.[30]

The Puritans were thus concerned that public worship regularly include prayer for the cause of Christ throughout the world, including world missions and the relief of the persecuted church suffering in Europe under Roman Catholicism and in the Middle East under Islam. Similarly, the Westminster Larger Catechism (1647) in its exposition of the Lord's Prayer (Q. 191), said, "In the second petition (which is, *Thy kingdom come,*) acknowledging ourselves and all mankind to be by nature under the dominion of sin and Satan; we pray, that the kingdom of sin, and Satan, may be destroyed, the gospel propagated throughout the world, the Jews called, the fullness of the Gentiles brought in."[31] The Westminster Standards shaped the piety of generations of British, North American, and Australian Reformed Christians, leading many into intercession for the world.

---

30. "A Directory for Publique Prayer, Reading the Holy Scriptures, Singing of Psalmes, Preaching of the Word, Administration of the Sacraments, and other parts of the Publique Worship of God, Ordinary and Extraordinary," in *The Westminster Standards: An Original Facsimile* (1648; reprint, Audubon, N.J.: Old Paths Publications, 1997), 10.

31. "The humble Advice of the Assembly of Divines...Concerning a Larger Catechism," 62, in ibid.

Thomas Boston (1676–1732) preached a series of sermons on the Westminster Shorter Catechism. In his sermon on "Thy kingdom come," Boston echoed the language of the *Directory* and the Larger Catechism. He said this petition in the Lord's Prayer teaches us that the duty and disposition of God's children is to desire His kingdom to come in, destroying the power of sin and Satan over men's hearts. "Every saint prays it down," he wrote. He said we are to pray for "the conversion of sinners to God, 2 Thess. 3:1, 'Pray for us, that the word of the Lord may have free course, and be glorified.' Converts are the church's children, for which she travails in birth, in her ministers and members, as naturally longing for the conversion of souls, as a travailing woman to see the fruit of her womb." This petition also requires us to pray for God to overcome Satan's opposition to the preaching and power of the gospel "and make the gospel triumph over them all." Likewise, Boston said, God's children must desire and pray for "the propagation of the gospel through the world, that it may be carried through all nations...that Christ may be King in all the earth."[32]

This pattern of praying was not merely a public formality, for it engraved itself upon the hearts of the people. The last words of English housewife Elizabeth Heywood (d. 1661) were a prayer "for the church of God, that the Jews might be converted, and that the gospel might be preached to the remainder of the Gentile nations."[33] May God make prayer for the nations so integral to our church's worship that it will even be included among our own last wishes.

### A Divine Missionary Book: The Holy Scriptures

The second Puritan method for praying for world missions was teaching people to pray the Scriptures. Matthew Henry wrote *Method for Prayer* (1710),[34] which followed the Westminster Standards in providing prayers for "the lost world," specifically for the

---

32. *The Complete Works of the Late Rev. Thomas Boston* (1853; reprint, Stoke-on-Trent, England: Tentmaker Publications, 2002), 2:578–80.

33. Murray, *The Puritan Hope*, 99.

34. See chapter 8 of this book.

spread of the gospel to foreign nations, the growth of the church by
many conversions, the salvation of the Jews, the relief of the Eastern
churches from Islamic oppression, and the blessing of the churches
in English colonies such as America.[35]

The key to Henry's method was putting the words of Scriptures
into the mouths of God's people. Henry wove together the words of
the Bible to impress upon the hearts of Christians in prayers such
as these:

> Let the people praise thee, O God, yea, let all the people
> praise thee.
>
> O let thy salvation and thy righteousness be openly
> showed in the sight of the heathen, and let all the ends
> of the earth see the salvation of our God.
>
> O give thy Son the heathen for his inheritance, and the
> uttermost parts of the earth for his possession; for thou
> hast said, It is a light thing for him to raise up the tribes
> of Jacob, and to restore the preserved of Israel, but thou
> wilt give him for a light to the Gentiles.
>
> Let all the kingdoms of this world become the king-
> doms of the Lord, and of his Christ.
>
> O let the gospel be preached unto every creature; for
> how shall men believe in him of whom they have not
> heard? And how shall they hear without preachers? And
> how shall they preach except they be sent? And who
> shall send forth labourers, but the Lord of the harvest?
>
> O let the earth be full of the knowledge of the Lord, as
> the waters cover the sea.[36]

As these selections indicate, the Psalms contain many expressions of God's dominion over all the earth and the future reign of
the anointed King over the nations. According to the design of the

---

35. *The Complete Works of the Rev. Matthew Henry* (1855; reprint, Grand Rapids: Baker, 1979), 2:48–49.
36. Ibid.

Holy Spirit, the Psalter is a missionary hymnal and prayer book. Calvin and the Puritans loved the Psalms and sang from the Psalter every day.

The call of the gospel sounds forth in the version of Psalm 2 that appeared in the Psalter of Sternhold and Hopkins (1560), used in Britain and North America for many generations:

> Now ye O Kings and Rulers all,
>   be Wise therefore and Learn'd:
> By whom the matters of the World
>   be Iudged and discern'd.
> See that ye serve the Lord above,
>   in trembling and in feare:
> See that with reuerence ye reioyce,
>   to him in like manner.
>
> See that ye kisse and eke [also] embrace,
>   his blessed Sonne, i say:
> Lest in his wrath ye suddenly,
>   perish in the mid way.
> If once his wrath neuer so small,
>   shall kindle in his brest:
> Oh then all they that trust in Christ,
>   shall happy be and blest.[37]

New England's *Bay Psalm Book* (1640) celebrates the triumph of the gospel over all the earth in this version of Psalm 98:

> Sing to the Lord a new song: sing
>   all the earth the Lord unto:
> Sing to Jehovah, bless his name,
>   still his salvation show.
> To the heathen his glory, to all
>   people his wonders spread.

---

37. *The Booke of Psalms, collected into English Meeter, by Thomas Sternhold, Iohn Hopkins, and others: conferred with the Hebrew, with apt Notes to sing them withal* (London: for the Company of Stationers, 1628; reprint, Columbus, Ohio: Lazarus Ministry Press, 1998).

> For great is the Lord, much to be praised,
>     above all gods in dread....
> Ye kindreds of the people all
>     unto the Lord afford
> Glory and mightiness also
>     give ye unto the Lord. [Ps. 96:1–4, 7][38]

Likewise, the Scottish Psalter of 1650 foresees a world redeemed by Christ, renewed by the preaching of the gospel, and rejoicing in God, in its famous version of Psalm 100:

> All people that on earth do dwell,
> Sing to the Lord with cheerful voice;
> Him serve with mirth, his praise forth tell,
> Come ye before Him and rejoice.[39]

The greatest means the Lord uses to teach His people to pray for the world is the Word of God. If we want people to be faithful in praying for the spread of the gospel throughout the world, we should fill our worship services with the words of *the* missionary book. Colossians 3:16 says, "Let the word of Christ dwell in you richly in all wisdom; teaching and admonishing one another in psalms and hymns and spiritual songs, singing with grace in your hearts to the Lord." The practice of singing the Psalms in public and family worship would help turn the church's inward focus outward to a world that desperately needs to worship the true God.[40]

---

38. *The Bay Psalm Book* (1640; reprint, Bedford: Applewood Books, 2002), 185–86.

39. *The Psalms of David in Metre, according to the Version Approved by the Church of Scotland, and Appointed to be Used in Worship* (Cambridge: Cambridge University Press, n.d.).

40. For a modern edition of the Psalms for church worship, see *The Psalter* (Grand Rapids: Reformation Heritage Books, 1999). On the historic practice of Psalm singing, which has largely fallen out of favor in the contemporary church, see Joel R. Beeke and Anthony T. Selvaggio, *Sing a New Song: Recovering Psalm Singing for the Twenty-First Century* (Grand Rapids: Reformation Heritage Books, 2010).

## Conclusion: "Walk over the vast ocean"

William Gurnall (1616–1679) asked, "Is there none, O man, that needs the mercy of God besides thyself?" In contemporary language, is there no one else that you want to be saved besides yourself? God gives us permission for our love to begin at home. So pray for your family. After that, consider what is happening in your neighborhood. Then pray for your community. Go on to pray for your nation, but do not stop there. As Gurnall said,

> Let thy prayers walk over the vast ocean.... Visit the churches of Christ abroad; yea, the poor Indians and other ruins of mankind that lie where Adam's sin threw them with us, without any attempt made as yet upon them by the gospel for their recovery, and carry their deplored condition before the Lord. Our Drake is famous for compassing the earth with his ship in a few years; thou mayst by thy prayers every day, and make a more gainful voyage of it too than he did.[41]

41. William Gurnall, *The Christian in Complete Armour* (1662–1665; reprint, Edinburgh: Banner of Truth Trust, 2002), 2:524–25. Francis Drake (1540–1596) was an English sea captain who circled the earth 1577–1580.

*Chapter 12*

# Prayerful Praying Today
———————————— c○つc○つ ————————————
JOEL R. BEEKE

> *Elias was a man subject to like passions as we are,*
> *and he prayed earnestly that it might not rain: and it*
> *rained not on the earth by the space of three years and*
> *six months.*
> —JAMES 5:17

The Scripture says Elijah "prayed earnestly." The KJV marginal notes provide the alternate translation that the prophet "prayed in his prayer." In other words, his prayers were more than a formal exercise; he poured himself into his praying. Bible commentator Alexander Ross says that idiom communicates intensity: "A man may pray with his lips and yet not pray with an intense desire of the soul."[1] You might call it "prayerful praying."

After studying the prayer lives of the Reformers and Puritans, I am convinced that the greatest shortcoming in today's church is the lack of such prayerful prayer. We fail to use heaven's greatest weapon as we should. Personally, domestically, and congregationally, the prayer we engage in is often more prayerless than prayerful. One-half of our calling as ministers and elders is prayer (Acts 6:4), but in reality we spend no more than 5 percent of our time in prayer.

---

1. Alexander Ross, *The Epistles of James and John*, The New International Commentary on the New Testament (Grand Rapids: Eerdmans, 1954), 102.

All Christians are called to pray (Col. 4:2). Is anything more essential, yet more neglected, among us than prayer?

The giants of church history dwarf us in true prayer. Is that because they were more educated, were less distracted by cares and duties, or lived in more pious times? No; undoubtedly, what most separates them from us is that prayer was their priority; they devoted considerable time and energy to it. They were prayerful men who knew how to take hold of God in prayer (Isa. 64:7), being possessed by the Spirit of grace and supplication. They were Daniels in private and public prayer.

We have already noted that Martin Luther (1483–1546) spent the best two hours of every day alone with God.[2] Luther's prayer life was legendary. When he was facing a day that was particularly challenging, Luther told his friends, "I have so much scheduled for tomorrow I must pray for that I must arise an hour earlier to have an extra hour alone with God." On another occasion, Philipp Melanchthon (1497–1560), Luther's most able and trusted assistant, overheard Luther praying aloud as was his custom, for Luther said he wanted even the Devil to hear what he was praying. Melanchthon exclaimed, "Gracious God! What faith! What spirit! What reverence, and yet with what holy familiarity did Master Martin pray!" Yet such prayer took tremendous effort and self-discipline. Luther readily confessed, "Praying comes close to being the most difficult of all works."[3] Though people unacquainted with spiritual praying may think it is easy to recite a few words to God, Luther said, "Prayer is a difficult matter and hard work. It is far more difficult than preaching the Word or performing other official duties in the church…. This is the reason why it is so rare."[4]

We must strive to grow in prayer. John Welsh (1568–1622) of Ayr, the God-fearing son-in-law of John Knox, prayed seven hours

---

2. Andrew Kosten, translator's introduction to *Devotions and Prayers of Martin Luther* (Grand Rapids: Baker, 1965), 5.

3. Ewald M. Plass, comp., *What Luther Says: A Practical In-Home Anthology for the Active Christian* (St. Louis: Concordia, 1959), 1081 [3451].

4. Ibid., 1088 [3476, 3478].

a day. He confessed, "I wonder how a Christian could lie in his bed all night, and not rise to pray." He kept his robe close to his bed because a night seldom passed when he did not rise to commune with his God in a private room. Often his wife would find him praying and weeping after midnight. When she encouraged him to come back to bed out of fear he would catch cold, Welsh responded, "Oh, my dear wife, I have the souls of three thousand to answer for, and I know not how it is with many of them!"

Our prayerlessness is the more tragic because of the tremendous potential of prayer. The Puritan Thomas Brooks (1608–1680) wrote, "Ah! How often, Christians, hath God kissed you at the beginning of prayer, and spoke peace to you in the midst of prayer, and filled you with joy and assurance, upon the close of prayer!"[5] The wife of Joseph Alleine said of her husband:

> At the time of his health, he did rise constantly at or before four of the clock, and on the Sabbath sooner, if he did wake. He would be much troubled if he heard smiths, or shoemakers, or such tradesmen, at work at their trades before he was in his duties with God; saying to me often, "O how this noise shames me! Doth not my Master deserve more than theirs?" From four till eight he spent in prayer, holy contemplation, and singing of psalms, which he much delighted in, and did daily practice alone, as well as in his family.[6]

In this concluding chapter, let us consider the problem of prayerlessness and look at some solutions. If we are faithful in our efforts to acquire more of the gift and grace of true prayer, we can be sure God will help us to "take hold of him" (Isa. 64:7).

---

5. Thomas Brooks, *The Works of Thomas Brooks*, ed. Alexander B. Grosart (1861–1867; reprint, Edinburgh: Banner of Truth Trust, 2001), 2:369.

6. Richard Baxter, et al., *The Life and Letters of Joseph Alleine* (reprint, Grand Rapids: Reformation Heritage Books, 2003), 106.

## The Problem of Prayerless Praying

Let each of us begin with ourselves. Does our personal use of the weapon of prayer bring us shame rather than glory? Is prayer the means by which we storm the throne of grace and take the kingdom of heaven by violence? Is it a missile that crushes satanic powers, or is it like a harmless toy that Satan sleeps beside?

We ministers are usually more concerned about our sermons and what our listeners think of them than what and how we pray. As laypeople, we are usually more concerned about communicating with others than with God. Where is our prayerful passion for the presence of God?

Our prayer life is often "closed for repairs," though little repair work seems to get done. Good intentions surface from time to time, but, as the saying goes, "The road to hell is paved with good intentions." Good intentions without repentance and persevering implementation of better habits lead only to further deterioration and unfruitfulness.

When our prayer life is boarded up, everything else begins to shut down. How can we live to God outside the prayer closet when we so seldom meet Him in the closet? In that tepid condition, we often mistake prayerless praying for prayerful praying. We forget that in both we come with empty hands to God's throne. Prayerless praying, however, comes with listless hands, while prayerful praying clings with one hand to heaven's footstool and with the other to Calvary's cross, stirring itself "to take hold" of God (Isa. 64:7). Prayerless praying freezes before reaching heaven, while prayerful praying pierces heaven and warms the soul.

What is the condition of your prayer life? Perhaps you have never experienced a powerful prayer life. You may repeat words of prayer in a religious meeting or over a meal. You may express yourself in elegant words or the stock phrases of conventional piety and yet be a prayerless person. You may cry out to God for some pressing need but never possess the Spirit of prayer. Prayer is the soul's breath to God in faith, hope, and love. Does your soul ever pant after God in Christ? If not, your spiritual life is lifeless. If you are prayerless in your prayer, you are still dead in your sins. You must cry out to God in repentance, begging Him to make you alive in Christ.

Perhaps you once prayed in your prayers but your need for such prayer has grown dull. Backsliding usually begins in the inner closet of prayer. You looked forward to times of prayer. You longed to be alone with the Lord, to pour out your heart to Him with all its needs, confessions, vows, thanksgivings, and praises. You spread those before the Lord with eagerness as if He knew nothing about you, and yet with the consciousness that He knew you better than you know yourself.

But gradually your prayer life began to disintegrate. Even before you were aware of it, your prayers became more a matter of words than heart-to-heart communion with God. Form and coldness replaced holy necessity. Before long, you dropped your morning prayer. It no longer seemed critical to meet with God before you met with people. Then you shortened your prayer at bedtime. Other concerns broke in on your time with God. Throughout the day, prayer all but vanished. Previously, you prayed less on your knees throughout the day than you did with your eyes open—on the road, at work or school, or wherever you went—because most of your prayers were spontaneous.

Perhaps formality and deadness in prayer have replaced power and access to God, causing the omission of prayer to seem more reverent than engaging in prayer. "My knees are still bowed, but where is my love, urgency, necessity, and dependency on God?" we ask. "Where are the ongoing intercessory petitions for my family and the church?"

The confessions of Thomas Adam (1701–1784) may resonate with you in this condition:

> I pray faintly, and with reserve, merely to quiet conscience, for present ease, almost wishing not to be heard.... Prayer and other spiritual exercises are often a weariness to me; a task, and a force upon nature. I am too well pleased with pretenses for omitting them; and when they are over, I feel myself at ease, as it were, like after the removal of a heavy weight.... Whenever

I attempt to pray for others, I am soon made sensible that I do it in a cold, heartless manner; a plain indication that love is not at the bottom. It is an awful moment when the soul meets God in private, to stand the test of His all-searching eye.[7]

We must confront our prayerless praying, confess it to God, and plead for the renewal of our souls in recognizing the value of prayer. Charles Bridges (1794–1869) particularly speaks to pastors about the need for revival in prayer, based on Acts 6:4, "We will give ourselves continually to prayer, and to the ministry of the word." He wrote:

> Prayer is one half of our Ministry; and it gives to the other half all its power and success. It is the appointed medium of receiving spiritual communications for the instruction of our people. Those who walk most closely with God are most spiritually intelligent in "the secret of his covenant." Many can set their seal to Luther's testimony, that he often obtained more knowledge in a short time by prayer, than by many hours of laborious and accurate study. It will also strengthen our habitual engagedness of our hearts in our work, and our natural exercises and capacities for it. Living near to the fountain-head of influence, we shall be in the constant receipt of fresh supplies of light, support, and consolation—to assist us in our duties, to enable us for our difficulties, and to assure us of our present acceptance, and a suitable measure of ultimate success.[8]

Prayer is no less important for laypeople. How can you find a godly mate, raise your children in the Lord, and do your work for the glory of God without prayerful prayer? All things in life, from marriage to meals down to the hour of death, are sanctified by prayer and the Word (1 Tim. 4:4–5). Petitions are our sails, and the Spirit provides the wind. Without the Spirit, our prayers are prayerless, and prayerless praying results in lifeless living. Prayer is the thermometer of our spiritual condition.

7. Thomas Adam, *Private Thoughts on Religion* (Glasgow: Chalmers and Collins, 1824), 68, 73, 76.

8. Charles Bridges, *The Christian Ministry with an Inquiry into the Causes of Its Inefficiency*, 3rd ed. (London: Seeley and Burnside, 1830), 193.

## Solutions for Prayerful Praying

It is far easier to generate guilt about prayerlessness than to solve the problem. It is far easier to feel bad about powerless prayer than to repent and obey. But as Paul says in 1 Timothy 4:7b, "Exercise thyself rather unto godliness." He adds in 1 Timothy 6:12, "Fight the good fight of faith, lay hold on eternal life." I thus plead with you to aggressively seek a more fervent and faithful prayer life. This will require you to take hold of yourself and God. Since the Reformers and Puritans were masters of prayer, I will quote heavily from them in suggestions for prayerful praying. Here are their solutions.

*Take Hold of Yourself for Prayer*

Prayerful praying does not happen automatically. Do not think that going to a conference, listening to a preacher, or reading a book will flip a switch inside you and make you a praying machine. You must exercise self-control, which is not a legalistic mandate but a fruit of the Spirit prompted by the cross of Jesus Christ (Gal. 5:22–24). We must look to Christ as the vine who can produce good fruit in us, get a grip on ourselves, and engage in disciplined prayer.

David took hold of himself in prayer. He did not wallow in depression but engaged in self-examination, saying in Psalm 42:5, "Why art thou cast down, O my soul? and why art thou disquieted in me? hope thou in God: for I shall yet praise him for the help of his countenance." David did not sink into thanklessness but rose to thank God in the midst of his troubles. In Psalm 103:2 he says, "Bless the LORD, O my soul, and forget not all his benefits."

Consider the following seven principles of how to take hold of yourself for prayer.

*1. Remember the value of prayer.* Seek to realize the value of unanswered as well as answered prayer. William Carey (1761–1834) labored as a missionary in India for eight years before baptizing the first convert from Hinduism to Christ.[9] Yet in those years Carey

---

9. Timothy George, *Faithful Witness: The Life and Mission of William Carey* (Birmingham, Ala.: New Hope, 1991), 131.

learned to live for the glory of God alone. He wrote, "I feel that it is good to commit my soul, my body, and my all, into the hands of God. Then the world appears little, the promises great, and God an all-sufficient portion."[10] God's delay became marrow for Carey's soul. "You must distinguish between delays and denials," said Thomas Brooks.[11] William Bridge went even deeper, saying, "A praying man can never be very miserable, whatever his condition be, for he has the ear of God; the Spirit within to indite, a Friend in heaven to present, and God Himself to receive his desires. It is a mercy to pray, even though I never receive the mercy prayed for."[12]

May God also sanctify us through seemingly unanswered petitions. Remember, in the waiting time between sowing and reaping, plants are growing. Though we may wait a long time before receiving an answer to some prayers, we must pray on, realizing that prayer itself as well as the trial of delayed answers helps our soul grow.

But if unanswered prayer is sweet, how much sweeter is answered prayer! "Good prayers never come weeping home," wrote Joseph Hall (1574–1656); "I am sure I shall receive either what I ask or what I should ask."[13] God knows what is best for His children. He never denies us anything that we ask for in humble submission and according to His will. So pray on. Refuse to leave the Lord alone. Keep before you the encouraging words of Thomas Watson (ca. 1620–1686): "The angel fetched Peter out of prison, but it was prayer that fetched the angel."[14] Beg the Lord to bring back the days of John Knox (ca. 1514–1572), when his enemies dreaded his prayers more than the armies of ten thousand men.

10. Ibid., 104.

11. Brooks, *Works*, 2:371.

12. William Bridge, *A Lifting Up for the Downcast* (1648; reprint, Edinburgh: Banner of Truth, 1990), 55.

13. Cited in John Blanchard, comp., *The Complete Gathered Gold* (Darlington, U.K.: Evangelical Press, 2006), 455.

14. Thomas Watson, *A Divine Cordial* (1663; reprint, Wilmington, Del.: Sovereign Grace Publishers, 1972), 18.

**2. Maintain the priority of prayer.** Apart from God, we can do nothing (John 15:5). John Bunyan wrote, "You can do more than pray, after you have prayed, but you cannot do more than pray until you have prayed."[15] He also said, "Pray often, for prayer is a shield to the soul, a sacrifice to God, and a scourge for Satan."[16] Charles Spurgeon (1834–1892) wrote to ministers, "Your prayers will be your ablest assistants while your discourses are yet upon the anvil.... Prayer will singularly assist you in the delivery of your sermon; in fact, nothing can so gloriously fit you to preach as descending fresh from the mount of communion with God to speak with men.... After the sermon, how could a conscientious preacher give vent to his feelings and find solace for his soul if access to the mercy seat were denied him?"[17]

Let us then value prayer as the chief means to assist us in our ministerial duties, reserving time for prayer before and after each church task. Struggle to avoid prayerless praying whether in private devotions or public prayers. Even if your prayers seem lifeless, do not stop praying. Dullness may be beyond your immediate ability to overcome, but refusing to pray at all is the fruit of presumption, self-sufficiency, and slothfulness. When even the outward form of prayer is gone, all is gone. It is easy to pray when you are like a sailboat gliding forward in a favoring wind. But you must also pray when you are like an icebreaker smashing your way through an arctic sea one foot at a time. No matter what, keep prayer your priority.

**3. Speak with sincerity in prayer.** Psalm 62:8 says, "Trust in him at all times; ye people, pour out your heart before him: God is a refuge for us." To pray with your mouth what is not truly in your heart is hypocrisy—unless you are confessing the coldness of your

---

15. Cited in I. D. E. Thomas, comp., *The Golden Treasury of Puritan Quotations* (Chicago: Moody Press, 1975), 210.

16. John Bunyan, *The Works of John Bunyan*, ed. George Offor (1854; reprint, Edinburgh: Banner of Truth Trust, 1991), 1:65.

17. Charles Spurgeon, *Lectures to My Students* (1881–1893; reprint, Pasadena, Tex.: Pilgrim Publications, 1990), 1:41, 43, 44.

heart and crying out for heart-warming grace. Sometimes a sincere prayer, such as Psalm 119, is long and carefully crafted. Sometimes a sincere prayer, such as Psalm 86:11b, is quite simple: "Unite my heart to fear thy name." Or consider Luke 18:13: "God be merciful to me a sinner." Either way, settle for nothing less than sincerity in your prayer.

Be encouraged to strive for sincerity in prayer by these words of Thomas Brooks:

> God looks not at the elegancy of your prayers, to see how neat they are; nor yet at the geometry of your prayers to see how long they are; nor yet at the arithmetic of your prayers, to see how many they are; nor yet at the music of your prayers, nor yet at the sweetness of your voice, nor yet at the logic of your prayers; but at the sincerity of your prayers, how hearty they are. There is no prayer acknowledged, approved, accepted, recorded, or rewarded by God, but that wherein the heart is sincerely and wholly. The true mother would not have the child divided. As God loves a broken and a contrite heart, so he loathes a divided heart.[18]

**4. Cultivate a continual spirit of prayer.** "Pray without ceasing," says 1 Thessalonians 5:17. This refers to the spirit, habit, and condition of prayer rather than the physical act of prayer. It refers more to praying with your hat on and your eyes open than to petitioning in private. Speaking specifically to ministers on this matter, Spurgeon wrote,

> If there be any man under heaven, who is compelled to carry out the precept—"Pray without ceasing," surely it is the Christian minister. He has peculiar temptations, special trials, singular difficulties, and remarkable duties; he has to deal with God in awful relationships, and with men in mysterious interests; he therefore needs much more grace than common men, and as he knows this, he is led constantly to cry to the strong for strength, and say, "I will lift up mine eyes unto the

---

18. Brooks, *Works*, 2:256.

hills from whence cometh my help." Alleine once wrote to a dear friend, "Though I am apt to be unsettled and quickly set off the hinges, yet, methinks, I am like a bird out of the nest. I am never quiet till I am in my old way of communion with God; like the needle in the compass, that is restless till it be turned to the pole."[19]

Continual prayer is the unexplainable spirit and art of communion with God, which is sometimes hidden from the wise and prudent but revealed to babes. Its wisdom often extends beyond form and words. Bunyan said, "When thou prayest, rather let thy heart be without words, than thy words without a heart."[20] Keep your heart in a praying frame towards God even when you cannot express your prayers in words.

One more thing I have found helpful in the task of continual prayer is that whenever you feel the least impulse to pray, do so. Even if you are in the midst of a difficult job that demands concentration, always obey the impulse to prayer. The impulse may be a groaning of the Spirit, and we must never consider the Spirit's promptings as an intrusion. Do not tell yourself to wait until it's more convenient; start praying immediately.

**5. Work towards organization in prayer.** The apostle Paul prayed constantly for believers and churches all over the world. Paul was a remarkably busy person whose life was full of conflicts and trials. Yet he maintained a system of prayer. We can follow his example by keeping prayer lists and, with God's help, using them to help organize our prayers. At times you will feel more burdened to pray for some than others, but press on even when you do not feel like doing so.

Divide your list into three categories: those you intend to pray for (1) every day, (2) every week, and (3) every month. A good friend in South Africa spends an hour or more on his knees in his

---

19. Spurgeon, *Lectures to My Students*, 1:41.
20. Bunyan, *Works*, 1:65.

study every morning from 5:00 to 6:00, interceding in this manner. My family and I are on his daily list. I cannot tell you how many times I have been encouraged by realizing that this brother is daily lifting up my worthless name to the Lord of Sabaoth. No wonder John Newton (1725–1827) considered his best friends to be those who prayed for him.

Pray through your church directory, dividing the list to cover a reasonable number of people each day. If you are a pastor, you will know their needs. Praying may be the most valuable work that a minister does. It may also be the most important ministry of church members.

Use other prayer directories to pray through a list of missionaries supported by your church or denomination. Read the e-mails and newsletters of missionaries you support and pray for them after you are done reading. Otherwise you might forget.

**6. Read the Bible for prayer.** One reason your prayer life may be drooping is that you have neglected the Holy Scriptures. Prayer is a two-way conversation. We need to listen to God, not just to talk to Him. We do not listen to God by emptying our minds and waiting for a thought to spontaneously come to mind. That's non-Christian mysticism. We listen to God by filling our minds with the Bible because the Bible is God speaking in written form. Our Lord Jesus Christ says in John 15:7, "If ye abide in me, and my words abide in you, ye shall ask what ye will, and it shall be done unto you."

When you read the Bible, do so with the intent of responding to God's Word with prayer. For example, read Ephesians 5 with its many commands for the church and marriage. This is rich material for prayer. Praise God for the love of Christ presented in verses 2 and 25. Turn the commandments into confessions of your transgressions of God's holy law. And bring the laws of God to Him, praying for God to write them on your heart and the hearts of others. Every Scripture passage is fuel for burning prayers.

**7. Keep biblical balance in prayer.** The Scriptures present various kinds of prayer: praise of God's glories, confession of our sins, petition for our needs (spiritual and physical), thanks for God's mercies, intercession for others (family, friends, church, nation, and the world), and our confidence that God is willing and able to answer what we have prayed. We have a tendency to favor some forms of prayer to the neglect of others. For example, you might gravitate towards intercession but neglect thanksgiving. Paul says in Philippians 4:6, "Be careful [or anxious] for nothing, but in every thing by prayer and supplication with thanksgiving let your requests be made known unto God."

Another person might delight in praising God but shy away from confessing sin, forgetting that the apostle John tells us that one mark of walking in the light of God is confession of sins and finding forgiveness from God through the blood of His Son (1 John 1:7–9). Periodically examine your prayers to see if they are out of balance, and give more time and energy to the areas of prayer you are neglecting.

*Taking Hold of God in Prayer*
Deep within us, we know that it is impossible to solve prayerlessness by our own strength. The sacredness, gift, and efficacy of prayer are far above human means. God's grace is necessary for prayerful praying. Yet grace does not passively wait for God to strike us with revival. We must seek grace by first seeking the Lord. David writes in Psalm 25:1, "Unto thee, O LORD, do I lift up my soul" (see also Pss. 86:4; 143:8). Paul commands us in Colossians 3:1–2, "If ye then be risen with Christ, seek those things which are above, where Christ sitteth on the right hand of God. Set your affection on things above, not on things on the earth." So direct your mind and affections towards our covenant God in Christ, and draw near to the throne of grace. Just as Jacob wrestled with the Angel of the Lord and would not let Him go until he was blessed, so we must grasp hold of God until He blesses us.

Consider three principles for taking hold of God in prayer.

***1. Plead God's promises in prayer.*** In His sovereignty, God has bound Himself by the promises He has made to us. Augustine said his mother prayed long for his conversion, pleading God's promises. She "urged upon Thee, as Thine own handwriting," for God in His covenant mercy chose "to become a debtor by Thy promises."[21] Psalm 119:25 says, "My soul cleaveth unto the dust: quicken thou me according to thy word." Thomas Manton (1620–1677), alluding to Augustine, wrote, "One good way to get comfort is to plead the promise of God in prayer.... Show him his handwriting; God is tender of his word."[22]

Some months ago, an elderly friend brought me a spiritual letter from my father, who passed straight from the pulpit to glory in 1993. My father wrote the letter in the 1950s, shortly after his conversion. "I thought you might like to have this," the friend said. "Like to?" I said, "I would *love* to have this." I sat down and read it immediately with great pleasure—it was so personal because it was my father's handwriting. How do you think your Father in heaven feels when you show Him His own handwriting in prayer?

The Puritans made much of praying God's promises back to Him. John Trapp (1601–1669) wrote, "Promises must be prayed over. God loves to be burdened with, and to be importuned [urgently pressed with requests] in, his own words; to be sued upon his own bond. Prayer is a putting God's promises into suit. And it is no arrogancy nor presumption, to burden God, as it were, with his promise.... Such prayers will be nigh the Lord day and night (1 Kings 8:59), he can as little deny them, as deny himself."[23]

Likewise, William Gurnall (1616–1679) wrote, "Prayer is nothing but the promise reversed, or God's Word formed into an

21. Augustine, *The Confessions of St. Augustine*, trans. E. B. Pusey (New York: E. P. Dutton, 1950), 93 [V.ix/17].

22. Thomas Manton, *The Complete Works of Thomas Manton* (London: James Nisbet, 1872), 6:242. Here Manton quoted Augustine in Latin (cf. *Works* 7:21).

23. John Trapp, *A Commentary on the Old and New Testaments*, ed. W Hugh Martin (London: Richard D. Dickinson, 1867), 1:121 [on Gen. 32:9].

argument, and retorted by faith upon God again."[24] He also urged, "Furnish thyself with arguments from the promises to enforce thy prayers, and make them prevalent with God. The promises are the ground of faith, and faith, when strengthened, will make thee fervent, and such fervency ever speeds and returns with victory out of the field of prayer.... The mightier any is in the Word, the more mighty he will be in prayer."[25]

*2. Look to the glorious Trinity in prayer.* Much prayerlessness in our prayers is due to our thoughtlessness towards God. Our prayers may come from the stress of an immediate need or crisis, or they may become mere habitual talking to ourselves. But God dwells in our prayers most when our minds most dwell on God. Therefore when you pray, meditate on how the gospel reveals the Father, the Son, and the Holy Spirit to draw sinners to God. Before rushing into your list of requests, bring to mind Scripture texts that speak of the glory of our God, and turn those texts into praise.

Ephesians 2:18 tells us how the three persons of the Trinity operate in our prayers, saying, "For through him [Christ Jesus] we both have access by one Spirit unto the Father." Prayer is like a golden chain that runs from the Father via the Son and the Spirit back to the Father again. It is decreed by the Father, merited by the Son, shaped into words by the Spirit, and sent back up to the Son, who, through His intercession, presents it as acceptable and pure to His heavenly Father. So lean heavily on the Spirit to help you compose your prayers and trust in Christ to make your prayers effectual. By the Son and the Spirit, your prayers will reach the ears of the God of Sabaoth.

John Owen (1616–1683) advised us to commune with each person in the triune God.[26] He did so based on 2 Corinthians 13:14:

---

24. William Gurnall, *The Christian in Complete Armour* (1662–1665; reprint, Edinburgh: Banner of Truth Trust, 2002), 2:88.

25. Ibid., 2:420–21.

26. John Owen, "Of Communion with God the Father, Son, and Holy Ghost" (1657), in *The Works of John Owen* (1850–1853; reprint, Edinburgh: Banner of

"The grace of the Lord Jesus Christ, and the love of God, and the communion of the Holy Ghost, be with you all. Amen." So in your prayer life, pursue a deeper and more experiential knowledge of the riches of grace in Christ's person and work, the glory of electing and adopting love of the Father, and the comfort of fellowship with God by the indwelling Holy Spirit. In this way, you will pray not just to receive God's benefits but to receive God Himself.

***3. Believe that God answers prayer.*** I fear that we often do not believe in prayer as we should. Psalm 65:2 says, "O thou that hearest prayer, unto thee shall all flesh come." We sincerely come to God only when we believe that He rewards those who seek Him (Heb. 11:6). The Lord Jesus taught that the life of asking is a life of receiving, especially of the graces of the Holy Spirit (Luke 11:9–13). The very nature of God as Father is to give to His children. On the other hand, James rebukes those who ask God for spiritual wisdom to face trials but do not trust Him to give it generously (James 1:2–8).

A man once set up a tavern next door to a church. The wild parties, late-night hours, sinful indulgence, and morning refuse from the bar so distressed the church that people prayed God would intervene. He did. A tornado took out the tavern and left the church untouched. The tavern owner took the church to court, claiming his loss was due to the congregation's prayers. Church members claimed innocence, saying that they had no responsibility in the tavern's destruction. The judge marveled that an unbeliever seemed to believe in the power of prayer more than the church folk did!

May we not fall under the verdict of Isaiah 64:7: "There is none that calleth upon thy name, that stirreth up himself to take hold of thee." Instead, we must bestir ourselves to take hold of the living God!

Truth Trust, 1965–1968), 2:1–274. This excellent book has also been published separately as John Owen, *Communion with the Triune God*, ed. Kelly M. Kapic and Justin Taylor (Wheaton, Ill.: Crossway, 2007).

## A Cautionary, Encouraging Conclusion

Prayer is amazing, glorious, delightful work. Yet apart from faith in Christ, prayer is also difficult, demanding, and in many ways impossible. There is not a believer on earth that cannot sympathize with that. So, though I may have bordered on the idealistic in this closing chapter, my aim is not to discourage you but to encourage you despite your convictions about your own lack of prayer.

I want to conclude with a caution: do not despair in your prayer life. Do not expect to become a Luther or a Welsh in prayer immediately—if ever. We need to be realistic as well. Luther's prayer life was legendary even in his own time, and Luther was a legend in many other ways as well. I am sure many of his colleagues, more ordinary men in every other way, achieved less than Luther did in their prayer lives. Luther also had the benefit of long years of training in the discipline of sustained prayer in the monastery. John Welsh's spiritual life was extraordinary if not unique even in his own time and place. Such men were indeed Daniels, but Daniel stood head and shoulders above any other man of his generation. And all of them—Daniel, Luther, Welsh, or whatever giant we may have in mind—had to start somewhere and grow into what he eventually became, often through long and hard experience. Learning to truly pray in our prayers is not just a matter of getting more intentional or focused or methodical in prayer. It involves trials, warfare, and the enabling Spirit of God.

Ask God to make you a praying Elijah who knows what it means to battle unbelief and despair, even as you strive to grow in prayer and grateful communion with God. Isn't it interesting that James presents Elijah as someone quite like you and me? He prayed in his praying, but he could also despair in his despairing.

I share these thoughts because idealism can crush us with its incessant and insatiable demands. The Christian life is not just about being hectored for not praying, giving, or witnessing enough. Though we do need to be goaded forward, we must not turn Christianity into legalistic drudgery, with a long list of chores to do each day. In many ways, thankfulness—especially thankful prayer—is often a better motive for everything. If you are a Christian, praise God that you have something invaluable that a non-Christian lacks—you have a place to go with every need and thanksgiving. Thank God for the throne of grace.

Luther often exclaimed how great and marvelous was the prayer of a godly Christian. How amazing that a poor human creature should speak with the almighty God in heaven and not be frightened, but know that God smiles upon him for Christ's sake. The ancients thus ably defined prayer as an *Ascensus mentis ad Deum*, a climbing up of the heart unto God.[27] Aim more for that than for very long prayers.

Pray for grace to believe and be thankful that God decrees, gives, hears, and answers prayer. If we truly believe these things, we discover the motivation we need to undertake the journey from prayerless to prayerful praying, becoming contemporary Elijahs who, like the Reformers and Puritans, truly pray in our prayers to our worthy triune God of amazing grace. He is always worthy of being worshiped, feared, and loved—even to all eternity.[28]

27. Martin Luther, *The Table Talk of Martin Luther*, ed. William Hazlitt (London: George Bell, 1900), 156 [CCCXXVIII].

28. For more meditations on how to strengthen your prayer life, see James W. Beeke and Joel R. Beeke, *Developing a Healthy Prayer Life: 31 Meditations on Communing with God* (Grand Rapids: Reformation Heritage Books, 2010).

# Select Bibliography
## Reformers and Puritans on Prayer

—————————————— ᏫᎧᏮᎧᏮᎧ ——————————————

## PRIMARY SOURCES

### Published

Andrewes, Lancelot. *The Morall Law Expounded, 1. Largely, 2. Learnedly, 3. Orthodoxly. That is, the Long-Expected, and Much-Desired Worke of Bishop Andrewes, upon the Ten Commandements: Being His Lectures Many Yeares since in Pembroch Hall Chapell, in Cambridge.... Whereunto is Annexed Nineteen Sermons of His, upon Prayer in Generall, and upon the Lords Prayer in Particular, also Seven Sermons upon our Saviours Temtations, in the Wildernesse.* London: Printed for M. Sparke, 1642.

Baker, Richard. *Meditations and Disquisitions upon the Lords Prayer.* London: Printed by Anne Griffin, 1637.

Ball, John. *A Friendly Triall of the Grounds Tending to Separation: In a Plain and Modest Dispute Touching the Lawfulnesse of a Stinted Liturgie and Set Form of Prayer, Communion in Mixed Assemblies, and the Primitive Subject and First Receptacle of the Power of the Keyes: Tending to Satisfie the Doubtfull, Recall the Wandring, and to Strengthen the Weak.* [Cambridge]: Printed by R. Daniel for E. Brewster, 1640.

Baxter, Richard. "Directions for Prayer." In *A Christian Directory.* Vol. 1 of *The Practical Works of Richard Baxter.* Ligonier, Pa.: Soli Deo Gloria Publications, 1990, pp. 483–92.

_____."Forms of Prayer and Praises, for the use of Ignorant Families that need them." In his *The Poor Man's Family Book*. London: Printed by R. W. for Nevill Simmons, 1680, pp. 339–86.

Boston, Thomas. *Discourses on Prayer*. Reprint, Edmonton, Alberta: Still Waters Revival Books, 1996.

Brooks, Thomas. *The Secret Key to Heaven: The Vital Importance of Private Prayer*. Edinburgh: Banner of Truth Trust, 2006.

Brown of Wamphray, John. *Pious and Elaborate Treatise Concerning Prayer; and the answer of Prayer*. Glasgow: Printed by John Robertson and Mrs. M 'Lean Booksellers, 1745.

Bunyan, John. *I will pray with the Spirit*. Edited by Richard L. Greaves. Vol. 2 of *The Miscellaneous Works of John Bunyan*. Oxford: Clarendon Press, 1976, pp. 227–86.

_____. *Pilgrim's Prayer Book*. Edited by Louis Gifford Parkhurst, Jr. Wheaton, Ill: Tyndale House, 1986.

Burgess, Anthony. *CXLV Expository Sermons Upon the Whole 17th Chapter of the Gospel According to St. John, or, Christs Prayer Before His Passion Explicated, and Both Practically and Polemically Improved*. London: Printed by Abraham Miller for Thomas Underhill, 1656.

Burroughs, Jeremiah. *Gospel Worship, or, The right manner of Sanctifying the Name of God: in general, and particularly in these 3 great ordinances: 1. Hearing the Word, 2. Receiving the Lord's Supper, 3. Prayer*. Morgan, Pa.: Soli Deo Gloria, 1993.

Calvin, John. "Prayer, which is the Chief Exercise of Faith, and by which We Daily Receive God's Benefits." In vol. 2 of *Calvin: Institutes of the Christian Religion*. Edited by John T. McNeill. Translated by Ford Lewis Battles. Philadelphia: Westminster Press, 1960, pp. 850–920.

_____. *Treatises on the Sacraments of the Church of Geneva, Forms of Prayer, and Confessions of Faith*. Translated by Henry Beveridge. Reprint, Grand Rapids: Reformation Heritage Books, 2002.

Clarkson, David. "Pray for Everything." In vol. 2 of *The Works of David Clarkson*. Edinburgh: Banner of Truth Trust, 1988, pp. 172–84.

Cobbet, Thomas. *A Practical Discourse of Prayer: Wherein Is Handled, the Nature, the Duty, the Qualifications of Prayer...with the Necessity of, and Ingagements Unto Prayer, Together, with Sundry Cases of*

*Conscience About It*. London: Printed by R.I. for Thomas Newberry, 1657.

Cotton, John. *A Modest and Cleare Answer to Mr. Balls Discourse of Set Formes of Prayer Set Forth in a Most Seasonable Time When This Kingdome Is Now in Consultation About Matters of That Nature, and so Many Godly Long After the Resolution in That Point*. London: Printed by R. O. and G. D. for Henry Overton, 1642.

Dod, John. *A Plaine and Familiar Exposition on the Lords Prayer*. London: Printed by M. D., 1635.

Downame, George. *A Godly and Learned Treatise of Prayer; Which both conteineth in it the Doctrine of Prayer, and also sheweth the Practice of it in the exposition of the Lords Prayer*. London: Printed by Roger Daniel for Nicolas Bourn, 1640.

Edwards, Jonathan. *A Call to United, Extraordinary Prayer*. Introduced by David Bryant. Reprint, Ross-shire, U.K.: Christian Heritage, 2003.

_____."God's Manner Is First to Prepare Men's Heart and Then to Answer Their Prayers." In vol. 2 of *The Glory and Honor of God*. Edited by Michael D. McMullen. Nashville: Broadman, 2004, pp. 77–106.

_____. "An Humble Attempt to Promote Explicit Agreement and Visible Union of God's People in Extraordinary Prayer, for the Revival of Religion and Advancement of Christ's Kingdom on Earth." In vol. 2 of *The Works of Jonathan Edwards*. Edited by Edward Hickman. Edinburgh: Banner of Truth Trust, 1974, pp. 278–312.

_____."Hypocrites Deficient in the Duty of Prayer." In vol. 2 of *The Works of Jonathan Edwards*. Edited by Edward Hickman. Edinburgh: Banner of Truth Trust, 1974, pp. 71–77.

_____."The Most High, A Prayer-Hearing God." In vol. 2 of *The Works of Jonathan Edwards*. Edited by Edward Hickman. Edinburgh: Banner of Truth Trust, 1974, pp. 113–18.

_____. "Praying for the Spirit." In *Sermons and Discourses 1739–1742*. Edited by Harry S. Stout, Nathan O. Hatch, and Kyle P. Farley. Vol. 22 of *The Works of Jonathan Edwards*. New Haven, Conn.: Yale University Press, 2003, pp. 211–23.

_____. *Praying Together for True Revival.* Edited by T. M. Moore. Phillipsburg, N.J.: P&R, 2004.

_____. "The Suitableness of Union in Extraordinary Prayer for the Advancement of God's Church." In *Sermons and Discourses 1743–1758.* Edited by Wilson H. Kimnach. Vol. 25 of *The Works of Jonathan Edwards.* New Haven, Conn.: Yale University Press, 2003, pp. 197–206.

_____. "The Terms of Prayer." In *Sermons and Discourses: 1734– 1738.* Edited by M. X. Lesser. Vol. 19 of *The Works of Jonathan Edwards.* New Haven: Yale University Press, 2001, pp. 768–91.

Elton, Edward. *Gods Holy Mind Touching Matters Morall: which Himself vttered in Tenne Words, or Tenne Commandements. Also Christs holy mind touching Prayer, delivered in that most holy Prayer, which Himself taught vnto His Disciples: discovered by the light of His owne holy writ; and delivered by questions and answeres.* London, Printed by A[ugustine] M[atthews] and I[ohn] N[orton] for Robert Mylbourne, 1625.

Erskine, Ralph. *The Sermons and Other Practical Works of Reverend Ralph Erskine, Dunfermline, consisting of above one hundred and fifty sermons; besides poetical pieces, also, fourteen sermons on prayer: to which is prefixed an account of the author's life and writings.* Aberdeen: George and Robert King, 1863.

Fenner, William. *The Sacrifice of the Faithfull, or, A Treatise Shewing the Nature, Property, and Efficacy of Zealous Prayer Together with Some Motives to Prayer, and Helps against Discouragements in Prayer: to Which Is Added Seven Profitable Sermons.* London: Printed for John Stafford, 1648.

_____. *The Spirituall Man's Directory Guiding a Christian in the Path That Leads to True Blessednesse, in His Three Maine Duties Towards God: How to Believe, to Obey, to Pray, Unfolding the Creed, Ten Commandements, Lords Prayer.* London: Printed by J. G. for J. R., and are to be sold by William Gilbertson, 1656.

Goodwin, Thomas. *The Return of Prayers.* Vol. 3 of *The Works of Thomas Goodwin.* Reprint, Grand Rapids: Reformation Heritage Books, 2006, pp. 351–403.

Gouge, William. *A Guide to Goe to God: or, An Explanation of the Perfect Patterne of Prayer, the Lords Prayer.* London: Printed by G. M[iller] for Edward Brewster, 1636.

Henry, Matthew. *A Method for Prayer.* Edited by Ligon Duncan. Greenville, S.C.: Reformed Academics Press, 1994.

Heywood, Oliver. *Closet-Prayer a Christian Duty, or, A Treatise Upon Mat. VI, VI. Tending to Prove That Worship of God in Secret Is the Indispensible Duty of All Christians…Together with a Severe Rebuke of Christians for Their Neglect of, or Negligence in, the Duty of Closet-Prayer, and Many Directions for the Managing Thereof.* London: Printed for Tho. Parkhurst, 1671.

Hill, Robert. *The Path-way to Prayer and Pietie.* London: Printed by Richard Hodgkinsonne, 1641.

Howe, John. *The Right Use of That Argument in Prayer from the Name of God on Behalf of a People That Profess It.* London: Printed for Brabazon Aylmer, 1682.

Knox, John. *The Book of Common Order: or the Form of Prayers and Ministration of the Sacraments, etc., approved and received by the Church of Scotland.* Vol. 6, Part 2 of *The Work of John Knox.* Edited by David Laing. Edinburgh: Printed for the Bannatyne Club, 1864, pp. 275–380.

_____. *The Form of Prayers and Ministration of the Sacraments, etc., used in the English Congregation at Geneva.* Vol. 4 of *The Work of John Knox.* Edited by David Laing. Edinburgh: Printed for the Bannatyne Club, 1855, pp. 141–214.

_____. *A Treatise on Prayer, or A Confession, and Declaration of Prayers* of *Selected Writings of John Knox: Public Epistles, Treatises, and Exposition to the Year 1559.* Dallas: Presbyterian Heritage Publications, 1995.

Love, Christopher. *The Zealous Christian: taking Heaven by Holy Violence in Wrestling and Holding Communion with God in Importunate Prayer in Several Sermons, tending to direct men how to hear with zeal and to pray with importunity.* Edited by Don Kistler. Morgan, Pa.: Soli Deo Gloria, 2002.

Luther, Martin. *Appeal for Prayer against the Turks, 1541.* Vol. 43 of *Luther's Works: Devotional Writings 2.* Edited by Gustav K.

Wiencke. Translated by Paul H. G. Moessner. Philadelphia: Fortress Press, 1968, pp. 213–41.

———. *Devotions and Prayers of Martin Luther*. Translated by Andrew W. Kosten. Grand Rapids: Baker, 1965.

———. *An Exposition of the Lord's Prayer for the Simple Laymen*. Vol. 42 of *Luther's Works: Devotional Writings 1*. Edited by Martin O. Dietrich. Translated by Martin H. Bertram. Philadelphia: Fortress Press, 1969, pp. 17–81.

———. *On Rogationtide Prayer and Procession, 1519*. Vol. 42 of *Luther's Works: Devotional Writings 1*. Edited by Martin O. Dietrich. Translated by Martin H. Bertram. Philadelphia: Fortress Press, 1969, pp. 83–98.

———. *Personal Prayer Book, 1552*. Vol. 43 of *Luther's Works: Devotional Writings 2*. Edited by Gustav K. Wiencke. Translated by Martin H. Bertram. Philadelphia: Fortress Press, 1968, pp. 3–45.

———. *A Simple Way to Pray, 1535*. Vol. 43 of *Luther's Works: Devotional Writings 2*. Edited by Gustav K. Wiencke. Translated by Carl J. Schindler. Philadelphia: Fortress Press, 1968, pp. 187–211.

Manton, Thomas. *A Practical Exposition of the Lord's-Prayer*. London: Printed by J. D. and are to be sold by Jonathan Robinson, 1684.

Mayo, Richard. *Krypteuchologia, or, A Plain Answer to This Practical Question, What Course May a Christian Take to Have His Heart Quickened and Enlarged in the Duty of Secret Prayer?* London: Printed by D. Maxwel for Thomas Parkhurst, 1664.

Owen, John. *The Work of the Holy Spirit in Prayer*. In vol. 4 of *The Works of John Owen*. Edited by William H. Goold. Edinburgh: Banner of Truth Trust, 1967, pp. 235–350.

Perkins, William. *An Exposition of the Lords Praier In the Way of Catechisme*. Edinburgh: Printed by Robert Walde-graue, printer to the Kings Maiestie, 1593.

*Prayers of the Reformers*. Compiled and edited by Clyde L. Manschreck. Philadelphia: Muhlenberg Press, 1958.

Preston, John. *The Saints Daily Exercise: A Treatise Unfolding the Whole Duty of Prayer: Delivered in Five Sermons Upon I Thess. 5, 17*. London: Printed by Elizabeth Purslow for Nicholas Bourne, 1633.

*The Puritans on Prayer*. Compiled and edited by Don Kistler. Morgan, Pa.: Soli Deo Gloria Publications, 1995.

Rutherford, Samuel. *The Power of Faith and Prayer*. Stornoway: Reformation Press, 1991.

Scudder, Henry, and Richard Sibbes. *A Key of Heaven The Lords Prayer Opened, and so Applied, That a Christian May Learne How to Pray, and to Procure All Things Which May Make for the Glorie of God, and the Good of Himselfe, and of His Neighbour: Containing Likewise Such Doctrines of Faith and Godlines, As May Be Very Usefull to All That Desire to Live Godly in Christ Iesus*. London: Printed by Thomas Harper, for Benjamin Fisher, 1633.

Sibbes, Richard. "The Knot of Prayer Loosed." In vol. 7 of *Works of Richard Sibbes*. Edited Alexander B. Grosart. Edinburgh: Banner of Truth Trust, 1982, pp. 229–52.

Traill, Robert. *The Lord's Prayer, in John XVII. 24 Discoursed on, in XVI Sermons*. London: Printed for N. Hillier, at the Prince's Arms, in Leadenhall-Street, over-against S. Mary-Axe, 1705.

Twisse, William. *A Brief Catechetical Exposition of Christian Doctrine: divided into Foure Catechisms, comprising the doctrine of the: two sacraments — Lord's Prayer — Ten Commandments — the Creed*. London: G. M. for Robert Bird, 1632.

Ussher, James. *A Method for Meditation, or, A Manuall of Divine Duties, Fit for Every Christians Practice*. London: Printed by T.W. and are to be sold by John Place, 1651.

*The Valley of Vision: A Collection of Puritan Prayers and Devotions*. Compiled and edited by Arthur Bennett. Edinburgh: Banner of Truth Trust, 1975.

Vincent, Nathanael. *The Spirit of Prayer, or, A Discourse Wherein the Nature of Prayer Is Opened, the Kinds of Prayer Are Handled, and the Right Manner of Praying Discover'd, Several Cases About This Duty Are Resolved from Eph. 6, 18...: Unto Which Is Added a Direction for the Attaining the Gift of Prayer, That Family-Duty May Not Be Omitted, nor Secret Duty Discouraged Through Inability of Utterance and Expression*. London: Printed for Tho. Parkhurst, 1674.

Wallin, Benjamin. *Exhortations Relating to Prayer, and the Lord's Supper*. London: Printed for John Ward, 1752.

Watson, Thomas. *The Bible and the Closet, or, How we may read the scriptures with the most spiritual profit* and *Secret Prayer Successfully Managed*, by Samuel Lee. Edited by John Overton Choules. Harrisonburg, Va.: Sprinkle Publications, 1992.

———. *The Lord's Prayer*. Reprint, London: Banner of Truth Trust, 1960.

Witsius, Herman. *Sacred Dissertations on the Lord's Prayer*. Translated from the Latin of Herman Witsius, with notes by William Pringle. Reprint, Grand Rapids: Reformation Heritage Books, 2010.

**Unpublished**

Edwards, Jonathan. "If a People in a Time of Sore Drought Acknowledge God and Turn from Their Sins which Procure this Judgment, and Go to God through Christ by Prayer and Supplication, 'Tis the Way for Them Both to Obtain the Temporal Blessing They Need" (1730). Beinecke Rare Book and Manuscript Library, Yale University, New Haven.

———. "It Becomes Saints in Cases of Special Difficulty and Calamity of God's Church, to Betake Themselves in an Extraordinary Manner to Prayer to God" (1750). Beinecke Rare Book and Manuscript Library, Yale University, New Haven.

———. "One of the Main Subjects of Christian Prayer Ought to be the Advancement of the Interest of Religion in the World" (1749). Beinecke Rare Book and Manuscript Library, Yale University, New Haven.

———. "The Prayers of Saints Is a Great and Principal Means of Carrying on the Great Designs of Christ's Kingdom in the World" (1742). Beinecke Rare Book and Manuscript Library, Yale University, New Haven.

———. "The Suitableness of Union in Extraordinary Prayer for the Advancement of God's Church" (1747). Beinecke Rare Book and Manuscript Library, Yale University, New Haven.

———. "There Is No Goodness in Praying, Though It Be Never So Earnestly, Merely Out of Fear of Misery" (1728). Beinecke Rare Book and Manuscript Library, Yale University, New Haven.

_____."'Tis in Vain for Any to Expect to Have Their Prayers Heard as Long as They Continue in the Allowance of Sin" (1739). Andover Newton Theology School, Newton Centre.

_____."'Tis the Duty of God's People to be Much in Prayer for that Great Outpouring of the Spirit that God Has Promised Shall Be in the Latter Days" (1746). Beinecke Rare Book and Manuscript Library, Yale University, New Haven.

## SECONDARY SOURCES

### Books

Barth, Karl. *Prayer and Preaching.* London: SCM, 1964, pp. 9–63.

Beck, Peter. *The Voice of Faith: Jonathan Edwards's Theology of Prayer.* Guelph, Ont.: Joshua Press, 2010.

Beeke, Joel R. "The Communion of Men with God." In *John Calvin: A Heart for Devotion, Doctrine, and Doxology.* Edited by Burk Parsons. Orlando: Reformation Trust, 2008, pp. 231–46.

Calhoun, David B. "Prayer: 'The Chief Exercise of Faith.'" In *A Theological Guide to Calvin's Institutes: Essays and Analysis.* Edited by David W. Hall. Phillipsburg, N.J.: P&R, 2008, pp. 347–67.

Davies, Horton."Puritan Prayer-Book." In *The Worship of the English Puritans.* Edited by Horton Davies. Morgan, Pa.: Soli Deo Gloria Publications, 1997, pp. 115–61.

_____."Puritans and the Book of Common Prayer." In *The Worship of the English Puritans.* Edited by Horton Davies. Morgan, Pa.: Soli Deo Gloria Publications, 1997, pp. 57–76.

_____."Set Forms or Extemporary Prayers?" In *The Worship of the English Puritans.* Edited by Horton Davies. Morgan, Pa.: Soli Deo Gloria Publications, 1997, pp. 98–114.

Duncan III, J. Ligon. "A Method for Prayer by Matthew Henry (1662–1714)." In *The Devoted Life: An Introduction to the Puritan Classics.* Edited by Kelly M. Kapic and Randall C. Gleason. Downers Grove, Ill.: InterVarsity, 2004, pp. 238–50.

Hall, Peter. *The Puritan Prayer-Book.* Bath: Binns & Goodwin, 1848.

Hayes, Alan L. "Spirit and Structure in Elizabethan Public Prayer." In *Spirit Within Structure: Essays in Honor of George Johnston on the Occasion of His Seventieth Birthday.* Edited by E. J. Furcha. Allison Park, Pa.: Pickwick Publications, 1983, pp. 117–32.

Hesselink, John. *On Prayer: Conversation with God.* Louisville, Ky.: Westminster, 2006.

Lehmann, Martin E. *Luther and Prayer.* Milwaukee: Northwestern Publishing House, 1985.

Lewis, Peter H. "The Puritan Casuistry of Prayer—Some Cases of Conscience Resolved." In *The Good Fight of Faith; Papers Read at the Westminster Conference, 1971.* London: Published by the Westminster Conference in conjunction with Evangelical Press, 1971, pp. 5–22.

McKee, Elsie A. "John Calvin's Teaching on the Lord's Prayer." In *The Lord's Prayer: Perspectives for Reclaiming Christian Prayer.* Edited by Daniel L. Migliore. Grand Rapids: Eerdmans, 1993, pp. 88–106.

Old, Hughes O. "Matthew Henry and the Puritan Discipline of Family Prayer." In vol. 7 of *Calvin Studies.* Edited by J. H. Leith. Davidson, N.C.: Davidson College, 1994, pp. 69–91.

Partee, Charles. "Prayer as the Practice of Predestination." In *An Elaboration of the Theology of Calvin.* Edited by Richard C. Gamble. *Articles on Calvin and Calvinism, Vol. 8.* New York: Garland, 1992, pp. 357–68.

Redding, Graham. *Prayer and the Priesthood of Christ: In the Reformed Tradition.* London: T & T Clark, 2003.

Rust, Paul R. *The First of the Puritans and the Book of Common Prayer.* Milwaukee: Bruce Publishing Company, 1949.

Williams, Roy. "Lessons from the Prayer Habits of the Puritans." In *Teach Us to Pray: Prayer in the Bible and the World.* Edited by D. A. Carson. Exeter, U.K.: Published on behalf of the World Evangelical Fellowship by Paternoster Press and Baker, 1990, pp. 272–85.

## Articles

Beckmann, D. N. "Praying the Catechism: A Prayer Based on the Larger Catechism's Exposition of the Lord's Prayer." *Presbyterion* 16, no. 2 (1990): 81–88.

Byars, R. P. "Eucharistic Prayer in the Reformed Tradition." *Worship* 77 (2003): 114–31.

Carr, Deanna M. "A Consideration of the Meaning of Prayer in the Life of Martin Luther." *Concordia Theological Monthly* 42, no. 10 (1971): 620–29.

Christoph Ehrat. "Jonathan Edwards' Treatise Concerning Religious Affections and Its Application to Prayer." *Crux* 24 (1988): 11–16.

Devereux, James A. "Reformed Doctrine in the Collects of the First Book of Common Prayer." *Harvard Theological Review* 58, no. 1 (1965): 49–68.

Garlington, Don B. "Calvin's Doctrine of Prayer: An Examination of Book 3, Chapter 20 of the *Institutes of the Christian Religion*." *Baptist Review of Theology* 1 (1991): 21–36.

Haykin, Michael A. G. "The Holy Spirit and Prayer in John Bunyan." *Reformation & Revival* 3 (1994): 85–93.

Hebart, Friedemann. "The Role of the Lord's Prayer in Luther's Theology of Prayer." *Lutheran Theological Journal* 18, no. 1 (1984): 6–17.

Kaufman, Peter I. "'Much in Prayer': The Inward Researches of Elizabethan Protestants." *The Journal of Religion* 73, no. 2 (1993): 163–82.

Kelsay, John. "Prayer and Ethics: Reflections on Calvin and Barth." *Harvard Theological Review* 82, no. 2 (1989): 169–84.

Kidd, Thomas S. "'The Very Vital Breath of Christianity': Prayer and Revival in Provincial New England." *Fides et Historia* 36 (2004): 19–33.

Kreider, Glenn R. "Jonathan Edwards's Theology of Prayer." *Bibliotheca Sacra* 160 (2003): 434–56.

Loggie, Robert D. "Chief Exercise of Faith: An Exposition of Calvin's Doctrine of Prayer." *Hartford Quarterly* 5 (1965): 65–81.

Matteucci, Stephen. "A Strong Tower for Weary People: Calvin's Teaching on Prayer." *The Founders Journal* (Summer 2007): 21–23.

Old, Hughes O. "Daily Prayer in the Reformed Church of Strasbourg, 1525–1530." *Worship* 52, no. 2 (1978): 121–38.

Russell, William R. "Luther, Prayer, and the Reformation." *Word & World* 22, no. 1 (2002): 49–54.

Stein, Stephen J. "'For Their Spiritual Good': The Northampton, Massachusetts, Prayer Bids of the 1730s and 1740s." *The William and Mary Quarterly* 37, no. 2 (1980): 261–85.

Tripp, Diane K. "Daily Prayer in the Reformed Tradition: An Initial Survey." *Studia Liturgica* 21 (1991): 76–107.

Ware, Bruce A. "The Role of Prayer and the Word in the Christian Life According to John Calvin." *Studia Biblica et Theologica* 12 (1982): 73–91.

## Dissertations/Theses

Bakke, Robert O. "The Concert of Prayer: Back to the Future?" D.Min. dissertation, Gordon-Conwell Theological Seminary, 1993.

Barber, Robert L. "The Puritan Connection Between Prayer and Preaching." D.Min. dissertation, Fuller Theological Seminary, 2000.

Beck, Peter. "The Voice of Faith: Jonathan Edwards's Theology of Prayer." Ph.D. dissertation, Southern Baptist Theological Seminary, 2007.

Coulibaly, Nouhoum. "Calvin's Teaching and Practice of Prayer." Th.M. thesis, Tyndale Seminary, 2009.

Etheridge, David C. "The Prayer of Confession in the Corporate Worship of the Reformed Tradition." D.Min. dissertation, Union Theological Seminary, 1993.

Fritsch, Lyle H. "A Survey and Critique of the Modern Reformed Theology of Prayer." M.Div. thesis, Concordia Theological Seminary, 1982.

Harris, John E. "Guidance in and Experience of Liturgical Prayer: As an Element of Personal and Communal Worship in the Reformed Tradition." D.Min. dissertation, Pittsburgh Theological Seminary, 2003.

Lambert, Thomas A. "Preaching, Praying, and Policing the Reform in Sixteenth Century Geneva." Ph.D. dissertation, University of Wisconsin-Madison, 1998.

Maurer, Hans W. "An Examination of Form and Content of John Calvin's Prayers." Ph.D. dissertation, University of Edinburgh, 1959.

Naeher, Robert James. "Prayerful Voice: Self-Shaping, Intimacy, and the Puritan Practice and Experience of Prayer." Ph.D. dissertation, University of Connecticut, 1999.

Najapfour, Brian G. "'The Very Heart of Prayer': Reclaiming John Bunyan's Spirituality." Th.M. thesis, Puritan Reformed Theological Seminary, 2009.

Pelkonen, John P. "Martin Luther's Theology of Prayer, Its Systematic Structure and Its Significance for Michael Agricola." Ph.D. dissertation, Duke University, 1971.

Rai, Kushal. "Work of the Holy Spirit as Intercessor and Comforter: The Experiential Benefits of a Believer." Th.M. thesis, Puritan Reformed Theological Seminary, 2010.

Roser, Timothy W. "Can God Be Persuaded? A Discussion of the Immutability of God in Luther's Catechesis on Prayer." Ph.D. dissertation, Concordia Seminary, 2005.

Serafini, Johnny C. "The Puritans and the Doctrine of Intercession, a Trinitarian View." M.Div. thesis, Puritan Reformed Theological Seminary, 2009.

Smuda, Thomas E. "The Effectual Nature of Confident Prayer Expressed in Selected Writings of Martin Luther." M.Div. thesis, Concordia Theological Seminary, 1980.

Williams, Roy W. "The Puritan Concept and Practice of Prayer." Ph.D. dissertation, University of London, 1982.

# Scripture Index

## OLD TESTAMENT

# Subject Index

calling and employment, prayer
during, 147–48
Calvin, John, 27–42, 69, 74,
113–14, 115, 207–08, 209,
210, 213
Cameron, John, 90n31
Carey, William, 207, 216,
229–30
carnal prayers, 132
Carr, Deanna, 4, 17
catechetical instruction, 2–3, 5
childlike reverence, 106
children of God, 164
Christ-centered prayers, 167
Christian life, 27, 121, 140, 239
Christology, 64, 194
Church of England, 112, 119
Claghorn, George, 190
Clarkson, David, 124, 126,
129, 136–37
cold prayers, 132
command and promise, 11
commandment, to pray, 47–48.
*See also* duty to pray
commands of God, 178
common prayers, 52
communion with God, 28–29,
98, 100, 107, 152, 161, 165,
190, 202–03, 204, 206
condemnation, 79
confession of sin, 153, 156–57,
235
confidence, 33, 35, 72–73,
125–26, 128, 171, 211
content, of prayers, 124–31
continual prayer, 232–33
Conventicle Act (1593), 112
conversion, 91
corporate prayer, 40
covenant, 33
Cradock, Walter, 114

daily bread, 77–78, 179–80
death, 150
Decalogue, 5, 8
decrees, 30–31, 75–76
deists, conversion of, 157
delay, in prayer, 60–61
delight, in God, 133, 135
deliverance, from sin, 183–84
denial, in prayer, 61–63
dependence on God, 147
depravity, 204
despair, in prayer life, 239
Diet of Worms, 6
Dietrich, Viet, 24
discipline, 39
discouragements, 41
disproportionality, in prayer,
132
Donaldson, Gordon, 56
dullness, in prayer, 231
Duncan, Ligon, 153, 157, 158
duty, 183
becomes delight, 133
prayer as, 7–9, 11, 205

Ebeling, Gerhard, 6
Edwards, Jonathan, 187–206,
213–14
effectiveness, of prayer, 31
election, 90, 103
Elijah, 223, 239, 240
Eliot, John, 207
Elizabeth I, 67–68
enemies, prayer for, 25
Erskine, Henry, 159
eternity, 150
evening prayer, 150–51

faith, 32–33, 38, 45, 60, 94,
196, 204
fall, 203

humility, 34, 72, 94, 106, 126
hypocrisy, 44, 61, 70–71, 78,
  82, 116, 137, 205, 231

ignorance, 125
image of God, 202
imprecatory prayer, 26
incarnation, 194
individual piety, 40
indulgences, 2
indwelling sin, 123
infirmities, 116, 122–23, 132,
  139, 212
intercession, 102, 153, 157.
  *See also* Jesus Christ,
  intercession of
irreverence, 100
Islam, 157, 217, 219
*I Will Pray with the Spirit*
  (Bunyan), 111–19

Jesus Christ
  adoption in, 163
  ascension of, 80, 92–93
  death of, 80, 196
  exaltation of, 90, 92
  humanity of, 195
  humiliation of, 90, 92
  intercession of, 37, 39–40,
    80, 87–89, 94–95, 108,
    196, 237
  meditation on, 58–61
  as mediator, 58–60, 84–95,
    128, 196
  resurrection of, 80
  satisfaction of, 86, 194
  victory of, 212–14
Jews, conversion of, 157, 219
Judson, Adoniram, 207
justification, 180

Keeble, N. H., 111
Kelynge, John, 113, 115
Kiffin, William, 109n1
kingdom of God, 74–75, 82,
  100, 107, 157–58, 212,
  213, 217
  as four-fold, 176–77
Knox, John, 43–65, 211, 224,
  230
Kosten, Andrew W., 1, 24, 26

Laing, David, 57
laypeople, prayers of, 228, 234
Lehmann, Martin E., 7
limited atonement, 90
Lloyd-Jones, D. Martyn, 189
Lombard, Peter, 92n35
Lord's Prayer, 3, 5, 6, 38–39,
  102, 105, 158
  Boston on, 173–84, 218
  Henry on, 145, 152
  Luther on, 19–20
  Perkins on, 69–82, 211–12
Ludwig, Leonhard, 24
lukewarmness, 137
Luther, Martin, 1–26, 74, 224,
  239, 240

MacDonald, D. D. F., 161
manner, of prayer, 12–17,
  99–100, 131–39
Manton, 121, 122, 123, 126,
  131, 133, 134, 236
Mary I, 53–54
Mary Stuart, 63
material needs, 78
M'Cheyne, Robert Murray, 158
McNeill, John T., 28
means of grace, prayer as, 162
Melanchthon, Philipp, 224
merit, 96, 97

# Contributors

———————— ∞∞∞ ————————

**Peter Beck** holds a Ph.D. in Church History and is assistant professor of Religion at Charleston Southern University.

**Joel R. Beeke** is president and professor of Systematic Theology and Homiletics at Puritan Reformed Theological Seminary and a pastor of the Heritage Netherlands Reformed Congregation of Grand Rapids, Michigan.

**Michael A. G. Haykin** is a professor of Church History at Southern Baptist Theological Seminary and a lecturer at Puritan Reformed Theological Seminary.

**Brian G. Najapfour**, a pastor from the Philippines, is a recent graduate from Puritan Reformed Theological Seminary (Th.M.) and a Ph.D. student at Southern Baptist Theological Seminary.

**Johnny C. Serafini** is pastor of the Heritage Reformed Congregation of Kinnelon, New Jersey.

**J. Stephen Yuille** is pastor of Grace Community Church, Glen Rose, Texas.

# Developing a Healthy Prayer Life
## 31 Meditations on Communing with God
*James W. Beeke and Joel R. Beeke*

978-1-60178-112-3    Paperback, 112 pages

Is your prayer life characterized by such things as sincerity, urgency, and delight? Engagement in prayer is a vital part of our communion with God, making a profound impact on our growth in grace. In this book, you will find thoughtful meditations on prayer in the life of the believer, as well as ample encouragement to cultivate this spiritual discipline in your own life. If you want to be more devoted to prayer, or simply want to assess the health of your prayer life, read this book. It provides both a helpful examination and a needed tonic for those concerned about growing in godliness.

"We have needed a book that comprehensively, yet simply, teaches us to pray, not by techniques (though some how-to's are helpful), but by uniting *prayer* in the presence of God with *life* in the presence of God; that shows us how dependent and reverent *living* arises out of dependent and reverent *praying*. *Developing a Healthy Prayer Life* is just the book to help us to unite our praying *and* our living in a Christ-honoring whole."

—Terry Johnson, Senior Minister of Independent
Presbyterian Church in Savannah, Georgia,
and author of *The Family Worship Book*

# Meet the Puritans
*Joel R. Beeke and Randall J. Pederson*

978-1-60178-000-3                    Hardback, 935 pages

*Meet the Puritans* provides a biographical and theological introduction to the Puritans whose works have been reprinted in the last fifty years, and also gives helpful summaries and insightful analyses of those reprinted works. It contains nearly 150 biographical entries, and nearly 700 summaries of reprinted works. A very useful resource for getting into the Puritans.

"As furnaces burn with ancient coal and not with the leaves that fall from today's trees, so my heart is kindled with the fiery substance I find in the old Scripture-steeped sermons of Puritan pastors. A warm thanks to the authors of *Meet the Puritans* for all the labor to make them known."

—John Piper, Pastor,
Bethlehem Baptist Church,
Minneapolis, Minnesota